CHAKRA MANTRAS

First published in 2006 by
Red Wheel/Weiser, LLC
With offices at:
500 Third Street, Suite 230
San Francisco, CA 94107
www.redwheelweiser.com

ISBN-10: 1-57863-367-2
ISBN-13: 978-1-57863-367-8

Library of Congress Cataloging-in-Publication Data

Ashley-Farrand, Thomas.
  Chakra mantras : liberate your spiritual genius through chanting / Thomas
Ashley-Farrand (Namadeva).
    p. cm.
  Includes bibliographical references (p.   ).
  ISBN 1-57863-367-2 (alk. paper)
  1. Mantras. 2. Chakras. 3. Self-realization—Religious aspects. I.
Title.
  BL560.A828 2006
  294.5'37-dc22
                              2006010358

Design by Gopa & Ted2, Inc.
Typeset in Weiss
Cover art © Gopa &Ted 2, Inc.

Printed in Canada
TCP

10 9 8 7 6 5 4 3 2 1

For Margalo, Satyabhama

CHAKRA MANTRAS

LIBERATE YOUR SPIRITUAL GENIUS
THROUGH CHANTING

THOMAS ASHLEY-FARRAND
NAMADEVA

WEISERBOOKS
San Francisco, CA / Newburyport, MA

CONTENTS

Acknowledgments

O BOOK IS EVER the work of just one person, and this one is no exception. My agent and friend, Liz Williams, is a moving force behind this book. Thank you, Liz. I am grateful to Red Wheel/Weiser Publisher Jan Johnson, for being so accommodating in allowing me to push back my manuscript deadline. Associate Publisher Brenda Knight's support was heartfelt and I am grateful. Managing Editor Caroline Pincus and her copyeditor helped greatly in smoothing out the manuscript, and I thank them for their assistance.

As always, my wife, Margalo Ashley-Farrand, helped with suggestions, comments, and corrections during the writing process. Years ago she gently encouraged me to write, even when I resisted. Her unending support through all my writing efforts is more appreciated than I can fully express.

Finally, Sadguru Sant Keshavadas (deceased) and Guru Mata, his widow and lineage holder, have blessed my spiritual work since 1973. An expression of gratitude seems absurd compared with what they so tirelessly and continuously give to me and so many others. So I just say in complete truth that without them this and my other works would not exist.

Chart of the Chakras and Attributes

Chakra	Chakra	Chakra	Chakra
Muladhara	Svadhistana	Manipura	Anahata
Principle	**Principle**	**Principle**	**Principle**
Earth	Water	Fire	Air
Devata	**Devata**	**Devata**	**Devata**
Indra	Varuna	Agni Deva	Vayu
Loka	**Loka**	**Loka**	**Loka**
Bhu	Bhuvaha	Swaha	Maha
Tanmatra	**Tanmatra**	**Tanmatra**	**Tanmatra**
Gandha (smell)	Rasa (taste)	Rupa (form)	Spasha (touch)
In body	**In body**	**In body**	**In body**
Base of Spine	Genital Center	Navel	Cardiac Center
Petals	**Petals**	**Petals**	**Petals**
4	6	10	12
Bijam	**Bijam**	**Bijam**	**Bijam**
Lam	Vam	Ram	Yam
Music note east	**Music note east**	**Music note east**	**Music note east**
Sa	Ri	Ga	Ma
Music note west	**Music note west**	**Music note west**	**Music note west**
Do	Re	Mi	Fa
State of Consciousness	**State of Consciousness**	**State of Consciousness**	**State of Consciousness**
Jagrat (or wakeful)	Swapna (or dream)	Shushupti (or deep sleep)	Turiya Jagrat (awake to higher consciousness)
Sheath or Kosha	**Sheath or Kosha**	**Sheath or Kosha**	**Sheath or Kosha**
Food (Annamaya)	Prana (Pranamaya)	Mental (Manomaya)	Intellect (Vijnanamaya)
Prana or Vital Air	**Prana or Vital Air**	**Prana or Vital Air**	**Prana or Vital Air**
Vyana (Excretion)	Apana (Evacuation)	Samana (Distributive)	Prana (Respiratory)
Shakti	**Shakti**	**Shakti**	**Shakti**
Dakini (Power holding Earth)	Rakini	Lakini	Kakini
Saguna Manifestation	**Saguna Manifestation**	**Saguna Manifestation**	**Saguna Manifestation**
Indra	Prajapati	Brahma	Vishnu

CHAKRA Vishuddha	**CHAKRA** Ajna	**CHAKRA** Sahasrar
PRINCIPLE Ether	**PRINCIPLE** Intelligence	**PRINCIPLE** Consciousness
DEVATA Saraswati	**DEVATA** Guru and/or Dakshini Murti	**DEVATA** Paramashiva
LOKA Janaha	**LOKA** Tapaha	**LOKA** Satya
TANMATRA Shabda (sound)	**TANMATRA** Buddhi (cosmic mind)	**TANMATRA** Prakriti (primordial energy)
IN BODY Cervical Center	**IN BODY** Brow Center	**IN BODY** Cerebrum
PETALS 16	**PETALS** 2	**PETALS** 1000
BIJAM Hum	**BIJAM** Om	**BIJAM** Sohum
MUSIC NOTE EAST Pa	**MUSIC NOTE EAST** Dha	**MUSIC NOTE EAST** Ni
MUSIC NOTE WEST So	**MUSIC NOTE WEST** La	**MUSIC NOTE WEST** Ti
STATE OF CONSCIOUSNESS Turiya Swapna (mystical vision)	**STATE OF CONSCIOUSNESS** Turiya Shushupti (direct perception, Savikalpa, Samadhi)	**STATE OF CONSCIOUSNESS** Turiya Turiya (Nirvikalpa, Samadhi)
SHEATH OR KOSHA Bliss (Anandamaya)	**SHEATH OR KOSHA** Soul (Individual)	**SHEATH OR KOSHA** God (All Souls and more)
PRANA OR VITAL AIR Udana (Transformative)	**PRANA OR VITAL AIR** Cosmic Ego	**PRANA OR VITAL AIR** Cosmic Mind
SHAKTI Shakini	**SHAKTI** Hakini	**SHAKTI** Shakti Katyayani
SAGUNA MANIFESTATION Rudra	**SAGUNA MANIFESTATION** Dakshina Murti (or Guru)	**SAGUNA MANIFESTATION** Parama Shiva

INTRODUCTION

HIS BOOK IS ABOUT our spiritual evolution. It is about the role and process of spiritual development and about the deeper truths that lie beneath our more relative selves. It is also a practical book, giving indepth guidance to the complex system of chakras and mantras—spiritual maps and tools for our higher development.

The material presented here will work for you regardless of what your spiritual ideal is or what your personal "spiritual mosaic" looks like. It will focus on the common spiritual anatomy we all carry and will lay out core Sanskrit mantras that will aid in various aspects of our spiritual development.

As we begin this journey, the most important initial idea I can express is that you are immortal. There was never a time you were not. There is never a time you will not be. Your immortal essence is referred to by many names: the soul, the self, *atman, jiva,* or lower *purusha.* These are but a few of the various names that refer to your personal inner divine flame of truth. That which you are. That which is imperishable. It is a part of you that is not actively involved in any of your worldly conditions; yet it watches and, in some hard-to-describe way, learns.

But even as that flame is your true self, there is another part of us that lives in this world that I call the Ego-Mind-Personality. It is not immortal. It experiences all of the pains and joys of life, and then dissolves, in its current form and expression, at the time of death. This day-to-day part of us also comes and goes from life to life; and an essence of what we have learned and attained in any one life goes forward from one life on to the next. The Ego-Mind-Personality can choose to evolve to a new, higher state of consciousness and being. It can become immortal if it chooses to embark upon a program of spiritual discipline that systematically leads to immortality. Through discipline it can evolve and grow until it eventually merges with the *atman* and becomes immortal.

If we look closely at what we know about various religions throughout human history, it would seem that the decision for the Ego-Mind-Personality to become immortal is a choice we will all make sooner or later, but, as yet, there is no definitive proof that this is so—we as a human family certainly have not yet gotten to that point en masse. But still, the major religions are trying to convey something important to us. And throughout history, the great spiritual figures have deemed the pursuit of this of the highest importance. The religions and spiritual teachers speak with one voice about our divine destiny, about immortality, about living a spiritual life, and about spiritual rewards. The details vary, but the essential message is the same: We are much more than we know, if we will but undertake the journey to achieve it.

To describe our common journey, it is helpful to use the map of powers, abilities, and potentials embodied in stories about some of the celestials that are told in various Hindu scriptures but principally in the Puranas. The marvelous abilities of the characters in these stories—both good and evil ones alike—can be likened to a periodic table of divine abilities and characteristics we will encounter as we progress. These stories can help define both the journey and what we may find along the way.

I will begin here by sketching out the general themes found in the rest of this work and some basic concepts that serve as foundational ideas for the chapters that follow.

According to both the Vedas and the Puranas, in the beginning at the supra-cosmic level, there was only a transcendent unity. There was one Being of which we were a part. Then, in a truly enigmatic decision, that Being decided to diversify itself. The idea of many individual parts was conceived, and individual souls sprang from that transcendental Being.

From that Being we have come. Ultimately, it is to that Being in its reality to which we will return.

The first step after the decision of that Being to become many was the establishment of each of us as individual beings. Even then, we were still in unity with that Cosmic Truth. We had only the thinnest of veils separating us from complete absorption into that Being. We had commenced a journey for reasons known only to our soul and that Great Being. When we have finished the first phase of that journey started long, long ago, we will reach the place of Great Decision discussed near the end of this book. No matter what our decision at that point, we will have evolved back into conscious contact with the state of Being from which we have come. We will have traveled up through the chakras, adding to our experience and knowledge.

Almost everyone who has even a nodding acquaintance with eastern spirituality has heard the word chakras. As energy processing centers in the subtle body located along the spine, they are traditionally taught as six in number with a seventh at the top of the head. In addition to these seven chakras, there are other esoteric chakras that are sometimes taught to advanced students. There are mantras and seed sounds that activate those esoteric chakras, and some of them contain keys to our spiritual progress.

The seed sound *Hrim*, for instance, is taught in both Hinduism and Tibetan Buddhism as the seed sound for the Hrit Padma, the "sacred heart" which is described in the Narayana Suktam as an eight-petaled lotus "two finger widths" below the Anahata (heart) Chakra. This chakra is described as that place in which the self, the soul, resides.

In Tibetan Buddhism, one mantra initiation into advanced spiritual practice involves the Kala Chakra, or wheel of time. This esoteric chakra, called the Lalani Chakra in Hinduism, is sometimes located just above the Vishuddha or throat chakra. But in another system, it is located in a different place in the head, above the Ajna Chakra, also called the third eye. In fact, there are a handful of different chakra systems that are defined and placed in different parts of our spiritual anatomy. Here I will use the most common system of chakra definitions and placement, while incorporating aspects of other systems I have been taught, and which I have tested since 1973.

My teacher, Sadguru Sant Keshavadas, taught that every organ and gland has a chakra of its own to help it process the energy that helps it function properly. The great Swami Sivananda noted that some yogic texts speak of 144 chakras in the body. And, the comprehensive chakra manual *Laya Yoga*[1], by Shyam Sundar Goswami, minutely describes many overlapping chakras systems and some esoteric schools that locate over 200 different chakras in the body. Sundar goes into such detail as to make the information nearly impossible to take in, especially for the average yoga student and even then for some advanced practitioners. That gives you some indication of the intricacy of this system of spiritual anatomy.

Other chakras in both Tibetan and Hindu systems are even less available to students in the West. The Soma Chakra in the forehead, the Manas Chakra in the back of the head, and other chakras scattered in various places in the body have energy processing abilities that are activated by mantras. Some of these mantras are given to everyone while others are usually given only to select students. All of which is to say that in examining the path that presents itself to the willing seeker, we must examine both traditional and a few more secret chakras.

In our spiritual journey, we will likely encounter conditions or obstacles that challenge us. We will be "burning up karma" and can experience all kinds of psychological, physical, and spiritual discomfort in the process. There are various spiritual practices to help us with these challenges. Hinduism has discovered the science of mantra to help invoke various spiritual energies that help dissolve difficulties. Mantras can also act as buffers to minimize painful karmic burn-off. These mantras resonate within the chakras, the major energy processing centers located along the spine in the subtle body. Throughout this book, I'll take you through not only the ways mantras can help you on your spiritual journey, I'll also provide you with the Sanskrit chants and the recommended number of recitations to provide support on the spiritual path.

My Seven Intentions for This Book

1. To present for your consideration a simple explanation of the system of chakras that exist in all of us. The system I present will be drawn from several of the dozens of systems that exist in the ancient texts from India. All of the research has been done by others, most of whom are great spiritual scholars as well as advanced practitioners. There is only one item in the discussion of the chakras that is original with me. It is my discussion of the function of the dramatic mythic character called Ganesha, and his chakra. Very great minds and spiritual practitioners have provided all the rest of the information.

2. To outline a general path of spiritual development that encompasses efforts conducted during more than one lifetime. The purpose of this spiritual development is to discover and therefore become consciously more of what you are and always have been.

3. To present energy-invoking tools called mantras that, when used, enable you to accumulate more and more energy leading to various "changes of state" in your organism, or that which you inhabit—your bodies, both physical and subtle.

4. To provide a description of, in as simple language as I am able, the journey to and place of "great decision," where we reach a fundamental evolutionary point of choice. From that decision, two great and divergent paths are presented to all of us.

5. To list some of the superhuman abilities that come, eventually, to us all. The great healers among us have unlocked some of these abilities and many of them have dedicated themselves to helping us. As part of the process, I will introduce you to several healers and their spiritual opening.

6. To offer several of the great healing mantras from India.

7. To convey stories from the great tales and epics of India that teach us something important or useful about our journey. And they are fun.

Spirituality does not have to be long-faced and serious all the time. Personally, I think the great ones told funny stories to their disciples.

I pray that God attends your every need on your magnificent journey.

Thomas Ashley-Farrand

Namadeva

March 2006

PART I

COSMIC CONCEPTS

CHAPTER ONE

BACKGROUND

 O ENSURE that we have some common understanding, I will need to provide and explain some foundational ideas and terms. If you are familiar with these ideas, you may want to proceed directly to the next chapter.

VIBRATION

When the sun shines upon us, we feel its warmth. We feel the vibration of heat upon our skin. Whether one regards the energy of the sun as a particle or a wave, in either case a vibrational effect is felt. It is the vibration of light reflected from objects that allows us to see. When we hear music, the same phenomenon is in play. We hear because of vibrations that we capture in the tiny chambered nautilus in our inner ear. It is composed of little hairs that vibrate when sounds reach them. You see how both sight and sound perceptions in our physical bodies are directly tied to vibrations.

Eastern spiritual texts speak about a subtle body that interpenetrates our physical body. Different schools and paths of spiritual study call this subtle body by different names. But mystics in those schools use the same language to discuss what goes on in that body. They all use the term "chakra" to describe energy processing centers located along the *shushumna*, or "spine" in the subtle body.

The *shushumna* runs from the base of the spine to the place at the top of the neck where the spine meets the head. On this path are the major chakras. It is in these chakra centers that energy is processed and distributed to both the subtle and the physical bodies. But what kind of energy are we speaking about?

There are well-known types of energy that we have devised instruments to measure: infrared, radio waves, microwaves, x-rays, and many other kinds of radiant energy. Although they cannot be perceived by the senses, they exist nonetheless. Over the last hundred years or so, we have grown increasingly adept at seeing these energy currents, measuring them and even harnessing them for our use.

The ancients have long discussed kinds of energy that exist and that we can process but for which we have not as yet devised any means of perception or measurement. There are skeptics who decry discussion and education about these hidden kinds of energy. They reason that if we cannot measure them, then they must not exist. Yet these same people think nothing of putting on suntan lotion to protect them from the burning rays of the sun that once we could not measure but now easily measure and employ means to lessen. Is it so hard to deduce that since we only recently "discovered" a vast array of energies that we now use, that there still might be a vast pool of energy kinds and types that we have not yet learned to measure?

CHAKRAS

Most of us are familiar with the major nerve ganglia located along the spine in our physical body. For example, we know that the solar plexus is located in the abdomen just below the stomach. For men, this is where the belly grows. In the subtle body, a powerful energy processing chakra called the Manipura Chakra is located here. Each chakra will be discussed in detail later. For now, please note that there are similar energy processing centers in the subtle body located in the areas of our sex glands and the anus, the thymus, heart, throat, and between the eyebrows at the third eye in the physical body. In all, there are six major chakras or energy processing centers located along the *shushumna* in the subtle body, with a seventh at the top of the head, corresponding to the brain in the physical body.

Each chakra looks like a flower or wheel, with petals or spokes that detail its composition. In fact, the very word "chakra" means "wheel" in Sanskrit. Each chakra has a different number of spokes or petals. All you need to know about chakras for now is that they process energy that flows into them. By processing the energy, they make it available for our use. That use can be simply to improve health or to empower special abilities that will appear over time.

SOUND

In the Gospel of John it says, "In the beginning was the Word. And the Word was with God and the Word was God." Talk about a powerful statement summarizing the power of sound!

In Genesis we find, "And God said, let there be light." Notice that the phrase does not say something like, "And God made light to shine." No, God produced light by *saying* something, by using the power of sound that only God could command. The clear conclusion is that light was not the original or highest. It was sound. From sound came light, according to Genesis. Since light comes from sound, sound is actually higher on the spiritual scale than light. This is why there are several classifications of sound in the Eastern scriptures. Each has a different kind of potency.

The chanting of mantras is called *Japa* in Sanskrit. In *Gayatri, The Highest Meditation,* Sadguru Sant Keshavadas refers to the Agni Purana as defining the word *Japa* thusly, "The syllable *'Ja'* destroys the birth and death cycle and the syllable *'Pa'* destroys all sins. Thus, that which destroys all the sins and puts an end to the birth-death cycle and liberates souls from bondage is *Japa.*" Within the performance of *Japa* there are several classifications:

Vachika Japa: Here one repeats the mantra out loud. The vibrations of this kind of chanting or *Japa* are very beneficial to the physical body. Disciplines focused on healing will find this approach very powerful.

Upamshu Japa: Whispering or muttered sound. Dedicated practitioners of mantra can often be seen seemingly talking to themselves. They
are really practicing Upamshu Japa. This practice helps the mantra
go deeply inside. The deeper one's practice penetrates, the more profound is the ultimate result.

Manasika Japa: This is the repetition of mantra formulas that is entirely
silent. If you are going shopping in a supermarket but still want to
continue your work with mantra, this is a highly recommended method.
You will not draw those perplexed stares and people will stop avoiding
you, believing that you are deranged.

The language used to describe these mantra practices is Sanskrit. In
some texts, Sanskrit has been called Deva Lingua or language of the
gods. Others have called Sanskrit the "Mother of Tongues." Latin and
Greek and all European languages borrow heavily from Sanskrit. For
example, Mater is Mother, and Pitra is Father.

Mantra

All of the above divisions of *Japa* can be applied to the study and practice of mantra. Mantra is a word that has taken root in the lexicon of
ordinary English conversation. Any phrase that is spoken several times
has become a "mantra" in colloquial speech. We have all seen examples
of this on the evening news. But I will apply the classically correct definition of the word.

Mantra is a Sanskrit word that describes a spiritual formula. This formula is exact and has been tested by the ancient *rishis* (sages) of old India.
Mantra formulas work in specific ways, bringing energy and consciousness into the spine, the *shushumna*, and to the chakras located along the
spine for a specific purpose, producing a specific effect. Since human
physiology, both physical and subtle, is the same in all people, the effects
of each specific mantra is well known among the adepts who have used,
and in some cases, discovered them. Physicians are able to diagnose and
treat our problems because our physical bodies are nearly the same.

They contain the same organs that operate in the same way, and have the same fluids that act in the same way. Similarly, our spiritual physiology is the same. Because of this, the ancients were able to know in advance which mantra formulas would produce what effect.

Mantra effects are so powerful that the science of mantra was intentionally hidden for thousands of years. Only in the last 150 years have mantra formulas started to be released throughout the world. Why now?

The answer is that more and more advanced students of the old masters have been born here in the West in the last fifty or so years, and more have been coming here and are taking birth today. One can only assume that this is because of one or more global crises that we are moving toward. The future of humanity is safeguarded, but that does not mean we will not have problems that we must navigate. But that, as they say, is a subject for another time.

Please take to heart, I believe there is a great variety of ways to access that knowledge within. I do not presume to say that Sanskrit or mantras represent the only or exclusive way of arriving at the grand human destiny. There are words that make me crazy. Those words are: Highest, Fastest, Best. Ultimately, there is that which is highest, fastest, or best for you. It might not be the fastest, highest, or best for your neighbor. When organizations or teachers announce that they have the highest, fastest, or best means for spiritual attainment, I roll my eyes. True messiahs are in much shorter supply than many organizations would have you believe. Competition among true spiritual teachers does not exist. Sadguru Sant Keshavadas used to say, with a twinkle in is eyes, "If Moses, Jesus, Krishna, and the Buddha got together, they would have a wonderful cup of tea with loving discourse among them. Outside, their followers would be trying to pluck out each other's eyes, arguing over who is the greatest. This was never the message of those great ones whom we follow."

Sanskrit mantras are the way that was taught to me, and which I have practiced intensely since 1973. I have had enough personal success with mantra methods that I can recommend and teach them. I make no other universal claims.

SANSKRIT

Mantras work directly in the chakras because there is an iron-clad relationship between the sacred language Sanskrit, chakras, and mantras. There are fifty letters in the Sanskrit alphabet. Although some scholars have included diphthongs (combinations of two or more letters in a logical pronunciation scheme) in the alphabet and arrived at fifty to fifty-four letters, most of the ancient texts use fifty as the number of letters.

Each solitary vibration of each letter is said to be represented by, or attuned to, a petal on one of the chakras. If you add up all the petals (or spokes) on the six major chakras located along the spine, or *shushumna*, you arrive at a total of fifty: the same number of letters as in the Sanskrit alphabet. This is no accident. Each petal vibrates in resonance with one of the petals on one of the chakras.

If you study the Shiva Sutras or the Lakshmi Tantra, you will come across a chapter that explains in detail "The Great Matrika" (Mother). The Matrika is described in both texts as "She who binds and she who sets free." The Matrika is revealed in both texts as the Sanskrit alphabet, the building blocks of all creation. The Matrika contains all the vibrations of the universe, physical as well as subtle (more on this in Chapter 24). She is literally the Mother of Creation. And all of her powers and vibrations exist in each of us as the petals of the chakras.

Suddenly the words of ancient mystical texts become more clear: "Man is the microcosm of the macrocosm," "The Kingdom of Heaven is within," "As above, so below," and others. Within us is a summary of everything. Granted that it is encoded. Granted that to access it will take great effort. Fortunately, some among us have received enlightened instruction and have made it available to the rest of us through both the oral tradition of the enlightened ones and the sacred texts that have been translated for our use.

REINCARNATION

The idea of past and future lives is a fundamental assumption in the discussion and methods contained in this book. This idea runs the gamut from controversial to loopy. But for me, there was an incident in 1975 that moved it from the theory column to the actual column.

As a temple priest in Washington, D.C., one of my responsibilities was to hold public meditations. They were scheduled for Wednesday and Saturday evenings. On most Saturday evenings no one would attend, which was just fine with me. With most residents out of the house and no one present for the public meditation, I would have some of my deepest personal meditations.

One particular Saturday, I had been sitting in meditation for about half an hour. I was way, way, way "out there" or "in there," as the case may be. In this state, somewhere I heard the doorbell ring. It rang once . . . it rang twice. . . And then somewhere in me it registered that everyone was gone, and I was the only person left in the temple.

At the time I was dressed in a dhoti and shirt. A dhoti is a wraparound piece of material like a sarong. I wore the white, sheer cloth around my waist, and covered my top with a long Indian shirt called a kurta. It is cool and comfortable.

As the realization of the doorbell and empty house percolated through to wherever I was, I concluded that I would have to arise to answer it. So I reached for my sword to steady myself as I got up. But as I started to rise, I discovered that my sword was missing, and I went into a momentary panic.

A samurai is never without his sword. A samurai sleeps with his sword. A samurai eats with his sword. A samurai has his sword by his side in meditation and at all other times. A part of him is in constant readiness. Again, a samurai is *never, ever* without his sword. I knew I had not set my sword down anywhere and yet, my hands slipped over to my left side where the grip always was and encountered thin air.

The motions of arising with a sword are so automatic that one does not even think about it. It's like driving a car. You just do it. When you arise with a sword, there is a fluid motion where one hand grabs the handle momentarily as you rise. When you are on your feet, the hand comes away and you are mobile. I had done it 100,000 times in exactly the same way. My sword was not on the accustomed left side of my waist where it always was.

Imagine getting in a car, entering the freeway, reaching 65 miles per hour, and then needing to suddenly stop. But when your foot goes over to find the brake pedal, it isn't there. You panic. It is not possible that there is no brake pedal. There is always a brake pedal, yet clearly it is not there. How can that be? This is how I felt.

I was already halfway to my feet, and my eyes opened as I glanced down at the floor to see if it possibly had fallen out somehow. By the time I was standing erect, I realized I was not in Japan. I was not a samurai. The hairs on my arms and the back of my neck stood on end. I understood that in the depths of my meditation, I had been in contact with another lifetime. And as I was coming out, I confused that life— just for a second—with this lifetime.

It is very difficult for me to adequately describe the intensity of the feeling. But the net result of the experience was that the idea of reincarnation went from *theory* to *fact* in a flash. For the briefest of time, I had been *in* that other life. It wasn't a dream. It wasn't a vision. I have called it a past life "bleed-through." I was a samurai. I knew how I had meditated as a samurai. I knew what my sword looked like—long and slightly curved with a white handle. (For you movie buffs, this experience was in 1978, long before the film *Highlander* came out. But my sword looked very much like the one Sean Connery had, and eventually gave to McCloud.) And I wore it on the left side of my saronglike garb. I knew what kind of case it was in. I could see everything.

Many things about that life were quite similar to what I was currently doing in this life. Except I was not in that life, I was in this one.

I answered the door. The person was at the wrong house.

But I had been given a gift through this "accident." That experience was a turning point for me. I knew beyond any doubt that reincarnation was factual.

The next step from that understanding was the realization of the power of our karma, accumulated over past lives.

KARMA

All of us have problems of one kind or another, and mantra practice can be a great aid to softening or even eliminating some problems. One of the most common problems is the presence of an obstacle to much needed abundance. But the curious thing is that the amount of work needed to make the problem go away varies widely from one person to another. Some people can work for 40 days and their ship comes in, so to speak. Others can work for months and make only a little progress. The reason for the differences in length of time to achieve results is karma.

Everything in life is Karma. Everything: your mate or significant other, your health issues, your employment and job status, your relative inner happiness or discontent. Everything. Classical scriptures from India divide karma into four types:

Sanchita Karma: This is the sum total of all of your karma. All of the conscious workings of your mind, the subconscious tendencies, your emotional predispositions and mental acuity, all accumulated from all of your previous lifetimes are covered by this all-inclusive Sanskrit term. It also encompasses all of your past actions—both good and bad—the results of which will be worked out in one lifetime or another.

Prarabdha Karma: The karma that you have chosen to work off in this lifetime is called Prarabdha Karma. It includes the position of the planets at the time of your birth. But as we all know, two people born at the same time and place will have different kinds of lives. So while it is true that the planets are very powerful influences in our karmic predicaments, other facets of our karma are always in play.

Agami Karma: The term covers immediate effects from present actions. You accost someone by shouting from your car and chances are they will shout back. This is Agami Karma in action.

Kriyamana Karma: This kind of karma describes your present willful actions that will influence future karmic return. It is with a nod to Kriyamana Karma that we find religious proscriptions for behavior. From the Ten Commandments to the Golden Rule, to the *Yamas* and *Niyamas* in Hinduism, which are the Ten Commandments and the Golden Rule lumped together in a Hindu version of the same proscriptions, to the Eightfold Path of Buddhism—all of these seek to improve the quality of future karmic return of previous actions and thoughts. These practices and proscriptions are a future karma improvement kit.

SHAKTI

In the East, the notion of shakti is taught as the feminine power of nature. This applies to any power you can name: thought, movement of your body, movement of the planets. Since the entire universe is said to be found within, then the source of all power must also be found within. It is, in the form of the kundalini shakti, located at the base of the spine.

Since we do not have infinite capacity to hold and process power, the conscious kundalini only releases that amount of power that we can safely handle. Mantra is a form of kundalini shakti. "Mantra is an aspect of kundalini, and it is in a sound-form. So mantra is actually kundalini in mantra form."[2]

SPIRITUAL TOOL KIT

Mantra, then, becomes a means of working with the spiritual energy that is all around us all the time. As we harness that energy through mantra practice—*Japa*—we can fulfill desires, create good karma and begin to neutralize bad karma. We can start a process of deep healing that may even resolve a mountain of unpleasant karma accumulated over many lives.

Using all these spiritual practices, we move steadily toward the next step in our spiritual evolution.

CHAPTER TWO

CONSCIOUS EVOLUTION

INDUISM AND BUDDHISM, which have a common root, present a strikingly similar view of the evolution of Being and Consciousness into the physical form of the universe, although they use different methods, images, and intellectual constructs. According to both Hindu and Buddhist beliefs, we were created first in nonphysical realms. Long before this physical universe—our home—appeared, our consciousness descended from the purely spiritual space it occupied into a mental realm, where mind could exist. Powerful spiritual ideas coalesced into understandable concepts of what creation looked like, and it ultimately materialized into the physical universe.

We descended to the physical plane to learn, grow, and evolve as physical entities, and then finally to return to the nonphysical existence from which we first appeared. By the time we return, however, we will have accumulated much knowledge about physical creation, about the joys and cares of living in physical bodies, about choice and consequence, about illness and recovery from physical, as well as mental and emotional difficulties. Although we will have triumphantly returned to that exalted state from which we came, we will be changed through our experiences and will have become something more, in some way that is difficult to define.

In the West, we speak of the *soul* as the essence of each person. In the East, this same essence is most often expressed as the *atman*. With some variation, Buddhists often refer to our real nature as something akin to *cosmic mind.* However, the origin of our souls or the genesis of the *atman* or cosmic mind is not so easy to track down. One must rely upon the myths and stories of India, where the beginnings of the universe and all of its inhabitants are presented in easy to grasp stories and fables.

MODERN PHYSICS AND CREATION

The monoblock theory of the creation of the universe, widely held in modern physics, holds that originally all of the matter in the known universe was compacted into a single mass at one location. The force generated by such a great mass concentrated in one place produced an explosion of great magnitude: the "big bang."

It scattered matter in all directions at a velocity close to the speed of light, producing the universe as we know it. As matter began to cool and coalesce, suns and planets and galaxies were formed, and the universe as we know it came into being. According to our current understanding of the laws of physics, there will come a time far in the future when that original impetus, generated by the explosion of the monoblock, will slow and finally come to an end. Matter will have slowed its headlong flight and eventually halt. This running down and dispersal of all the matter and energy in the universe, what science calls "entropy," will also cause suns to expand in their dying gasp and consume the planets, even as black holes increase their size and engulf stars and whole galaxies. Essentially, the universe will come to an end like a wound-up clock exhausting its spring.

You may have noticed something is missing from this theory. Since science tells us that something cannot come from nothing, where did the monoblock come from? The common answer from physicists and chemists is, "We don't know." Some scientists do attempt explanation through the use of what has come to be known as "string theory" that postulates the existence of multiple universes. But there still has been no definitive explanation of where that monoblock came from.

The venerable spiritual texts and teachings from the Vedic tradition do offer an explanation through the same stories and fables that explain the origin of the soul or *atman* we each carry. The legend of Narayana explains the creation of the universe and mankind as it has been passed down through scripture and story for countless generations in India. When the journey of the soul or *atman* comes to an end with all its attendant accomplishments, it will most assuredly have been worth it. We each will have reached a new phase of divinity and immortality that grew, seemingly unsuspected, from that original impetus.

Descended from the very highest levels of the created universe, where consciousness and power are one, into successively denser and denser states of existence, the soul has followed the original impetus of a being called Narayana. The story of Narayana is discussed in more detail in Chapter 6. It then began a quest via a journey of involution to learn about materiality. The initial part of the journey finally comes to an end at the base of our spine. Here our individual evolution now commences with all of its experiences, choices, consequences, and distractions toward that state which we left so long ago.

Our wondrous soul also contains the essence of compassion. Since the evolving consciousness will experience both pain and enjoyment while occupying a physical form, the soul-*atman* empowers that consciousness with two gifts. The first is free will or choice. Exercising this gift, individual consciousness may embrace, evade, or put off until another time specific experiences to be encountered and lessons to be learned. It also may select some particular path from among many options back to union with Narayana. The second gift is a "device" that allows the individual consciousness to operate in the relative world of materiality. Called the *ahamkara* in Sanskrit, it is the ego that can choose *how* and *whether* to grow and evolve while in the physical universe. The lowly ego is even offered the priceless gift of becoming divine, should it choose to consciously evolve.

Through spiritual growth, the human ego can attain immortality by joining with the *atman* to become something new it could never have anticipated. The ancient Indian mechanism for the ego to accomplish this journey is called *Ganesha* or *Ganapathi* in the Hindu faith. The Ganesha-Ganapathi chakra (operating as a phantom chakra) has its permanent residence in the first of the six chakras located at the bottom of the spine. These centers represent a hidden map for our common journey back up the spine to that divinity from which we have come.

But how did we come to have such an opportunity? How did the chakra system come about? The answer may astound you and challenge your credulity.

CHAPTER THREE

THE COMPLAINTS OF THE EARTH

HE STANZAS OF DYZAN form a foundation for H.P. Blavatsky's two-volume metaphysical masterpiece, *The Secret Doctrine.*[3] Yet much of what they impart is unknown to students and practitioners of techniques employed to promote spiritual growth. The stanzas begin with an amazing dialogue between the earth and the sun, in which the earth is complaining that she cannot get enough spiritual energy for her advancement. Modern science has taught us, of course, that the earth is way out on a spiral arm of the galaxy, so we know our home is very far away from the center of the galaxy which is ablaze with fusions of stars and an abundance of light. But when the Stanzas of Dyzan were written thousands of years ago, there were no scientific records to explain what the location of the earth was nor the amount of light it receives. So records of ancient complaints of the earth, understood in this context, are remarkable.

The physicality of light is only one of the qualities of light. We know from the nimbus of the saints in pictorial renderings, from the halo of the Christ and the Buddha, from the light surrounding the carriers of the Ark of the Covenant, as well as from other spiritual sources, that light has spiritual qualities as well as physical ones. In fact, accumulations of spiritual light seem to go hand in hand with spiritual evolution. So it is not surprising that *The Secret Doctrine* focuses on the spiritual dimensions of the earth's complaints.

Hearing the woes of the earth, the sun (the Great Shining One) agrees to carry the complaints of the earth to the higher realms. In the midst of this conversation that takes place over thousands of years, the stanzas report that the earth rolls over on her side before continuing the conversation. I read this and thought, "Well, there is a clear reference to a pole shift if ever I saw one!"

The earth was not patient. Taking matters as her own responsibility, she began to create beings on her own. Dinosaurs were the result. Powerful forces in both the physical and spiritual realms did not view the experiment favorably. Boom! An asteroid or comet hit the earth and the giant creatures disappeared in a cosmic flash.

Meanwhile, in the higher realms, a spiritual council determined that the earth should, indeed, get help for her evolutionary progress. A highly evolved race of spiritual beings was asked to help. They declined saying that although the goal was a noble one, giving this kind of aid was not their job or province. Blavatsky declares that we know these beings today, mythically, as the angels who refused God.

Another race of spiritually advanced beings volunteered to help, lending their light to the creation of a race of beings that will help the earth evolve. Their plan was that this race of beings, human beings, would act as a step-down transformer. They would receive energy of the highest and finest sort in a receptacle capable of holding sublime consciousness at the crown of their structure. They would then step-down the energy through successive centers, until the base of the organism was reached. This energy would be in a form that the earth could use in her evolution.

The major chakras in the human subtle body are ruled by the basic elements—both physical and nonphysical. Starting from the sixth chakra at the brow center and moving down the chakras, the following is a list of the elements that are the essence of the chakras:

Sixth .... Mind
Fifth .... Ether
Fourth .... Air
Third .... Fire
Second .... Water
First .... Earth

According to the Stanzas of Dyzan, the finest spiritual energy comes into the crown chakra and is stepped down, chakra to chakra, until it reaches our base chakra, ruled by the earth principle. Here, that energy that started in our crown chakra is now in a form that the earth can use for her own evolutionary progress. Nowhere is the innate nobility that humans feel about themselves referred to in the initial stages of creation. Our importance was only highlighted by the function for which we were designed. Interestingly, though, some very old spiritual concepts are reflected in quite a different way than we are used to thinking about them. "Man is created in the image of God." Yes, that certainly can be applied in a cosmic sense. "As above, so below." Yes, this can also be true, but in a way quite apart from our usual manner of thinking about it.

But from the initial description in the Stanzas of Dyzan, humanity had no real importance of its own. We were designed, essentially, as a tool for the earth. A step-down transformer is nothing more than a tool, something one uses when necessary, and then discards or lays down when not in use.

Fortunately, consideration of us as a species does not end there. The stanzas go on to explain, through lengthy explanations that go into Volume II of this nearly 1500 page work, that the original council decided, as part of our construction, we would be naturally sentient, or self aware. Now sentience is different from intelligence. A plant demonstrates a certain kind of intelligence as it grows naturally toward the sun. One can call it instinct but, viewed in a broad context, instinct is merely one kind of intelligence. Animals also demonstrate intelligence: the dog chasing a thrown stick, a cat rubbing against our leg, fish with their noses pointed toward the top of an aquarium waiting for the food they know will eventually arrive. All of these activities involve intelligence of a kind, but sentience is different.

Sentience means self-awareness. Sentience means an understanding of oneself as a being in the universe. Sentience means thought and reflection.

That long-ago, faraway council, described by the stanzas, realized that it had created a race of sentient beings for a specific purpose and then essentially discarded them. This was not right. No standard of ethics or morality can justify the discard of a sentient race. So it was further decided that this race of beings would be given the opportunity to become that for which it was the vehicle, if it should so choose.

Now, the humble purpose for which we were created was turned upside down. If we started by receiving the very finest of energy from the highest place in the spiritual as well as physical planes of the universe, then we could also be that, become that, evolve to that. Different ball game. Journeying from the humble to the sublime was now part of our birthright, if we *chose* to do so.

Understandably, the earth began to get attention from other more advanced beings in the spheres of light above.

CHAPTER FOUR

THE PRICELESS OPPORTUNITIES IN HUMAN BIRTH

HERE ARE SUPERNATURAL REALMS where spiritual delight surpasses anything in the everyday mind of humanity. We are largely unaware of these realms and their spiritual treasures, save through scriptural references from the various religions. As the Stanzas of Dyzan, the Vedas, the Puranas and other spiritual texts reveal, there are many such realms. But however glorious they may be, two things become evident the more one studies these scriptures. First, only one or two realms even approach the highest ones. The rest are somewhere below the highest. Second, although the lifespan of such beings who inhabit them may be extraordinarily long, most are not immortal. With few exceptions, the sublime egos with which they conduct their sentient lives do not exist forever.

Now comes this new species on the earth that, because of the purpose for which they have been created, has the opportunity not only to reach the highest plane of consciousness but also, through the mechanism of its sentience, its ego, it has the opportunity to become immortal. Given this, quite understandably, some of these celestial beings concluded that if they wanted to increase their spiritual lot and have the ability to become immortal, they would have to incarnate on Planet Earth.

The current popular mindset believes that if a being that is advanced in some way wants to come to earth, it must do so in a mechanical contraption of some sort, like a flying saucer. But truly evolved beings would not have to resort to such primitive devices. They could just be born here. Again, there is ample evidence that this is true, even if it is more difficult for us to comprehend. We understand "mechanical" far better than "spiritual."

Jesus was said to come to Earth through Immaculate Conception. In The Ramayana, Rama and his brothers arrived through the vehicle of a fire ceremony that produced a ball of divine substance that became Rama, Bharata, Lakshmana, and Shatrugna, who grew in the wombs of three women, one of whom had twins. In the Vedas and Puranas, various beings appeared through other than ordinary means. Markandeya, Dattatreya, and other entities appeared through spiritual means, springing from esoteric knowledge and practice.

If one follows various scriptures and is willing to think outside the box of mechanical devices, beings from other realms have been coming here for a long time. And they know what the potentials are when they take a human birth. Indeed, in Hindu and Buddhist scriptures one finds again and again the idea that even the gods (small "g," of course) desire human embodiment.

WHY DO THEY COME?

There are two reasons they desire to come to earth. First, they can improve their position in the universe through their spiritual efforts. Scriptures from India and Tibet are replete with stories about yogis and lamas of various ranks meditating in caves for a dozen years or more, during which time they advance rapidly. The celestials know the potential contained in human birth, while most of us do not. Knowing what they can achieve, they advance rapidly.

The records of the being who became the very first Shankaracharya indicate that he was a prodigy. He became a swami, a monk, at age twelve. Madvacharya, another prodigy, when just a toddler went to various temples and declared that there was one great truth contained in all the idols. When his father would give him spiritual teachings every morning, Madva would interrupt his review of the previous day's lesson and tell his father, "You taught me that yesterday. Teach me something new." Ramanujacharya, similarly, understood the feminine nature of power at a young age. He was so advanced that he corrected an interpretation of scripture by his teacher while still a very young man. The teacher was so upset he plotted to kill the young student, but later he became the student of his former student.

These are not ordinary people. And there are beings in human embodiment, as this is written, who are not ordinary. For example, there is a class of beings in India called Jagad Gurus. Although I discuss gurus in more detail in a subsequent chapter, for now I will briefly discuss Jagad Gurus.

Jagad means "world" and guru means "that which dispels darkness." So Jagad Guru roughly translates as an enlightener of the whole world. It is a staggering concept. By the Grace of God I have met three different Jagad Gurus: two from the Shankaracharya tradition and one from the Madvacharya tradition. In Chapter 27 I will tell of one of those meetings. For now, let me state that meeting a Jagad Guru is a life-altering experience. Aside from the actual experience of meeting such a person, there comes the understanding of how little we in the West know about truly advanced spiritual beings. Let me also observe that it is easy to conclude that these great beings are probably not from this realm. They do not come from earth, even though they are walking around here in human bodies.

They come here to take advantage of the opportunity afforded by human birth to advance very rapidly on a spiritual level. There is also another reason. Once in human form, they see the potential of the species as a whole. They get a glimpse of what we will eventually become and they decide to help. They render aid through the power of their presence. They give help individually to those whom they meet in their spiritual work. They are able to recognize one another, so each Jagad Guru appoints his own successor while they are both relatively young. And even as they render aid and bless the world, they hide most of what they are able to accomplish spiritually. They hide their accomplishments, because they are humble and because they do not want to overshadow the evolving humans who might become too intimidated to continue the strenuous work toward individual spiritual evolution, if they understood too much about the level of attainment a Jagad Guru embodies. Any ostentatious display of their knowledge and extent of their divine abilities would only get in our collective way.

HUMANITY IS UNIQUE

So the great ones who come to earth put their shoulder to the wheel of human evolution, even as they also evolve themselves. They see, they understand, and they help. Because the very nature of our form is constructed to contain, access, and transmit to the earth the very highest vibrations (the highest consciousness and states of being contained by sentience in the universe) we are unique.

We can evolve and grow in ways that most humans understand through a somewhat hazy awareness, and the opportunities are profound.

CHAPTER FIVE

GODS AND GODDESSES

OR MOST OF US, the journey from being individual beings united with the consciousness of the universe into and through the labyrinth of physical existence and then back to union with an all-pervading consciousness appears to be a strictly intellectual exercise. However, stories of the Hindu gods and goddesses with their struggles between good and evil make understanding this journey easier. They richly illustrate many positive and negative aspects of consciousness that humankind has in common with these divine beings.

As we follow the evolution of our own individual consciousness, learning and retelling these myths and stories from the Puranas can be useful. Spiritual teachers of India tell ancient stories whose characters represent various (and sometimes conflicting) ideas, forces, and concepts. Instead of dry principles set within a tableau of spiritual laws and metaphysical constructs, we have a rich cosmology composed of stories, myths, and legends that catalogue the very creation of the universe and the appearance of individual souls. They make the interrelationships clear, even if the spiritual or scientific facts are not detailed. Mystical ideas that explain the soul's role in the interplay of consciousness and power within our everyday existence are similarly conveyed by these stories.

Some spiritual teachers of great attainment have taught us that each of the gods and goddesses in the Vedic pantheon are anthropomorphized principles that represent a quality that exists in each of us.

Although any one of those qualities may be only barely evident, or even dormant, the potential for us to develop these qualities is certain. Other teachers say that these great beings in the Vedic pantheon exist in some form of reality, and interact with humanity through both meditation and incarnation, meaning they actually get born here to do certain work. Whichever of these scenarios is true, all of the teachers from various philosophic camps speak about the greatness that each of us can attain.

We have among us talented mathematicians and musicians, poets and engineers. Each person who demonstrates genius in his or her field has combined a latent predisposition for it with a great deal of hard work. Notwithstanding the genes that may indicate massive talent for this or that ability, the achievement of greatness in any field is usually hard won. Talent and perspiration make a potent mixture.

Similarly, each god and goddesses, at the very least, represents a great spiritual status of a particular kind that we may also achieve. But the same ingredients apply to reach the state they represent. These are: talent and effort. Through diligence and effort we may achieve some measure of what the divine ones have attained. I believe talent without character and discipline is like a petrified flower. It has substance and duration and perhaps even beauty of a sort, but it does not grow. It is frozen in place.

None among us is "average." Each of us has the power to achieve stupendous spiritual heights, manifesting qualities of one or more of the Hindu gods and goddesses. In this context, the words of Jesus resound in our ears as he tells the disciples, "Know ye not ye are gods?"

To the genuine Hindu and Buddhist spiritual seeker, this idea is so well understood and accepted that it is taken for granted. The recent history of India overflows with towering flesh and blood spiritual teachers of great attainment, some of whom we have heard about in the West, who taught a few chosen disciples who then taught many others. I am referring to Paramahansa Yogananda (and his lineage of great gurus), Paramahansa Muktananda (as well as his guru, the great Bhagavan Nityanananda), Sadguru Sant Keshavadas, Swami Sivananda of the

Divine Life Society, Satya Sai Baba, Ananda Mayi Ma, Ramana Maharshi, Brahmananda Saraswati, Neem Karoli Baba, the Dalai Lamas, and Karmapas, to name just a few.

SECRETS REVEALED

Through these and other spiritual giants, we in the West have been exposed to the vast spiritual knowledge that previously had remained hidden in India and Tibet for many centuries. It is only recently in the last hundred and fifty years that much of this knowledge has been revealed to Western seekers. Some of this knowledge rests upon a foundation of practice of Sanskrit mantras. These spiritual formulas of immense specific power are matrices of sound energy. They have the capacity to bring the power represented by the gods and goddesses to each of us. If we combine the talent within our "spiritual genes," with dedication and effort, the promise of those "genes" can be realized as "genius."

Our understanding of the chakras and their potency in our lives has come through the promulgation of Indian and Tibetan views of ways to approach spiritual matters. Issues of health, perception, power, and service to humanity in our culture are now being met with new ideas and new methods for expression. Yoga postures (*asanas*), Sanskrit mantras, and Vedic philosophy have profoundly affected our culture, influencing thinking from the university classroom to the local YWCA.

Throughout the myriad influences of the Eastern disciplines and concepts, a single idea echoes in the fringes of conscious understanding and subconscious assumptions: "We are much more than we currently know." And we can become that "more" through study and effort. There are ancient paths we can tread to realize our spiritual destiny. We can develop to such a high level that we approach the lofty consciousness and power represented by the gods and goddesses from old India. It is our spiritual birthright.

MOUNT UP, PILGRIM

Each member of the Hindu pantheon has a vehicle upon which he or she rides. Usually the vehicle is a bird or animal that contains certain qualities that help it manifest the principle it transports. For example, Shiva, the Hindu figure that represents the concept of consciousness, has Nandi the Bull as his vehicle. Nandi, carrying Shiva, demonstrates the inexorable nature of consciousness. Just as a bull is nearly unstoppable in any common way, the consciousness of the universe is inexorable in its march to self-fulfillment. The image of the bull encapsulates an idea of power of movement that is massive, yet casual at the same time. Only when challenged does the bull pose a threat. Similarly, the very consciousness of the universe proceeds inexorably even while it is challenged. Black holes, colliding galaxies, and on a more personal earthly scale, earthquakes and pole shifts qualify as challenging physical events. Whether on a large scale or smaller planetary scale, these events are just as unstoppable as Nandi the Bull.

In another example, Subramanya, the eldest son of Shiva and Parvati, has the peacock as his vehicle. As an early representation of individual consciousness, the Subramanya principle with its peacock vehicle is a most beautiful, yet carefully hidden map of how the consciousness of an individual being moves "down" into a physical existence from a transcendent place of consciousness and is united with all creation. By examining the peacock we can access a deeper meaning of Subramanya, who is most often referred to as the god of war. In his deeper spiritual significance, Subramanya stands as the highest possible individual attainment of consciousness. Beyond that state there is only the complete absorption and unity with absolute Being. There are mantra formulas and strategies that will supercharge our efforts to reach that high state of individual consciousness.

But what is the source of that higher state of consciousness? Something cannot come from nothing, so what is the source of both the universe and that sublime state of consciousness towards which we are headed?

CHAPTER 6

NARAYANA

N A REALM beyond the laws of physics, beyond the minds of humans, beyond the ken of any save the most highly spiritually advanced, lies a reality completely different from the one we inhabit. There, a divine being called Narayana sleeps. Narayana exists in a realm governed by a type of mental activity altogether different from the one we currently are engaged in. *This* universe, the realm *we* call home, does not exist at all in the realm that Narayana occupies. There, the galaxies as we know them are not even a cosmic conjecture. Sentient beings are far from conception. But as Narayana sleeps, this four-armed androgynous being prepares to create our universe. When he dreams, he generates the stuff of our universe where we will be players in a divine drama.

The epic of Narayana describes his dream and the creation of the world. As the dream opens, a lotus flower blossoms from Narayana's navel and starts to grow. It grows and changes until it resembles an egg from which ultimately hatches a four-faced masculine being called Brahma. Brahma experiences an overwhelming urge to create and multiply. From within him the great feminine energy embodied as the goddess Saraswati speaks through his mind, and the cosmos is born. Saraswati is Brahma's power, the feminine energy of creation. Creatures of every form and description come into existence, and the "play" of the universe unfolds. In this story, Narayana is divine Beingness, Brahma is Mind that experiences desire, and Saraswati is Divine Speech, which is not unlike the power contained in the opening phrase of the Gospel of John, "In the beginning was the word," or God's divine command in Genesis, "Let there be light."

Brahma is the creative principle of the universe that emerges from the navel lotus of Narayana. Brahma is a metaphor for all of creation: its laws, its inherent consciousness and intelligence, as well as its consciously manifested potencies which operate through sages, saints, rishis, *devas*, celestials, bodhisattvas, and divine beings of various nature, temperament, and description. Narayana is the name given in stories and in Hindu scriptures to that which is the sum and substance of all the manifest and unmanifest realms. Narayana is that which is neither created nor destroyed but which precedes the creation, life, and destruction of the universe. Brahma's creative urge operates through the form of this expanding universe for trillions of years, until it dissolves back into Narayana. This is not unlike the scientific view where the universe becomes spent and subsequently absorbed into black holes where it disappears altogether. Narayana, however, is neither created nor destroyed. And this cycle of creation repeats itself, as following the destruction, later, another Brahma appears to begin the process again.

The term "Brahma" does not appear in the Vedas. Its creation stems from the Sanskrit word "Brih" which means "to grow" or "to expand." By growing from the navel lotus of Narayana, this has also become known as the Golden Egg of Creation, sometimes called Hiranyagharba. *Brahma is the name for the principle which creates the manifest realms.* The Vedas proclaim in the Purusha Suktam that "three quarters of this universe are in indestructible realms above. Only one quarter of this universe appears and disappears, comes and then goes." That one-quarter is where we, in our Ego-Mind-Personality, are operating. Brahma is all of it.

SHORT BRAHMA MANTRA

Practicing the mantras of Brahma can make one a rishi or sage. Over time, the mysteries of creation unravel and reveal themselves. This short mantra proclaims the wholeness of the universe, as well as one's identification with all of it. Speaking it regularly in mantra meditations eventually cements one's identity with a unified universe.

Aham Brahmasmi
[Ah-huhm Brah-mahs-mee]

NARAYANA TEACHES HIMSELF NEW THINGS

In the various stories and scriptures pertaining to him, Brahma's progenitor, Narayana, is called several things of a personal nature rather than a cosmic nature: "a flame existing within the bosom of us all, but not of the physical universe," "the supreme soul," "the Soul of all the souls," "the cause and repository of being and consciousness," "that Being of which we are a part that 'bodies itself forth' to protect the pious and the good within this universe," "the guru (spiritual preceptor) of all the worlds," and more. We will explore Narayana in a personal way further when we take up the subject of the Hrit Padma in a subsequent chapter, but for now we rejoin Narayana's sublime slumber.

During his sleep, Narayana has set forces into motion and now watches as the laws of creation begin to operate through Brahma. It is fascinating. Great as Narayana is, by watching all that Brahma consequently sets into motion, Narayana is experiencing spontaneity and, yes, even learning of a sort. Narayana participates in the drama of his dream by placing himself squarely in the center of it, even while Brahma and his power Saraswati are engaged in creating the universe.

In Narayana's dream, two seemingly paradoxical things are happening simultaneously. The spheres of the universe are being formed, and individual beings are being created. As each new being is created, Narayana simultaneously installs a small bit of himself inside it. Now each being is just the tiniest bit separated from him while still being a part of him. He places a small, thumb-sized blaze of pure spirituality that is his own divine substance into the spiritual heart of every person and entity.

Narayana's self-insertion into the dream-drama of our universe pro-
duces two things. First, in the small piece Narayana gave of himself to
sentient beings, there is now a state of bliss, called *ananda* in Sanskrit.
This bliss is actually the first stage of an illusory separation between
Narayana, lying in the inky blackness outside the universe, while
Narayana as the soul-*atman* is our own divine essence.

The soul realizes that it is part of the great being Narayana. However,
it is also aware of the slightest veil of separation between it and the rest
of Narayana in another realm. This piece of Narayana understands that
while it is embodying a seemingly separate existence, it knows that it is
part of Narayana. This knowledge of itself produces a state of ecstasy,
bliss, also called *ananda*.

At the same time, feeling that it is somehow separate makes it the
"appreciator" of this state of ecstasy. It is the beginning of a distinction
between "self" and "other." The *ananda* state of consciousness is what we
humans experience either just before merging with the great divine, or
just after separating from it. The fact of our apparent separation
produces the concept of us as "individual experiencers."

This is the beginning of sentience. After all, sentience is also based
upon the idea of separation: separation from the other parts of this reality and separation from other beings, in this case, apparent separation
from Narayana. Ultimately, the whole idea of sentience rests upon a
division between self and other things or persons, often called "duality."
So, then, at the point where sentience appears, the plot thickens.

Narayana dreams a universe that is musically unscored. The dream
will write its own melody and accompaniment spontaneously. With a
satisfied snore, Narayana wills his individual essences in the dream, our
souls, to begin a journey of accumulating experiences that will ultimately become a descent into material existence. Individual souls will
begin to form layers around themselves that become energy processing centers called chakras. Some of these individual beings are created
with a bit more of the substance of Narayana. They will become the
great sages, celestials, and Maha Siddhas, who understand the nature of
the creation of the universe. They understood at the dawn of time the

mystical statement: "I am in the Father and the Father is in Me." Simultaneously, in this way, the whole universe is formed and each individual being takes shape.

The supreme state of blissful union of individual self with Narayana takes place in us at the seventh spiritual center or Sahasrara Chakra at the top of the head. This state of total union, in which individuality does not appear, then gives way to a lower superconscious state that while still sublime is now experiencing still more separation from Narayana in his discrete realm. The new and still glorious individual consciousness is the closest that our individual consciousness may come to its full expression without rejoining or merging back again into Narayana, the source.

But there is one small difficulty with the separation of the individual self from the all-encompassing reality. So far we have looked at the evolution of the universe from what is a Vaishnava point of view. There are similar viewpoints by followers of Shiva and Shakti, for instance. In the Vaishnava view, Narayana is usually seen, both mystically and scholastically, as the highest point of Vishnu (the preserver). Never mind that the Narayana Suktam, the ancient hymn describing Narayana, declares that "He is Brahma, Vishnu, and Shiva. He is Supreme." Never mind because certain scriptures describing Shiva call Him supreme. And certain others call Shakti—the great Universal Feminine Force—supreme. The truth is, they are all correct. But it is also true that each earthly group of souls, following each of the paths, declares that its way is best, highest, fastest, or some other expression of exclusive supremacy. And so we have the endless squabble of religion and the bickering of sectarianism. But mystic truth, like a well-cut diamond has many points of view. All of them are accurate in their own context.

TRUTH IS ONE

In his book, *Siva and His Worship*, Swami Sivananda, founder of the Divine Life Society, explains very early in the text that "The higher Vishnu as Narayana, and the higher Shiva are the same."[4] As long as there is form, he explains, they are identical. So it does not matter if we call this Being, from which the universe has come, Narayana or Shiva. By any name we call it, it is what it is. The formless, however, is another matter. The great Sivananda calls it *Paramashiva*.

In *Laya Yoga*, by Shyam Sundar Goswami, *Paramashiva* comes up in reference to Narayana, "Narayana is Parama Shiva — Supreme Consciousness. He is Infinite and All, and so, he is beyond the universe of mind-matter. But when he is in concentration, being established in his own secondless *sattvic* form, he is also conscious of the Beingness of his own power, which, as Supreme Power, is one and the same with him."[5]

Since Narayana as Vishnu takes incarnation in many forms for the preservation and restoration of Dharma, I have chosen to refer to this being as Narayana. The Narayana Suktam listed below is a sacred hymn to Narayana.

This is the mantra of Narayana:

Om Namo Narayanayah
[Om Nah-moh Nah-rah-yah-nah-yah]

This mantra affirms the existence of the immortal self living in a mortal body.

NARAYANA SUKTAM
HYMN TO THE SPIRITUAL FLAME
WITHIN THE SACRED HEART

The Narayana Suktam is a song to the Universal Self which resides in all beings and which is the desired end of all worship. The last verse clearly states that it is Brahma, Vishnu, and Shiva all in one. Narayana is all forms of the Hindu Trinity in one. It is the threefold flame of the esotericists, burning in the paricarp of the sacred heart. The sacred heart is an eight-petalled lotus called the Hrit Padma, located just two finger-widths below the heart center or Anahata Chakra.

1) *Om Shahasra Shirsham Devam Vishwaksham Vishwa Shambhuvam;*
   Vishwam Narayanam Devam Aksharam Pararam Padam.

We meditate on Narayana who is infinite consciousness, self-effulgent witness, cosmic being who is the Self of all the selves, who forms the cosmos and who is indestructible and the Supreme abode of Peace.

2) *Vishwataha Parama Nityam Vishwam Narayanam Harim;*
   Vishwa Mevedam Purushas Tadvishwa-Mupa-Jivathi.

We meditate on Narayana whose essence lies beyond this universe. Yet He is the close one, eternal, all pervading Truth and forgiver of all errors. Not only is He the support of this entire universe, he is in reality this universe itself.

3) *Patim Vishwasyat-meshwaram Shashwatum Shivam Achyutam;*
   Narayanam Mahajneyam Vishwatmanam Parayanam.

We meditate on Narayana who is the Lord of the Universe, substance of all the souls, eternal abode of blessedness, invincible, the Universal Soul, the highest object to be sought after and the Supreme abode of rest.

4) *Narayana Param Brahma, Tattwam Narayanah Paraha;*
   Narayana Paro Jyotir Atma Narayanah Paraha;
   Narayana Paro Dhyata Dhyanam Narayanah Paraha.

Narayana is the ultimate creator and the supreme principle of Truth which pervades everything. Narayana is the Light Eternal, the Cosmic Self seen through the individual self. Narayana is the ultimate object of all meditation. Indeed contemplating Narayana, there is no other meditation.

5) *Yacha Kinchit Jagatsarvam, Drishyatae Shruyatepi Va;*
   Antarbahischa Tatsarvam Vyapya Narayanah Sthithaha.

Whatever is seen or heard, Narayana is that which pervades the within and without of everything.

6) *Anantham Avyayam Kavin Samundrentam Vishwa Shambhuvam;*
   Padmakosha Pratikasham Hridayam Chapya-dhomukham.

We meditate on Narayana in the budding lotus in our sacred heart, for He is the infinite, invulnerable and omniscient life of all lives. All blessings come from Him.

7) *Adho Nistya Vitasyante Nabhya-mupari Tishtathi;*
   Jwalamala Kulam Bhati Vishwasya-yatanam Mahat.

Below the root of the throat chakra and twelve inches above the navel center is the mystic sacred heart. There shines Lord Narayana surrounded by a garland of flames.

8) *Santatan Shilabhistu Lambatya Kosha Sannibham;*
   Tasyantae Sushiram Sukshmam Tasmin Sarvam Pratishtitam.

There one sees the heart's lotus, surrounded by all of the sheathes of existence and thousands of *nadis*. Near it is the subtle channel of the spine (*shushumna*), wherein the Universe is made manifest.

9) *Tasya Madhye Mahan-agnir Vishwachir Vishwa-tomukhaha;*
   Sogra Bhugwi Bhajantishtan Aharama-jaraha Kavihi;
   Tirya Gurdhwa Madhash-yayi Rashmya-yastasya Santata.

In the *shushumna* at the navel center is a brilliant all-encompassing cosmic fire. This fire digests the food, nourishes the body, and distributes energy to all parts of the body. This nature of this fire is wisdom and it is inexhaustible, spreading its rays all over the body.

10) *Santapayati Swam Dehama-pada-talamastakaha;*
   Tasya Madhye Vahnishikha Aniyordhwa Vyavishithaha.

This cosmic fire keeps the entire body warm with the life principle, yet in its midst there is an even subtler flame facing upwards.

11) *Nilatoyoda Madyasta Vidyulle-kheva Bhasvara;*
   Nivara Shuka-vattanvi Pita Bhaswat-yanupama.

This flame shines as a silver-white line of electricity emerging from a center of dark blue clouds.

12) *Tasya Shikhaya Madhye Paramatma Vyavasthithaha;*
   Sa Brahma, Sa Shivaha, Sa Harihi, Sendra Soksharaha
   Paramaha Swarat.

And in the midst of this flame, Narayana is established. Beyond this universe, yet manifesting himself within it, He is indestructible. Verily He is Brahma, He is Shiva, He is Vishnu and Supreme.

13) *Vidya Buddhi Dhanaish Varya Putra Poutradi Sama Padaha*
   Pushpanjali Prada Nena Dehime Ipsitam Varam
   Mantra Pushpam Samarpayami.

We ask now for knowledge, pure intellect, wealth and prosperity, progeny and material happiness. Please bestow the same unto us. So saying, we offer these mantras flowers to you.

14) *Om Namo Narayana Vidmahae, Vasudevaya Dhimahi, Tanno Vishnum*
   Prachodayat.

May we realize this Narayana the indwelling being who is the spirit of all. May we meditate upon the Vishnu aspect of this Great Being and thus become illumined ones.

SUBRAMANYA AND GANESHA-GANAPATHI

Shiva and his sons Ganesha and Subramanya are stars in the drama of our evolution. The Subramanya vehicle, the peacock, serves as a metaphor through which Subramanya manifests. When the male peacock is just walking along, we think we understand his beauty because there are a few visible feathers of various hues. They are pleasant looking enough, and the spine of bright hues coming from the headband he wears is interesting and colorful but not really spectacular. But when the peacock spreads its multicolored fan, an entirely new and previously hidden dimension of beauty, color, and design comes into view. If we have not seen such a thing before, the unfolding of a peacock tail fan can be almost confounding in its appeal.

With a similar dramatic appearance, like Subramanya the soul moves down from the crown chakra at the top of the head into the rest of the brain, where the peacock's tail of the chakras appears. Later it will move into the body. In the brain, the soul or *atman* understands itself as a separate conscious entity creating a new physical form. When our individual *atman* was totally immersed in Narayana, it was in a state of consciousness *in unity* with the consciousness of the entire universe. We were as a cup poured into the ocean. Although the cup of our individual existence stood ready, the contents of our being was immersed in the great water of the ocean, nonseparate, part of it. When the cup dips into the oceans and brings up a portion of the water, separation occurs. The water in the cup is now separate from the water of the ocean.

In like manner, when our individual being is resting in the crown chakra, we know nothing of self and other. There is no separation. There is only Narayana and the bliss of absorption in it. Then the center of our being dips downwards into the rest of the brain, and we become aware of our individual existence because we experience separation from Narayana. We understand the potential offered by individual existence. A divine ego forms, and we become self-aware and cognizant of others who are also self-aware.

This self-awareness is akin to the few feathers of the Subramanya's peacock. As being descends further from the head into the spine, the magnificent potential of the chakras comes into full view, one by one, stunning in the potential of their capabilities through the elements that predominate in each: mind, ether or space, air, fire, water, and finally earth. Vast spiritual abilities become self-evident. Time and space become baubles hanging from the tree of our individual existence like so many ornaments and brightly colored lights. With the entrance of the soul into the brain and moving to the base of what will become our head, the peacock's fan begins to spread. Power and consciousness previously hidden from view become magnificently apparent as the chakras come into view, one by one. The soul does the equivalent of a mirthful chuckle and seemingly says to itself, "Just think of the possibilities!"

From the Subramanya state of consciousness in the head just below the crown chakra, where our highest individual superconscious awareness operates, we descend into the successive dimensions of familiar reality represented by the chakras and the elements that predominate or rule them.

First stop is the Ajna Chakra at the brow center where overall unity is established, insuring that all levels of subsequent creation will be integrated into this place of consciousness. From here spring the pairs of complementary opposites: male and female, hot and cold, yin and yang, and so on. Forms of spiritual electrical currents come into being and vehicles for containing and directing them are created: the masculine current *ida*; the feminine current *pinagala*; and the *shushumna* or spine. The latter will hold centers called chakras that correspond to the great levels or spheres of the manifest universe. Then the *atman* slips into the newly created spine and begins its descent toward materiality.

Second stop is the Vishuddha or throat chakra, where time-transcending ether is born. From the Vishuddha Chakra, all the principles of matter-yet-to-become-manifest are seen in perfect harmony, as well as the construct of "time" in which these forces will play out for billions and billions of years. Famed mystic Edgar Cayce was able to reach this state while in deep sleep. Viewing time and space on a single canvas,

Cayce was able to direct people to obscure cures, even to the extent that journeys to country stores were made by the faithful who found a specific "blue bottle behind the can in the middle of the third shelf."

Next, the soul descends with perfect consciousness into the Anahata Chakra or heart center. For reasons known only to them and to other superconscious entities, certain classes of beings stopped their descent here. They became the immortal celestials that, from time to time, interact in the realm of human affairs. A majority of souls, however, continued to descend into the realms of matter to experience and learn. The *atman* observes that the heart center provides the best possible vantage point for learning and observing the play of materiality. A small eight-petaled chakra called the Hrit Padma is formed just below the Anahata Chakra or heart center into which the soul settles as it continues to create the rest of its spiritual vehicle, the human subtle and physical bodies.

One by one, the lower chakras come into existence: the Manipura Chakra at the solar plexus and the Swadhisthana Chakra at the sacral plexus. Finally, the earth is reached at the bottom of the spine with the creation of the Muladhara Chakra at the coccygeal plexus. Here, the creative power of the very universe itself rests in each human individual. Having reached this place, the divine feminine power (kundalini shakti) obeys the primal desire of the involving consciousness and goes into a semi-sleep mode, weaving a resting place in three turns of spiral power that can be seen at the base of everyone's spine by the clairvoyant adept.

Now, the soul has completed the first phase of its directive from Narayana. It has "involved" into a state of individual existence in a material universe. Involution is complete. The divine essence, shimmering like a flame, rests in the sacred heart; here this light "not of this world" always shines.

There is a saying in metaphysical circles, "Evolution presupposes involution." Through the soul's decent into our human incarnations, through involution, Narayana as the *atman*, our divine essence, will begin to learn the lessons of "materiality." At once completely detached yet totally involved, the soul watches in perfect serenity as this new thing, the human body with its subtle energy body and dormant feminine power, functions in the world. Pain and pleasure are merely poles in a spectrum of experiences. Rich or poor, healthy or disabled, intellectually gifted or dull unto stupidity, the soul-*atman* holds the ultimate unfolding of life with equanimity. In the meantime, the reins are passed to the Ego-Mind-Personality where the process of decision-making, of choice and ensuing consequence, and determination of our karma begins.

PART II

GANESHA
SENTIENCE, SHAKTI,
AND WILL

CHAPTER 7

COSMIC REALITY REVISITED

HE ANCIENT HINDU SAGES said long ago that this world or reality as we know it is illusory, that it does not really exist in the way we think of it or the way we perceive it. Texts of the various paths within Hinduism speak with one voice on this subject: What we agree upon as reality is an illusion. As a scientifically oriented society we have openly scoffed at this idea. The universe, as we perceive it and interact within it, is quite real. Our senses confirm this fact. Our scientific data from various instruments confirm this fact. From Galileo, Newton, Neils Bor, Enrico Fermi, Albert Einstein, and myriad others, our scientists have confirmed this fact for us. Our reality is anything but illusory. It operates according to certain laws that have been verified again and again. The ancient Hindu sages were dismissed as cloudy-headed mystics living in a primitive society with no "hard" scientific data to rely upon.

The ancient ones have also said with one voice that the nature of power is feminine, not masculine. Consciousness is masculine but it is powered by feminine energy. Without the power of the feminine, consciousness would not manifest at all. Nor would the universe itself. The universe would be an idea, mere potential that has not come to fruition due to the lack of power to make it so.

When the Great Feminine power enables consciousness, the universe itself is born. The sages conclude with the idea that this very universe is the "body" of Divine Mother. The ancient sages, teaching through many different movements and schools, have stated that without understanding and working with the instruments of power related to the Great Feminine, spiritual freedom cannot be obtained. Through one spiritual discipline or another, one may obtain some miraculous abilities, but those too are eventually revealed as illusory. True spiritual progress at higher levels is directly tied to an understanding of and facility with tools of spiritual development pertaining to the Great Feminine, "She who binds and She who sets free." We are bound, the ancients teach, when we have no knowledge of Her. We are on the path to freedom when we work with Her, using the ancient spiritual practices that reveal Her mysteries and methods.

This idea may seem far-fetched. For a male-oriented mentality that pervades much of western culture, the idea of power being a feminine attribute is absurd, even laughable. We see the power of our male sports heroes every day. The idea that the very nature of power could be feminine is immediately dismissed, even if it should be presented for consideration. To a closed mind, power could not possibly be feminine.

Hmmm . . . But Maybe . . .

As we entered the Twentieth Century, science discovered molecules that had long been hinted at by ancient philosophers and thinkers from before the renaissance. Then we cracked the atom and began to delve deeper and deeper into its component parts, piece by piece. When we finally confirmed the structure of the simplest atom, the hydrogen atom, we found something interesting. The lone item circulating the nucleus, an electron, was really a particle of energy. It had structure, form, movement—yet it was not matter in the normal understanding of the term. It was really structured energy. This idea was revolutionary. Structure, form, and movement are terms that apply to something that has a solid existence, but the electron does not. It only appears that way.

The mysteries kept on coming the deeper we pried into the secrets and structure of the atom. The nucleus of the hydrogen atom seemed, at first, solid and thus scientifically comforting. But this was false comfort, based more upon desire than on unfolding scientific discovery. The solid nucleus of the atom gave way to an ever-smaller world of particles that, like the electron, were composed of energy. Patterned energy, structured energy, measurable energy, but like the electron, there was nothing called matter present. There were only ever-finer patterns of structured energy. Matter, as we were trained to think of it, did not and does not exist.

Adding to the unfolding wonder inherent in these discoveries was the larger structure these patterns of energy produced. Between the electrons circulating the nucleus of any atom are vast amounts of space. Places where nothing at all exists. At deeper and smaller levels within the nucleus, the same phenomenon exists. There are indescribably tiny pieces of structured energy and vast stretches of space, relatively speaking.

In a sweeping overview, any atom is a thing composed of patterns of structured energy and vast reaches of space. When we examine a block of wood, for instance, we assume it is solid and occupies space. It has density, strength, can be sanded, cut, whittled, shaved, and joined with other pieces of wood to create great structures. It obeys the laws of physics just as any other item of matter does. Yet, strictly scientifically speaking, there is very little, miniscule in fact, substance there. It is almost illusory.

Astonishingly, the deeper we delve into matters atomic in nature, the closer we come to the conclusion arrived at through meditation by the ancient Hindu sages. This reality is founded on illusion. There is really nothing we call matter that exists. There are only patterns of energy in smaller and smaller configurations. The whole universe is composed of patterns of structured energy that manifest in a variety of ways. The whole universe is energy. The ancient sages told us this long ago in the mists of time. They also said that this whole universe is the body of Divine Mother, "She who binds and She who sets free."

Modern physics, or even metaphysics, has not been able to definitively show that the nature of power is feminine. Nor has it been proven that the nature of consciousness is masculine. But there is a wealth of scriptural and experiential evidence to suggest that these concepts are accurate. Also, the ancient ones were unerringly correct about the nature of our apparent reality, so it would not seem a great stretch to assume that they were also correct about the nature of power and consciousness as well.

In joining the two ideas, power must empower something that can contain and/or use it, just as consciousness must derive its operation from some form of energy. The two are interdependent, just as fire and its power to burn are indissolubly joined.

So modern science is coming around to a view of the universe that the ancient sages explained to their students. When we look at the earth and the solar system, we see that both are mostly space. Students in antiquity just accepted these conclusions from their teachers. Now, we have science to confirm these facts through a different and more understandable methodology than meditation or direct spiritual perception. Modern physics and chemistry can clearly demonstrate through experiments what the ancients were saying. Matter is merely an overlapping series of patterns of structured energy. Together, they form the very cosmos in all of its dimensions.

In mythological terms, these energy patterns are Ganesha-Ganapathi.

CHAPTER 8

AFTER THE BEGINNING

THE APPEARANCE
OF GANESHA-GANAPATHI

ONCE THE UNIVERSE came into existence, according to the ancients, successive levels of reality began to appear. The first four levels are nonphysical and permanent. The next three levels are the reality we inhabit. This idea is encapsulated in a series of verses found in the Rig Veda called the Purusha Suktam. This scripture in both transliterated Sanskrit and translation can be found on pages 56–59.

Soon after the creation of the universe, sages and perfected beings of great understanding were also created. So great was their intellect, they quickly arrived at the logical conclusion that something cannot come from nothing. Thus, there must be something—a primal cause—from which this universe has come. Joining their great intelligence with intuition, they reasoned that if there was something that created this universe, it was somehow still in contact with this universe. If so, it could be contacted. So those two great, slightly different classes of hugely advanced beings, called the Maha Siddhas and the Celestial Sages, devised a fire worship ceremony (*yajna*) in which this primal force outside of the known universe could be contacted and invoked. Here is the Purusha Suktam (Hymn to the Transcendental Overself) with translation.

The Purusha Suktam can be recited for study, prayer, or contemplation.

THE PURUSHA SUKTAM
HYMN TO THE TRANSCENDENTAL OVERSELF
FROM THE RIG VEDA

Hari Om Sahasra Shirsha Purushaha Sahas Rakshaha Sahasrapat
Sa Bhumim Vishwato Vritwa Atyatista Dashangulum

The Primal person has a thousand heads, a thousand eyes, a thousand feet. Pervading the entire universe He transcends everything (is twenty fingerwidths above, which means transcendental).

Om Purusha Evedum Sarvum Yadbhutum Yaccha Bhavyum
Utamritatwa Syeshanaha Yadanni-nati Rohati

All this is the Supreme Person—that which was and that which will be. He is the Lord of immortality. He shows this as he grows by the food, whereas he is the essence of it.

Om Etavanasya Mahima Ato Jyayamscha Purushaha
Padosya Vishwa Bhutani Tripad-asyam-ritam Divi

The existence of the universe in all three periods of time (past, present, and future) is the manifestation of the glory of this Primal Person. He is also beyond and greater than the universe. This entire universe with all its creatures is only a quarter of that great truth. Another three-quarters is above in the realms of light that are indestructible.

Om Tripadurdhwa Udait Purushaha Padosyeha Bhavat-punaha
Tato Vishwang Vyakramat(u) Sashanana-shane Abhi

The invisible three-fourths effulgence of this Cosmic Person is established in realms of light. Only his one-fourth effulgence appears and disappears here. In this manifested one-fourth power, the Primal Person pervades all the living animals—those who manifest hunger and thirst—and in all inert matter as well with its various names and forms.

Om Tasmad Viradajayata Virajo Adhi Purushaha
Sajato Atya-richyata Paschad-bhumi Matho Puraha

This universe of varied forms emerged from this (Purusha) primal person. Holding the cosmos as his body, the Supreme Being manifested. He created the celestials, animals and human beings, and the earth by his own power, even though he remained transcendental.

Om Yatpurushena Havisha Deva Yajna Matanvata
Vasanto Asya Sidajyam Grishma Idhma Shara Dhavihi

Later. To propitiate this Cosmic Truth, the celestials made a symbolic mental fire-sacrifice. To this fire-sacrifice, spring became the oblation, summer became the holy grass, and the rainy season became the main offering.

Om Tam Yajnam Barhishi Proukshan Purushum Jatama-grataha
Tena Deva Ayajanta Sadhya Rishayascha Ye

They installed the Cosmic Person over the holy grass and invoked him there, the One who was before the creation and the object of the great fire-sacrifice. Thus, the Celestials and the perfected beings, joining together, performed the mental fire-sacrifice; the great meditation, keeping him as the main oblation.

Om Tasmadyajnat Sarvahutaha Sambhritum Prashadajyum
Pashumstamschakre Vayavyan Aranyan Gramyascha Yei

There emerged a curd that contained the ghee (melted butter) from the altar of the fire-sacrifice in which the Cosmic Being was the highest oblation. Later, birds that fly, animals of the forest, and the animals that move in the villages were created.

Om Tasmadyajnat Sarvahutaha Richaha Samani Jajnire
Chandamsi Jajnire Tasmat Yajus-tasma-dajayata

All mantras known as *Rik, Yajus, Samas,* and *Gayatri* emerged out of that altar in which the Self of all the selves was the main oblation.

Om Tasmadashwa Ajayanta Ye Ke Cho Bhaya-dataha
Gavoha Jajnire Tasmat Tasmadjata Ajavayaha

Horses, animals having two-lined teeth, cows, goats, sheep and the like were born of this cosmic sacrifice.

Om Yat Purushum Vyadadhuhu Katidha Vyakalpayan
Mukhum Kimasya Kau Bahu Ka Uru Pada Uchyete

Into how many parts did they divide this Cosmic Being when they decided to pour Him as the main oblation? Which is his face? Which are his arms? His thighs and feet?

Om Brahmanosya Mukhamasit Bahu Rajanyaha Kritaha
Uru Tadasya Yadvaishyaha Padbhyam Shudro Ajayata

Brahmins (priests) emerged from the mouth, Kshatriyas (warriors and rulers) from the arms, Vaishyas (tradespeople) from the thighs, Shudras (people of service) from the feet of this Cosmic Person.

Om Chandrama Manaso Jataha Chakshoho Suryo Ajayata
Mukha-dindra Schagnishcha Prana-dwayur-ajayata

From His mind emerged the moon, the sun from His eyes, Indra Lord of the first heaven and Agni the fire God, from His mouth. Vayu (the air), emerged from his breath (*prana*).

Om Nabhya Asidantariksham Shirshno Dyau Samavartata
Padbhyam Bhumir-dishaha Shrotrat Tatha Lokan Akalpayan

Atmosphere emerged from his navel, the Sphere of Light (*Dyuloka*) from his head, Earth from his feet, directions from his ears. Thus, the celestials (*devas*) created all the spheres (*Lokas*) from his cosmic body.

Om Saptasya Sanpari Dhayaha Trisapta Samidhaha Kritaha
Deva Yadyajnum Tanvanaha Abhagnum Purushum Pashum

For this sacrifice seven meters are the boundaries, twenty-one princi-ples are the oblations. To this sacrificial pillar, the gods bound the Cos-mic Truth itself by the cord of mantra for their realization. (This mantra stanza symbolizes that all spiritual disciplines end with Self-realization.)

Om Yaj Naena Yajna Maya Janta Devaha, Stani Dharmani Prathamanyasan
Tey Hanakam Mahimanaha Sachantae Yatra Purve Sadhyaya Santi Devaha

Thus the ancient gods worshipped the God of gods mentally through sacrifice. The techniques used in that Yajna (sacrifice) became the law of life. The meditation on this Cosmic Prayer of the Cosmic Form of God leads devotees to the highest heaven where the angels and mas-ters dwell.

Purusha Suktam Japa Dhyanam Samarpayami

We chant this mantra prayer to that Cosmic Being as a form of offering.

From these verses we can see three important ideas: (1) The tool of Sanskrit mantras was used to both invoke and tie or harness the primal cause of the universe within our reality. (2) The use of Sanskrit mantra tools was structured in such a way that future generations of sentient beings could use these tools (mantra formulas) to achieve a level of being similar to the great ones who constructed the ancient mental fire ceremony in the first place. (3) The Gayatri Mantra, a Sanskrit formula for invoking the complete vibrations of the realms of light, emerged from this ancient primordial and mental fire ceremony.

MYTH AND SYMBOL

The value of myths and stories lies far beyond the enjoyment they characteristically bring to those who read, tell, or listen to them. The epics from India characteristically contain great ideas in the form of characters. These characters, by their interaction, show how great concepts and forces combine, clash, and sometimes form new ideas and forces. Shiva and Parvati are examples of primary characters in grand stories about life in the universe.

Shiva is consciousness everywhere in everything. Parvati is energy everywhere in everything. There are stories of how Parvati sees Shiva in her dreams, even as a young child, and knows that she is for him. She knows that they are to be married and become one. She knows she is meant to empower Shiva. Without her, Shiva is in an unmanifest condition. The universe is an idea that has not yet been born. She empowers even the idea of the universe. Ultimately Shiva and Parvati will be married on a grand scale. The concept of the relationship between energy and consciousness is powerful and thought provoking.

OVERLAYS OF CONSCIOUSNESS

In you and me, we have the patterned energy of the atom overlaid by the components of a molecule, overlaid by the pattern of a cell, overlaid by the components of an organ in the physical body that is composed of those cells, overlaid by the system in which the organ resides, and so forth. It is only after several levels of energy pattern overlays that we get to the complete physical human body. And then we have the astral or etheric body that interpenetrates the physical body. It also has its form of subtle energy.

Here we are equally concerned with consciousness. And just as is the case with energy, there are overlays of consciousness. There are also parallel structures of consciousness. To keep from confusing energy patterns with structures of consciousness, I will call the structures in consciousness *frequencies*. A collection of frequencies I will refer to as *bandwidth*.

There are significant differences in frequencies at every level of consciousness. That is to say, the fundamental consciousness, the frequency of a cell, is different from the consciousness of an organ, just as the patterns of energy are different. Yet, strictly speaking, we cannot have one without the other. If there is no consciousness, the cell will not exist. Similarly, without the energy, the cell will not exist. They operate together just as fire and its power to burn. Fire and burning power operate together, we cannot separate them. And in an identical way, we cannot separate energy from consciousness.

There is a difference in the types of consciousness between cells and organs. The consciousness needed for an organ to operate is more complex and at a different frequency than a cell. Think of it this way, the lowly cell has the ability to operate on its own, yet it easily links up with other cells and even different kinds of cells to compose an organ. It exists quite easily within a hierarchy of both energy and consciousness as part of an organ, system, and human, while maintaining a certain autonomy.

But frequencies of consciousness are not merely associated with physical structure. The very nature of sentience includes the idea that we can voluntarily decide to explore different frequencies. We can choose to expand our bandwidth. When it comes to our personal evolution, this idea becomes critical when we decide that there are other dimensions to consciousness than what we learn in school or even in church.

It is useful to explore the general idea of frequencies and bandwidth using ideas with which we are already familiar.

COMMONLY ACCEPTED FREQUENCIES AND BANDWIDTH

When I speak to you here, I am using a language (English); a body of experience (spiritual); an approach in context (mystical); that we all share together. I do not have to explain what meditation is, or prayer, or any of the many things we share. This is because, in the realm of consciousness, we are on the same or similar frequency. I can speak plainly to you because our consciousness tuners are all dialed to the same position, as it were.

At some other time we might discuss some other topic, say movies or television. This is an entirely different realm of human experience. Thus, it has a different frequency. But because we have the same kinds of tuning range, we can easily match frequencies and discuss a topic with a completely different vibration.

This all seems matter of fact until we branch out a bit more. Have you ever been to a convention in a professional field completely different from your own? Lets say it's very, very different. Let's say it's a convention involving scientific exploration of communication devices involving television, telephone, the Internet, and so forth.

If we enter a working session at one of these conventions, one of the first things we would notice is that we don't understand what they are talking about. We understand the words, because they are speaking in English. They may occasionally use words like "television" or "telephone," but we still do not have the faintest idea of what's being said. This is because they are operating in a frequency that is not part of our individual bandwidth.

Oh, we know the English language, so we have a general idea of what the carrier wave is, but that is about it. The convention could also be about tailoring. We might attend a session and become completely lost as the language, expressed in tailoring terms, overwhelms us in short order. Once again, we may understand the words and syntax, but we would have no idea what they are talking about. They are operating on a different frequency.

The human brain has a huge, huge capacity for variations of frequency. Children learn the various cultural frequencies at home, in school and through television and movies. But as schooling becomes more advanced, the brain must build its ability to work in different frequencies. As we study in high school, college, graduate school, as well as trade and professional schools, we are adjusting our brain to use new frequencies. The process of learning creates new pathways in the brain. The neurons fire and jump across different gaps, new connections are formed as we grasp new ideas and learn new vocabulary. It is almost the equivalent of a cell multiplying until it becomes an organ. We build in our brain the capacity to operate on completely different frequencies within the general human bandwidth. Yet there are still vast bandwidths of frequencies that we have not developed.

Within just the United States, we have innumerable subfrequencies. Doctors, lawyers, teachers, auto mechanics, interior designers, dentists, all have their own professional language. Yet, interestingly, a doctor educated in Spanish has already created the frequency of that profession. If he or she comes to the United States they will simply learn the communication language and are ready to begin practice because they have already established the frequency of medicine in their brains.

There are many, many different subfrequencies. Countries, professions, religions, cultures, and general occupations all have their own frequencies, and these can overlap.

All of these frequencies together, plus many more, are what is called Shiva. Shiva is all forms of consciousness, wherever it may be found. And it can be found wherever there is energy. The state of consciousness to which we are seeking to evolve must involve the archetype that is called Shiva. That is to say, we must move beyond our usual frequencies to other, more advanced, more spiritual frequencies.

CONSIDER THE POSSIBILITIES

There is a frequency for planet Earth, a frequency for the sun, and another for the solar system which is a different layer of consciousness —a frequency that is distinct from a planet, just as a cell is distinct from the organ. These frequencies are so far outside any of the frequencies that we humans are accustomed to using that we have no idea of how these layers of consciousness operate. What does the sun "think?" We have no idea if it thinks at all, let alone what it thinks. If it does think, of what order of magnitude are its thoughts? How does the sun, for instance, measure time? Or distance?

It seem unreasonable even absurd to contemplate such thoughts . . . until we view them from the mystical side of humanity.

The ancient sages have told us that we can become any frequency of the universe. The old teachings, first transmitted orally and then later written down, state that we are the universe in microcosm. The esoteric texts confirm this with the testimony of those who have achieved the heights. Some of these texts give techniques for adding new "frequencies" to our bandwidth. For if all consciousness is Shiva and if we can become it all, then there is no part of the universe that we cannot eventually "tune in to" or build corresponding frequencies to in ourselves. We just have to know what to do.

The thousand-petaled lotus at the top of the head, the Sahasrara Chakra is the final state of achievement in what we are calling universal bandwidth. Once we have reached a certain point in our development, the kundalini energy, divine mother, shakti, the power of God, the holy spirit comes up the spine and instantly increases our bandwidth. We now understand, see, perceive, and participate in the universe in a new way. First, we move only a few steps. It is all the capacity we have at the moment. As we progress, our bandwidth will continue increasing, step by step, stage by stage, until our bandwidth is increased a millionfold.

The expansion of our bandwidth is so different from anything we have known previously that even lower stages defy description, leaving the mystics shrugging their shoulders as they try to describe it, their eyes looking around searching for a way to say something meaningful.

At every different chakra, the bandwidth expands to include new potentialities, bringing new perspectives into our reality. Within each chakra are multiple levels of expansion that allow for an orderly progression of conscious evolution. Step by step, chakra by chakra, we add to our bandwidth. New frequencies are added according to our capacity to receive and process them.

Finally, we reach the Ajna Chakra at its place centered just above the eyebrows where the unity of everything becomes manifestly real. Where previously we may have experienced certain frequencies as discordant, we now understand them as a symphony of cosmic dimensions. Everything fits in its own way. The Ajna Chakra is the place where cosmic consciousness is achieved. The unity of the entire cosmos is experienced. There is no discord, only tonic chords registering what most of us cannot see or hear at our present level of development.

Mystic author Alice Bailey explains in many of her books that when the human soul is liberated, there are a number of choices for additional evolution, further expansion of bandwidth that can be made. One can, for instance, enter the *deva* line of evolution. This is a nonhuman, conscious, sentient energy form that we only dimly perceive in our common human bandwidth. We know that plants and animals and even we, ourselves, have rudimentary *devas*, little energylike beings, that watch over our everyday health. But the topic is much deeper, broader, and more profound than that. We humans have the potential bandwidth in our spiritual construction to enter the *deva* line of evolution and grow in ways so different than those we are used to thinking of, that we have no vocabulary for this at all. That frequency has not been built in our present form, but the potential to grow in the bandwidth has been included among the possibilities for the expansion of consciousness.

Another choice the soul has is to ensoul and develop a planet. Yes, you too can become a Jupiter or Saturn eventually, if you like. The potential bandwidth for that activity exists within you. At the time and place of Great Decision discussed near the end of this book, you have the option of choosing such a path. Of course, many of us will choose the path of Earth Service, helping the Earth and her inhabitants to mature and develop spiritually. Others will elect to dissolve into the great ocean of Shiva and Shakti and become something beyond our capacity to contemplate.

Saints and sages have evolved to a point where they can exist between physical incarnations in a completely conscious state and in a realm that is yet another frequency available to us, if we choose to go that way. We can decide to become sages of such developed knowledge and consciousness that our bodies may come and go according to physical laws but our frequencies of consciousness have learned how to transcend the limitations of a single birth. We may decide to become saints and find our consciousness in complete harmony with matter and energy anywhere, as we serve the ends of conscious evolution with both knowledge and compassion, transcending the limits presented by a single incarnation.

A Different View

We can view the process of charting our spiritual evolution by expanding our thinking to contain an understanding of consciousness that is nearly infinite in its bandwidth of frequencies. Some frequencies overlap, while others may take arduous effort over several lifetimes to achieve. Our brain and chakra system contains the spectrum of possibilities that can actually be made manifest. Mostly it lies dormant but ready to be activated. Scientists routinely say we use less than 5% of our brain power. The rest is just there waiting for us.

The soul, a complete repository of all potentiality, is the place where the higher stages of the journey will be traveled in concert with the Ego-Mind-Personality. The first part of our common journey takes place through the lower charkas. Our choices and the exercise of decision combined with willpower determine the speed at which we progress through them toward the higher chakras and the ultimate goals of enlightenment and self-realization. Thankfully, divine grace often moves us toward opening new paths to higher or different frequencies. I will take up this discussion a bit later in the section of this book about Gurus and Jagad Gurus.

There is no secret of creation that cannot be made known to us. There is no level of physical or nonphysical creation to which we cannot attune ourselves. In this light, the catch phrase, "Be all you can be" takes on a whole new meaning.

There are many different ways to expand our bandwidth. Prayer, spiritual study, hatha yoga, service to humanity, service to a self-realized master, devotional music, scientific breathing (*pranayama*), an attitude of "search for truth wherever it may lead" all expand our bandwidth.

There are powerful mantras that will produce expansions of consciousness and increases in bandwidth. There are mantras that will help one through the intermediate stages of our common journey up the spine. Among the many mantras taught both here and in India there are several that stand out. The one that most sums up and contains all of the frequencies of all the chakras and all the realms is the Gayatri Mantra, discussed in Chapter 20 . And during the journey, we will face some trials and hurdles. The Ganesha-Ganapathi mantras help us overcome obstacles.

GANESHA GITA

Om Namo Vishnu Swa-rupaya
Namaste Rudra Rupine
Namaste Brahma Ruppine
Namo Ananta Swa-rupine

Om Salutations to you, O Lord Ganesha. You are (the form of) Vishnu, the form of Rudra (Shiva), and the forms of Brahma and the various forms of the infinite.

1. *Shive Vishbau Cha Shaktau Cha*
   Surye Mayi Nara Dhipa
   Ya-bheda Buddhi Yoga-ha
   Sa Sam-yag Yogo Mato Mama

   Aha-meva Jad-yas-mat
   Sri Jami Pala Yami Cha
   Kritva Nana Vidham Visham
   Sam Harami Swa-lilaya

King Varenya, there is no difference among Shiva, Vishnu , Shakti, Surya, and Myself. To know that we are One is to realize Truth. This I call Samyag Yoga. Assuming different forms I create, sustain, and dissolve endless universes by my Lila (divine play).

2. *Ahameva Maha Vishnu*
   Ahameva Sada Shivaha
   Ahameva Maha Shaktir
   Ahameva Aryama Priya

   Ahameko Nrinam Natho
   Hataha Pancha Vidaha Pra
   Ajnanan Mam Na Jananti
   Jagat Karana Kara-nam

Dear King, I am Maha Vishnu, I am Sada Shiva, I am Maha Shakti and I am the Sun God. I am the supreme master of all beings, and in ancient times I, Myself, manifested in the five forms as Vishnu, Shiva, Shakti, Sun, and Ganesha: That is Myself. I am the cause of the origin of the universe. Due to ignorance of my true form, they know me not.

3. *Matto Gnirapo Dharani Matta Akasha Marutan*
   Brahma Vishnus-cha Rudras-cha Loka Pala Disha Dasha
   Vasa-vo Mana-vo Ga-vo Mana-vaha Pasha-vopi Cha
   Saritaha Sagara Yaksha Vrikshaha Pakshi Gana Api

It is from me that fire, water, earth, sky, and wind, Brahma Vishnu, Rudra, celestials, ten quarters, Vasu, and other guardian deities, Manu (the father of men) human beings, the bovine race of cattle, all animals, rivers, oceans, yakshas, demi Gods, trees, the entire plant kingdom, and the entire bird kingdom have been created.

> 4. *Tathaika Vim-shat-chi Swargo Nagaha Sapta Vanani-cha*
> *Manush-yaya Parvata-ha Sa-dhyaha Siddha*
> *Raksho Ganas Tatha-ha*
> *Aham Sakshi Jaga Chakshur Alipta-ha Sarva Karma Bhihi*
> *A-vikaro A-pameya A-ham A-vyakto Vish-wago A-vyaha*

Similarly, heavenly abodes, the reptile kingdom, the seven islands and forests, mountains, Sadhyas (angels) and Siddhas (perfected beings), Rakshas (demons) are created by me. I am the solar deity, the witness of this world. I am detached and beyond all karma. I am beyond duality, causeless, the unmanifested, all pervading, indestructible principle.

> 5. *Ahameva Param Brahma*
> *Ayaya Ananda Atmakam Nripa*
> *Moha-yat Akilam Maya*
> *Shresh-tan Mamana Rana-mum*
>
> *Ajno Avyeyo Aham Bhuta Atmanan*
> *Adi-resh-wara Eva Cha*
> *Astay Tri-gunam Mayam*
> *Bhavami Bahu Yonishu*

I am the Supreme Reality, formless and blissful. Highly evolved ones also get deluded by my maya, the illusory power. I have no birth, I am indestructible, I am the self (*atma*) of all beings and am Eshwara, the Supreme Lord of all creation. Making my maya or energy as the excrutrix, I myself manifest in the form of all beings.

6. *Adharmo Pachaya Dharma Pachayo Mi Yada Bhavet*
   Sadun Sam-rakshitam Dustam Stha-ditum
   Sam-bhava Mya-ham
   Uchidya Adharma Nicha-yam Dharmam
   Samstha Payami-cha
   Hanmi Dus-tams-cha Dai-yams-cha Nana Lila Kara Muda

Whenever unrighteousness predominates and virtues decline, then for the protection of the saints and the good, and for the destruction of wicked demons, I take incarnation. I shall uphold and restore Dharma by uprooting unrighteousness. Such are my different Lilas of bliss.[6]

CHAPTER 9

THE CREATION OF GANESHA-GANAPATHI

MONG THE MAIN CHARACTERS in the story about the creation of Ganesha is Shiva. He is consciousness in all of its various phases and manifestations; the all-inclusive bandwidth within which all frequencies are contained. Wherever consciousness is found, Shiva will also be found. Because his bandwidth extends to all sentient (as well as nonsentient, as in plants and animals) consciousness, his domain includes not only the celestial planes where great sages and saints dwell but also the nether realms inhabited by ghosts and goblins, and the evil or negative entities that oppose the celestials at every turn and compete with them for dominance. Because Shiva's bandwidth includes all of these things, he is not limited to consciousness within a single individual body. Shiva also represents the soup of primordial consciousness from whence arose developing life on Earth (and elsewhere), the superconscious state that we, as discrete individual sentient entities, will all reach at some time.

THE CREATION OF GANESHA

As our story opens, we join Shiva, the principle of consciousness, and Parvati, the all-pervasive feminine principle of power at home. Before they entered the material world of duality, consciousness and power were united as a single entity-force. Now, Shiva is the masculine aspect, the total bandwidth of consciousness that inhabits all matter and all beings. And Parvati is the power of the universe inherent in all matter and all beings. We find them living as husband and wife.

Shiva spends a large part of his time seeing to the various affairs pertaining to dynamic consciousness. Parvati, working from home, lends her power to all living things, including Shiva himself, creating beauty and splendor as part of her subtle responsibilities. Together, they play out the drama of duality.

As part of his retinue, Shiva commands a number of *ganas* or powers, seen as servants who do his bidding. One day, as Shiva was heading off to work, Parvati asked for one of his *ganas* to stand watch while she took a bath. Shiva assigned a *gana* to the task and left.

Parvati approached the *gana* where he stood on the porch and instructed him that no one should enter the house while she was bathing. So saying, she went inside and began to draw her bathwater. As it flowed into the inviting tub, Parvati added to it flowers and substances to make it both rejuvenating and fragrant.

Before he had gone very far, Shiva realized that he needed to take some items with him that he had left at home. Turning around, he retraced his way and climbed the steps of his house. There, his *gana* stopped him.

"Halt!" said the *gana*, holding forth his outstretched and upright palm. "You may not enter while mistress Parvati is bathing."

"Are you mad, young *gana*? This is my house and you are my servant. Stand aside." So saying, Shiva brushed him aside and entered his house to pick up the articles for which he had returned.

Still drawing her bath, Parvati heard the "clump, clump" of Shiva's calloused feet and left the bath to investigate. Seeing her husband, she addressed him with some annoyance. "Why are you here? I left instructions not to be disturbed while conducting my bath. Even though one of your *ganas* was to stand guard, here you are tramping about the house as if I had said nothing and had no guard at all."

Arrogantly, Shiva had not taken her request seriously and now merely laughed with a regal toss of his head. "He is my *gana*, and he will surely not prevent me from entering my own house."

Shiva found the situation amusing, but Parvati was visibly annoyed. "If your *gana* will not do the job for which he was appointed he is useless to me. Go now, both of you." As Shiva left with his *gana* Parvati retired to her sitting room to think

Pondering the procession of events, it became clear to Parvati that she must have her own *gana*. Concluding thus, she took saffron, unguents, and a scraping of her skin, and with her matchless power created a beautiful young boy Ganapathi, (also called Ganesha). Giving him a staff similar to the one Shiva himself carried, she instructed the boy to keep anyone from entering while she was bathing and retired anew to her bath. Secure in the knowledge that finally she was protected from untimely visitation she fell asleep.

Several hours passed and Shiva returned to his house, only to find a strange young lad standing on the porch holding a staff similar to his own. Bounding up the steps, Shiva was only slightly surprised when the lad met his path squarely and blocked his way. "My mistress says you may not enter while she is bathing."

Shiva forbore the lad's ignorance and spoke. "This is my house, boy. I will enter whenever I desire." He started to move forward. Without warning, the young lad swung the staff and knocked Shiva off his feet. Completely surprised, Shiva fell down clumsily and rolled off the porch. Then he got irritated. Bounding up the steps, he became determined to explain in no uncertain terms who he was and what the consequences would be if the boy resisted him further. As he reached the top step, the boy's staff crashed into his abdomen and he fell, off balance once again. Now he was angry. Taking his own staff and stamping it three times on the ground, he stood steely eyed as a host of powerful *ganas* gathered in an instant. Shiva spoke to them in clipped tones. "This youngster seeks to block me from my home. Dispatch him at once."

What Shiva had not yet comprehended was that Parvati had invested the boy with a substantial measure of her own power. Even though Shiva's *ganas* rushed him in groups of five and ten, one swing of Ganapathi's staff in a circular motion scattered them senselessly around the front yard. For nearly an hour the *ganas* rushed the boy who defeated their every effort without even becoming winded. As the dawn of comprehension began to break over Shiva's countenance, he lifted his hand in a gesture—"cease attacking."

Changing tactics, Shiva gently asked the boy if he knew who he was. The boy responded that he neither knew who Shiva was nor cared. He had his instructions from his mother. Shiva's eyes rose. He now understood. Regaining his patience, he told the boy that he, Shiva, was really his Father and that the house he guarded was Shiva's own home. Still the boy refused him entry. Shiva shrugged and strode towards his doorway.

The boy met him at the door in one bound and smashed Shiva across the chest. Shiva, now prepared and entirely unscratched, threw the young lad twenty feet out in front of the door. Waiting not even one second, the lad bounded back to the door and took up combat with Shiva. Even though to all observation the battle was fierce, it was not. Though the boy was trying his best to defeat Shiva, Shiva was not even half trying. He could have dispatched the boy in one second, but did not since, in essence, this was his son, even if in name only. The boy, by contrast, was trying his best to defeat Shiva.

While the two battled, a crowd had gathered near the house. All manner of celestial persons stopped to see what the fighting was all about and who was involved. Some even took to wagering on the outcome. Shiva was not unaware of the crowd, and it bothered him. After a lengthy exchange of blows he allowed himself to be thrown some thirty feet away from the house. He landed, quite by his intention near Vishnu, another member of the Masculine Trinity to which he belonged.[7]

Pretending to recover his breath from the stress of battle, Shiva related his dilemma to Vishnu. "I am caught fighting someone who does not know who I am and who will not resign," he complained to Vishnu.

Vishnu nodded agreement. "Yes. And if you lose, the whole divine assembly will know that you are no longer invincible. You can imagine the furor *that* would create. Every would-be hero in the quadrant would come looking to get a piece of you to bolster his reputation." Vishnu shook his head. "You must put an end to this, and quickly."

Shiva was not pleased at these remarks, even though he understood quite well that they were true. "This boy was created by my wife. He not only has her power, but can you imagine Parvati's wrath if I dispatch the boy without her knowledge?"

"Then tell her," Vishnu responded.

"How can I, if I cannot even enter my own house?"

"Fine," Vishnu responded, "Become a divine wimp. I don't care."

Shiva laughed loudly and the trees shook. "If my wife heard you say that, you would become cooked meat for the crows in three seconds flat. Why don't you *yell* that last remark?"

"Not a chance." Vishnu made little designs in the earth with his toes. "You have no choice but to destroy the boy. Divine Law says that any being with the boy's power must be created by the two of you. If he defeats you with his mother's power alone, the Law will be broken. The Cosmos will not run correctly. There is no choice."

Shiva nodded. "Unfortunately, you make good sense. I will do it."

Shiva picked himself up off the ground and strode up to the boy who was readying to do battle. With one glance from Shiva's third eye, the boy's head was cut off. Partially disintegrated, it fell to the ground still smoldering. The earth shuddered briefly. A shriek was heard.

Out of the bath rushed Parvati. She was nearly red with rage. The celestials who had gathered to see the fight scattered like sparks driven from a raging fire and disappeared from view. "What have you done to my boy?" Parvati began to resemble Kali, the destroyer of negative ego, as her tongue extended from her mouth and she played with the thought of reducing Shiva to divine mush on the spot. Next, she looked like Durga, the divine protectress, as her eyes became fiery and little weapons grew from her body and then disappeared.

Shiva joined his palms and began to speak. "Oh Divine Shakti, who is the body of this universe itself, please hear my words. My first mistake was arrogance. When you requested my *gana* to keep guard over you, I did not take it seriously. For that I most humbly apologize. As for the divine boy you created, your *gana* was more attractive than any other in creation. His beauty was matched only by his devotion to you. So great was his dedication to you, his mother, he would not even let me into my own home. He would not recognize me as man of the house. I was reduced to begging for entrance into the realm which I created."

Parvati interrupted him, only the least bit placated. "Then why have you destroyed one of such beauty and devotion?

Shiva responded. "Suppose that I created a divine woman nearly equal to you in beauty, with unimaginable power, whose only job was to keep you from your home. What would you do?"

Parvati snorted. "If you try that, she will be reduced to a cinder in shorter time than it will take to create her."

Shiva agreed. "And a just act it would be as well. It is in such a condition that I found myself when confronted with the boy. I tried to reason with him and told him who I was. I asked for entrance, but he would hear none of it. If you had but said to him to let me in when I returned, he would be with you now. But you were not happy because my *gana* failed you, so you created him and did not tell him to let me in. Just what did you expect me to do?

Parvati saw Shiva's point. Her anger faded somewhat. "Yes, what you say is correct." She paused. "But I request you bring him back to life immediately."

Shiva replied. "I could do that but he has no head . . . it was . . . uh . . . Damaged."

"Then give him a new one," said Parvati.

Shiva thought a moment. "Since the head you gave him is gone, I cannot now create a new one. Neither can I take life from another to give him a new head. But to satisfy you I will give your *gana* a new head from the first creature that I encounter who has just died. I will bestow upon the boy with the new head my blessing of the highest consciousness. The body you have given him will hold a huge measure of your great power. Thus, together we can imbue that being with life like no other."

Parvati agreed on condition that it be done quickly.

Shiva said, "Let us go for a walk."

They began to walk through the countryside. After only a few minutes, they came across a young elephant that was dying. When it expired,

Shiva took the head and ran back and placed it on the body of the divine boy. Immediately the being sprang to life and bowed down to his divine parents. The celestials sang and the countryside was abundant with verdant growth. Even insects withdrew and all was harmonious as Ganapathi, who is also known by the name Ganesha, was born. And although Parvati was delighted, she did ask, "Did it have to be an elephant?"

The larger head, Shiva improvised placatingly, was needed to contain the huge amount of divine knowledge and wisdom he had given the boy. Further, the huge ears would keep fanning to allow only good deeds to reach his ears. The piercing eyes would look through to the very soul of any being who approached. And the trunk gave him a mysterious organ of action unknown to any other divine being.

Parvati, nearly satisfied, had one more request. "Make him as dear to you as your own son should be." Shiva agreed and took the young elephant-headed lad in his arms. "You shall be the remover of obstacles. With the lowly rat as your mount, you shall exalt that humble vehicle beyond what any may imagine. To insure this, you will soon come to be regarded as first among all celestials. I shall arrange events to bring this about. So be it." Parvati was completely happy.

SYMBOLISM

Power alone cannot create. It also takes intelligence and will. Thus, Parvati alone cannot create a sentient self-aware universe. Shiva must add his all-inclusive bandwidth if a being is to be created that contains the consciousness of the universe. You might ask how the universe can be considered self-aware, sentient. The ancient answer is that just as something cannot come from nothing, the highest state of cosmic consciousness must already be contained in the universe for it to be attainable.

In human beings, the force of Ganesha-Ganapathi is found at the base of the spine very near to the root of the kundalini shakti. This place is called the Ganesha *Loka*.

GANESHA LOKA

Ganesha's abode is called *Swananda Dhama* (the Abode of Bliss) and is created by a partial manifestation of his shakti called *Kama Dayani Yoga Shakti*. He can be approached as either *Nirguna* (formless) or *Saguna* (with a form).

Even though he is all pervading, he still manifests a distinct transcendental personality. Although dwelling in his abode, he protects the various *Lokas* (spheres or levels) of the universe and his devotees. There are some who dwell in the *Loka* with him free of hunger, thirst, sickness, to carry out his behests.

Swananda Dhama has four gates. Each gate is guarded by two attendants called *Parshadas*, bringing their total to eight. Each is short in stature, compassionate, but very powerful, and having four arms. In two hands they hold weapons and in the other two hands they hold a stick and the *Tarjani Mudra*—thumb and forefinger joined showing the soul's unity with God.

At the Eastern Gate are *Avigna* and *Vighna-raja* who hold a hatchet and a lotus. At the Southern Gate are *Swaktra* and *Balaram* holding sword and shield. The Western Gate is guarded by *Gaja-karna* and *Go-karna* holding bows and arrows. *Su-saumya* and *Shubha-dayaka* guard the North Gate. They hold a lotus and goad. There are also two great shaktis (powers) that guard the abode of Ganesha. They are *Tajovati* (brilliance) and *Jwalini* (the power to blaze forth).

Chinta Mani Dwipa (island of the wish-jewel) is called Ganesha's abode. In it there is a magnificent garden called *Kalpa Upavana* (garden of wish-fulfilling trees) where Ganesha can wander and contemplate the universe and its wonders.

In the work Sharada Tilaka, the *Chinta Mani Dwipa* (island of the wish-jewel) is discussed. "Among the seven oceans there is one called the *Ik-shurasa Sagara* (Ocean of Sugarcane Juice). In it the beautiful island of the *Chinta Mani Dwipa* dwells. It rises from the ocean and its waves constantly salute Lord Ganesha who dwells there in *Swananda Dhama*. All celestial trees like *Mandara*, *Parijata*, and others are in his garden called *Kalpa Druma*

Upavana. Every stone, plant, bird, flower, and other things on that island have consciousness and constantly sing the glory of Lord Ganesha.

"The landscape looks crimson. In the center of the island there is a mystical tree called the *Parijata,* which is conscious and sings the glories and praises of Ganesha in all seasons. At the foot of the tree is a great altar called *Maha Pita.* On the altar is a great lotus. In the midst of the lotus is a *shat-kona* (six-pointed star), in the midst of which is a *tri-kuna* (triangle). The supreme power of Ganesha is established in that triangle, who can be seen (by the skilled adept) sitting there. Meditating on Ganesha in that setting, one will be blessed with his *Darshan* (mystical appearance accompanied by divine grace)."

Chinta Mani Dwipa should not be regarded as an ordinary island. It is inconceivable to the human mind. But the heart can see this place. The triangle is in us at the base of the spine in the Muladhara Chakra. To that island, all the *nadis* in our system are connected in the subtle body. It is the source of energy and procreation as well. That is where we can find Ganesha. He is part of our own self at all times and in all situations.

CHAPTER 10

GANESHA-GANAPATHI: THE PRINCIPLE OF UNITY

N ADDITION TO BEING a figure representing cosmic consciousness, Ganesha-Ganapathi is also the principle of unity. Leaving aside the modern speculation regarding string theory with its multiple universes, the universe is—by definition—unified by its status as a single thing, a solitary entity. But Ganesha is other things as well. In addition to embodying the principle of unity, he is also the ruler of individual powers and the source of an individual's power. He is the unifying force found within us and throughout the universe.

We can begin our understanding of this principle by taking apart the two Sanskrit words "Ganesha" and "Ganapathi." First, Ganesha. In Sanskrit *gana* has two meanings: "power" and "group." *Esha* means "ruler." This means that Ganesha is simultaneously a ruler of a group and a ruler of power. In the stories pertaining to him, he is the ruler of any group and the lord over any set of powers, as the principle of unity. Next, Ganapathi. *Pathi* means spouse in the sense of "compliment of." Because the Sanskrit word *Ganapathi* means the "spouse of power," this elephant-headed figure is a function of consciousness that accompanies power. In the other context of the word *gana*, Ganapathi is the "spouse of the group," which denotes the unifying principle that accompanies any group. It is important to distinguish here between a group and a collection of individuals. They appear the same on the surface, but they are not at all the same. In a collection of individuals, the members have nothing that necessarily provides a cohesive bond. However, in a group, there is some common purpose involved, some reason the individuals have gathered or are connected.

So in one meaning Ganesha is said to be the "ruler of power." Since in the story Ganesha defeated all the other *ganas,* it is fitting that he be called the ruler of all powers.

His mother, the Great Feminine, has bestowed a huge amount of power on this creature who is then called the very compliment of power, a title that might well have been given to Shiva as consciousness. But in the story, Shiva willingly agrees to have this title awarded to Ganesha and adds to it his own blessings. Ganesha will then represent the unification of the various powers and divisions of consciousness that we as humans carry within.

Since *gana* means group, now Gana-esha becomes "group ruler." As Gana-pathi he is also the "spouse or compliment of the group." These are powerful ideas. A singular power bestowed with supreme consciousness by his father, Shiva, Ganapathi has been awarded a position that is at once the "ruler of any group" in general, and specifically the "ruler of any group of powers or abilities."

WHERE TWO OR MORE ARE GATHERED

It is common knowledge in Vedic Hinduism that the Ganesha-Ganapathi principle is automatically involved when there is more than one of anything that is part of something else. This principle holds true no matter how large or how small the elements in question. For instance, in the example of the hydrogen atom discussed earlier, there is one electron and one proton. These bits of structured energy form a new substance we call hydrogen. Because more than one thing is involved, the Ganesha-Ganapathi principle is automatically present. Operationally, Ganesha-Ganapathi is the unifying force and ruler of the new "thing" that is formed as a group. The new thing can be an atom, molecule, compound, engine, team of coworkers, or solar system as a collection of planets that form a new entity. Creating unity among separate things or consciousnesses is the province and task of Ganesha-Ganapathi.

In the human body, the same Ganesha-Ganapathi principle applies. Atoms form cells that compose organs. An organ is a group of cells working together in a common process. But each organ is also part of a system, such as the cardiovascular, digestive, reproductive, endocrine system, and so forth. The various members of each new "group" work together as part of a common process. Each organ is a collection of individual cells now working together as part of a single process, even though each cell has a primitive consciousness of its own. The new entity, the organ, also has a consciousness that is specific to its function. This means that there are several overlays of consciousnesses. There is atomic consciousness overlaid by molecular consciousness, further overlaid by organ consciousness.

But the overlay of layers of consciousness does not stop here. Organs are parts of systems that collectively have a primitive form of consciousness that allow members of the system to work together intelligently to perform their part of the common process, be it digestion, reproduction, or whatever. All of these systems are interconnected, acting as one system, which we recognize as a human being.

So a human being is, in effect, a vast collection of intelligent (or conscious) subsystems functioning together in a marvelous and mystical way. The Ganesha-Ganapathi principle is in operation at every level. When the cells form a new organ, Ganesha-Ganapathi is the unitary consciousness and presiding power of the organ's task. When the organs come together and form a system, Ganesha-Ganapathi is again the unifying power and presiding consciousness of the group entity. This whole idea is strikingly similar to the Christ who is recorded as saying "Wherever two or more are gathered, there I am." And like the Christ, Ganesha-Ganapathi is a Son of God that performs a specific function in our spiritual evolution.

Let's return to our story to see how Ganesha-Ganapathi came to be worshipped first among the celestials.

Race around the Universe

Shiva and Parvati were now at peace once again, but the crowd had again gathered curious to see the strange, new, elephant-headed entity.

Suddenly from among the denizens of consciousness a voice was heard. "Now there is yet another divine being! Mortals will soon develop religious ceremonies. Who shall be considered the first divine being to be recognized in such ceremonies? Who shall be first among us?" the voice asked insistently. "We need some order, this is all getting ridiculous!"

Looking at Parvati, Shiva immediately understood both the voice and the problem. He quickly answered to forestall a minor revolt. "That sentiment is quite correct. We need to determine who will be first among us in matters of ceremonial observance. Therefore, I propose a race around the universe." This idea was met with enthusiasm. Continuing, Shiva suggested that the members of the gathered assemblage each race around the entire universe three times. The first to complete this race would be crowned the winner, with the reward that the winner would be honored first in any divine ceremony or general undertaking from that time forward.

Each of the celestials headed toward his or her "mount." The Sanskrit term for mount is *vahan*. But strictly speaking the *vahan* is the means of manifestation for the thing it carries.

Subramanya climbed onto his peacock; Vishnu mounted his eagle. Each sat astride his or her own divine animal or bird vehicle for the duration of their competitive journey. An official starting point was determined and once all the contestants were lined up, Shiva held his trident aloft as a "get ready" signal. Suddenly, he dropped it and shouted, "Go!" Almost immediately all of the celestials were out of view, except one—Ganesha-Ganapathi.

Riding his *vahan*, a rat, Ganesha-Ganapathi went only a few strides down the platform that led out into the cosmos and stopped. "What nonsense!" He muttered acridly. "I haven't a chance."

"What's the matter?" asked Shiva.

"Everyone has a faster vehicle than I do. There is no way that I can compete with Vishnu or my brother Subramanya or any of the others. I might as well stop right here." With a sigh, Ganesha-Ganapathi stopped his trek and sat sadly astride his rat.

"My boy, your mother and I have given you every advantage," Shiva chided him. "You have both *siddhis* (magical powers) and *buddhi* (divine, self-aware intelligence). Is there no way you can think your way out of this apparent problem?"

Ganesha's head snapped up. "What do you mean? What are you trying to say? Is there something I can do? C'mon, gimme a break, here!"

"As a judge in the race, I cannot show you any favoritism. I just think you should use your head, that's all." Shiva was visibly disappointed.

Ganapathi knew he was missing something, some bit of information that contained an answer to his problem. But what was it? He decided to review the available facts: The celestials all wanted to be the first one honored in divine affairs and assemblages. To determine who would be first, a race three times around the universe would be held, with each celestial riding on his or her own particular mount. Since he was large and his vehicle, the rat, was tiny, his journey would be ponderously slow. Finally, the race had been devised by his parents, who would not be participating, but only presiding.

Somewhere among these essentials was a key to this mystery. What could make him go faster than the others in the race? It was not possible to change the laws of local physics for him alone; his father would never allow such a thing. That was out of the question. If he took a shorter route, he would not be fulfilling the terms of the race, so that was out, too. He could use a different mount, but that would disqualify him. What could it be?

He thought, then, of asking his mother. Maybe she could offer him a clue. As he started to go to her, limping along on his rat. Shiva smiled broadly and muttered, "I think he's got it."

A shock went through Ganesha-Ganapathi. When he rode toward his mother, his father believed he had finally "gotten it." Gotten what?

Everything slowed down as Ganesha reviewed the data in his head and he and his rat lumbered toward Parvati. When he came within three strides of his mother, she turned around suddenly and beamed at him. In the flash of her beatific smile he "realized" his way to victory.

Without losing even a single stride, he rode his rat round and round the smiling figure of his mother. When he had completed three trips around her, Shiva went to him and, beaming to himself, placed a golden crown on Ganesha-Ganapathi's head, declaring him the winner.

Soon some of the speediest of the celestials began arriving back from their three laps around the universe. The first to arrive, Subramanya riding his peacock, noticed the crown of victory on Ganapathi's head and let out a cry of disappointment and irritation. "Hey! He didn't pass me. How come he's the winner?"

The next celestial concluding the race had a similar reaction. "Old trunk face never passed me!" In a few moments there were a dozen or more clamoring for an explanation or crying "Foul!" and "Fixed!"

Shiva raised his hands to quiet them down. "As you can see, I have declared Ganesha-Ganapathi the winner. Now let him tell you why he qualifies as victor."

With that, all turned to Ganesha, who spoke clearly and with great devotion. "This entire universe is my Divine Mother. Her body is the divine energy of the cosmos displayed in the illusion of forms. And yet, my Divine Mother also sits here in front of us all. Thus, by going round my mother three times, I have traversed the farthest corners of this universe. By going round her three times, I have gone round this universe three times. It cannot be otherwise." He ended with a quiet question. "Who among you can call me wrong?"

The celestials all joined their palms in the greeting. "Salutations to the divine Ganesha-Ganapathi!"

Subramanya, chief of the celestial army, spoke for them all. "Oh Ganesha, your wisdom shines like a thousand suns. While we egotistically strode around this cosmos, you have allowed the devotion of your heart to shine into the mind, and light the spark of intuition. Truth has opened to you. Truly you deserve to be first among us. For Parvati is verily this entire universe in a single person. Salutations to Ganesha-Ganapathi. Salutations to Parvati, Divine Mother and body of the Cosmos. Salutations to Shiva, consciousness everywhere in everything."

And from that day to this, Ganapathi is honored first among all the celestials in any ceremony or before beginning any endeavor. In any ceremonial honoring any of the Hindu Pantheon, a Ganesha-Ganapathi mantra is the very first mantra uttered.[8] When a new house is being considered, Ganesha-Ganapathi mantras are chanted and ceremonies performed. If there is some family or business difficulty, Ganesha-Ganapathi mantras are chanted and ceremonies observed. If any obstacle or trouble should appear, Ganesha-Ganapathi mantras spring to the lips of millions upon millions of devout Hindus all over the world.

The chanting of the mantras begins to break down the obstructing or disharmonious energy pattern that is interfering with the desired end or goal. Although the practice is as old as the sandy soil turned over for centuries by patient ox-driven plows, the concepts are as contemporary as those found in the modern use of twenty-first century tractors.

ANCIENT WISDOM IS TODAY'S SCIENCE

To review ideas presented in a previous chapter, in modern physics we know that every particle of matter can be divided again and again until we finally arrive at intricate patterns of energy that are illusive and ephemeral. What we call "matter" cannot be pinned down in any comforting way. Although we have discovered laws that govern the behavior or properties of matter under a variety of conditions, the "substance" of matter itself is nowhere to be found. It is astonishing to consider that spiritual teachers of old India understood this phenomenon without having the benefit of modern scientific methods of proof.

As the Hindu tradition tells us, Shiva and Parvati — energy and consciousness dancing together—created the universe. The ancient Greeks had a word that expresses the same idea in a slightly different way:

bylozoism, which means "life at every level." The Greeks saw the continuum of matter as alive from the smallest particle up to the largest boulder, planet, or sun.

If we, today, understand that the universe is essentially intelligent energy, then it does not matter if that understanding manifests in complex mathematical formulas or in the neighboring wheat field. We all still must behave according to laws consequent to our reality.

CHAPTER 11

GANESHA-GANAPATHI: THE EXTERNAL UNIVERSE FOUND WITHIN

N ANCIENT DICTUM OF METAPHYSICS is that "Man is the microcosm of the macrocosm," meaning that man is the entire universe in miniature. This same idea is reflected in the Biblical statement, "Man is created in God's image." By this we understand that a human being, when fully developed spiritually, will manifest divine attributes that God bestowed upon humankind as its birthright. Jesus and Moses each demonstrated miraculous powers by showing control over the forces of nature. Jesus even stated, " . . . and greater things shall ye do." His words imply that the kind of miracles he performed, and more, can be done by others.

Whether in the healing energy utilized by authentic healers or in the medical prescriptions given from the deep trance of mystic Edgar Cayce, the upper reaches of an expanded human potential peek out at us from everywhere in religious literature as demonstrated by various individuals. These individuals live among us in every era, and they, as well as we, contain the inherent capability to attain similar high states of consciousness and ability.

From the myths of India, the story of Ganesha-Ganapathi provides an ancient key to our spiritual development. Our evolution back to cosmic consciousness is possible because the entire universe is contained within, as clearly represented by Ganesha-Ganapathi, the "Lord of Cosmic Consciousness."

As already discussed, without the combination of the masculine and feminine polarity, the universe is no more than a divine idea that is potential, but not yet actualized. When the great masculine intelligence and universal bandwidth unites with the infinite feminine creative power, the universe is born.

Ganesha-Ganapathi is also born of the union of the supreme masculine and feminine principles. He is the unifying consciousness of the universe, operating with both volitional power and self-knowledge.

The two great powers of Ganesha-Ganapathi are expressed as his "wives" or his "spouses." The idea of spouses is consistent with the concept of the nature of power as feminine. These powers or "wives" of Ganesha-Ganapathi are *siddhi* and *buddhi*.

SIDDHI IS DIVINE POWER

When people practice spiritual disciplines with regularity over time, certain changes in their perceptions occur. Sometimes they have new abilities, such as clairvoyance. They may become psychic. Others may manifest profound healing abilities. Still others may find that they have some new ways of interacting with life based upon a blossoming understanding of the law of consequence, or karma. There is nothing extraordinary about this. Anyone may test this statement in the laboratory of his or her own life. Such abilities are part of the spiritual birthright of us all. While the scriptures of most of the great world religions also make this claim, in Hinduism this idea is explicitly expressed as the varieties of spiritual power that automatically accompany an expansion of consciousness. Some are found vested in sages and saints such as described by Paramahansa Yogananda in his classic *Autobiography of a Yogi*. There are two categories of these abilities called *siddhis* and *tushtis* that are commonly discussed in a variety of texts. The following list of "Great Abilities" will show you the various attributes associated with *siddhis* and *tushtis*.

SIDDHIS

Anima:	The ability to become atomic in size
Mahima:	The ability to become larger in size
Lagima:	To become light as air
Grima:	To become heavy
Vayapti:	To spread or move and materialize in many places
Prakamya:	To fulfill desires at will
Eshitva:	Lordship over millions of souls
Vashitva:	The ability to attract anything

TUSHTIS

Bhuta Bhavishaya Jnana	Knowledge of past, present, and future
Dura-Dristi	Clairvoyance
Dura-Shravana	Clairaudience
Parakaya Pravesha:	Entering into another's body
Kaya-Vhuha	Materializing simultaneously in many places
Jiva Dana	Bringing the dead back to life
Jiva Krana	Causing the death of anyone at will
Sarga Krana	Creating new worlds or galaxies
Arga Krana	Destroying that which has been created

MINOR SIDDHIS
(WITH SOME DUPLICATION FROM ABOVE)

1. Freedom from hunger and thirst
2. Freedom from the effects of heat and cold
3. Clairvoyance
4. Clairaudience
5. Control of the mind
6. Able to take any form
7. Animate a dead body
8. Death at will
9. Playing with Devas after first seeing them

10. Fulfill desires at will
11. Knowledge of past, present, and future
12. Move beyond the pairs of opposites
13. Prophecy
14. Turn base metals into gold
15. Taking multiple bodies for the purpose of working out karma
16. Jumping power of a frog
17. Destroy sorrows and diseases
18. Knowledge of one's past lives
19. Knowledge of the clusters of stars and planets
20. Power of perceiving the *siddhas*
21. Master of the elements and of the *prana*
22. Can move to any place
23. Omnipotence and omniscience
24. Can rise in the air and stay there as long as desired
25. Can point out where various treasures are hidden

BUDDHI IS DIVINE WISDOM

Ganesha's second "wife" is *buddhi*. As divine self-aware intelligence governed by wisdom, *buddhi* (from whence derives the idea of a *"Buddha"* and, eventually, Buddhism) is an outgrowth of universal understanding. The mystics of India taught that cosmic consciousness is a state wherein we are dynamically "at one" with the form and consciousness of the universe. This unity with universe will automatically make universal understanding available to anyone who achieves it. Thus, *buddhi* will always accompany cosmic consciousness.

So the divine attributes (wives) which accompany Ganapathi are: *siddhi*, the ability to accomplish within himself (that is, anywhere within the entire manifested universe) and *buddhi*, the wisdom to know what to do, when to do it, and how to accomplish it. In this light, Ganesha-Ganapathi signifies the idea of an entirely sentient universe on the one hand, and the sentient universe specifically contained within the human potential on the other.

Although sentience on such a scale that it includes the entire universe may seem incomprehensible to our human ego in its everyday state, great states of self-realization have been achieved for centuries by souls striving to attain them. A multitude of sages and saints over the centuries have brought forth within themselves states of existence explicitly described in various mystical texts. And these texts contain amazing similarities in their descriptions of these higher states. Whether following a path pertaining to Shiva or one dedicated to Lakshmi, the four states of consciousness and the levels within them are described in remarkably similar language whether these states are described in the Puranas (mythic stories) or Tantras (texts on paths to spiritual attainment).

LEVELS OF CONSCIOUSNESS

Jagrat (Waking State): The state of consciousness in which most of us live our lives.

Swapna (Dream State): The dream world we inhabit during sleep and remember upon awakening.

Aviveko or *Shushupti* (Deep Sleep): That level of sleep wherein even the dreams do not occur. The mind does not function even in the dream state. Only the *prana* is active.

Turiya: The higher state of consciousness that emerges from its eternal hiding place within. One cannot reach it directly by effort, but we can prepare ourselves through spiritual practices so that that omnipresent and eternal state of consciousness emerges from its place in the background of our consciousness.

Three states of *Turiya*:

Turiya Jagrat: The activity of the normal mind ceases, and supermind emerges.

Turiya Swapna: The person crosses the boundaries of limitation of knowledge and enters the realm of unlimited knowledge.

Turiya Shushupti: In this state one perceives that everything is composed of some form of shakti.

Turiyatita: A state of uninterrupted divine rapture where the I-sense in the normal ego connection does not exist. All distinctions, including those between immanent and transcendent disappear.[9] The great, true Sadgurus are in this state. Dattatreya, widely regarded as the first Sadguru on record, was once asked to discuss the significant spiritual differences between *dvaita* (dualism) and *advaita* (nondualism). He replied that if one was still concerned with these kinds of distinctions, one still had a ways to go.

Since Ganesha is said to be approachable as either a formless entity, or through his cuddly form seen in illustrations, then realization of states of consciousness attained through him must be one of the three states of *Turiya*, or of *Turiyatita*. Whatever state of consciousness we individually achieve, our work begins and ends within ourselves for we are the entire universe in miniature.

MICRO EXPRESSION OF GANESHA

The outworking of Ganesha-Ganapathi in you and me requires a deeper look at our spiritual physiology. In humanity, Ganesha-Ganapathi has a spiritual physiological location that is really only a starting point.

In the Muladhara Chakra, at the base of the spine in the human subtle body, sits Ganesha-Ganapathi. As Sant Keshavadas states in his book, *Lord Ganesha*, "Ganesha's abode is called *Swananda Dhama* (the Abode of Bliss) and is created by a partial manifestation of his shakti called *Kama Dayani Yoga Shakti*. He can be approached as either *Nirguna* (formless) or *Saguna* (with a form). . . . The triangle [his Island abode] is in us at the base of the spine in the Muladhara Chakra. To that Island, all the nerves (*nadis*) in our system are connected in the subtle body. It is the source of energy and procreation as well. That is where we can find Ganesha. He is part of our own self at all times and in all situations. Even though he is all pervading, he still manifests a distinct transcendental personality."[10]

Even though the Ganesha *Loka* within is carefully described at a certain inner location, his influence is said to spread everywhere, because at this location at the base of the spine, there are channels that lead to every portion of the physical and subtle components of human anatomy. Thus, his operation is not static (operating only from a single place) but dynamic. It moves from place to place within us depending upon the needs and state of development of the organism.

I call this activity of Ganapathi a phantom chakra that moves from place to place inside us. It starts its journey closest to the kundalini shakti, the Great Feminine power source at the base of the spine. At this location, it is entirely consistent with Ganesha-Ganapathi's creation in the myths pertaining to him. He is devoted to his mother, meaning he has access to the kundalini shakti and can use her power at will.

The key to understanding Ganapathi's moving nature lies in viewing the relationship between where our consciousness is now and to where it will evolve with his help. He is often called the Lord of Cosmic Consciousness. That does not imply that he is cosmic consciousness, but rather that he empowers something that attains it. That something is our Ego-Mind-Personality.

THE RAT

In the story of the race around the universe, Ganesha's vehicle is the rat. Now if Ganesha-Ganapathi is a symbol for cosmic consciousness, what could the rat possibly be? This tiny, humble, feral, glitteringly intelligent rodent symbolizes our everyday Ego-Mind-Personality, or *ahamkara* as it is called in Sanskrit. We all try to satisfy our ego wants and ego needs everyday, but we are often spiritually small and devious in the way we go about fulfilling those desires. Just like a rat.

The venerable *I Ching*, the Chinese oracle-in-a-book, states that to achieve spiritual progress one begins with "uncompromising truthfulness with oneself." Engaging in just a little of this practice discloses some of the ignoble, selfish, negatively self-serving qualities of our ratlike ego, as we go through life constantly seeking a position of advantage or superiority over conditions and other people.

Most of us decided early in life to seek some kind of advantage or superiority over life conditions and other people as a way to survive. The
seemingly natural attempt to advance over the pack is programmed into
us. We learn it all at home and in school at a very early age. But this
assumption and corresponding conduct based upon it will not lead us back
to that divine place from which we have come. The image from ancient
Hinduism of the ego as a rat is quite appropriate.

But why should cosmic consciousness sit astride a rat? It seems like a cosmic joke until we understand it in a larger context: Even our humble ego can
have a great destiny if it submits to the divine. We can attain the highest wisdom, *buddhi*, and the vast spiritual ability to accomplish called *siddhi*, but to
do this the ego must become the *vahan*, the vehicle for something greater.

That small creature in us, that at first avoids the light, can become the
vehicle for that which the Ego-Mind-Personality is striving to attain. The
rat now becomes noble. It is the ratlike Ego-Mind-Personality that awakens
to conclude that there is more to life than eating, sleeping, mating, and fulfilling desires. It is that same part of us that picks a path of evolutionary
progress and starts to work. This is the part of us that performs discipline,
continues to strive, has noble ambition, receives the grace of God, and eventually achieves immortality.

The Ganesha-Ganapathi principle sits astride the rat of our ego, and
helps it, guides it, sometimes scolds it, rewards it as they ride together from
lowly self-serving ignorance, to a transformed state where the ego becomes
divine and experiences the bliss of cosmic consciousness. The ego achieves
this through the Grace of the Great Feminine that created the Ganesha-
Ganapathi entity in the first place and then empowered it. Because the
intelligence and wisdom springing from great and benevolent consciousness was requisite to its function, Shiva also blessed the elephant-headed
one and insured that he was the first among the celestials. With the power
of the kundalini shakti at the base of the spine at his disposal, and the
omnipresent consciousness of Shiva constantly with him, Ganesha-
Ganapathi can now commence that task for which he was created: l
eading the ego back to its position of individual cosmic consciousness,
back to its source.

To understand the magnitude of this task, it helps to consider the multiple nature of the human ego.

WHO AM I NOW?

The ego interacts with the universe through the mind, personality, appetites, desires, goals, strategies, and a host of other qualities that are almost never in agreement with one another. To a person with a weight problem, there is an I who wants to eat far too much. But there is another I who wants to lose weight. These two I's are both part of the ego but are in direct conflict with one another.[11]

We encounter the idea of multiple I's all the time as we navigate through life conditions. The smoker who wants to stop has a difficult time mastering the I who wants to continue puffing away. The person who drifts from job to job is in conflict with the I who wants a steady worklife.

The problem we experience with all of our ego I's is that there is no unity among them. There is no master I who makes all the other I's behave according to some overriding value system or criteria upon which the I's can agree, or with which they will conform. The result is conflict. Although the conflict is within, it usually plays out in the drama of our unfolding lives.

The person who longs for a meaningful relationship but serially sabotages it is in a state of inner disagreement and turmoil. If all the I's within agreed that a single, steady, fulfilling, and meaningful relationship was desirable and possible, it would happen in the outer world. But for a variety of reasons best left to psychologists to unravel, there is no inner agreement. Conflict and strife among conflicting parts of ourselves that all claim to be I is the standard for most of us in life.

Following the path offered by Ganesha-Ganapathi, however, the unification of all the various I's into a coherent unity can be accomplished bringing peace and mental clarity, and ultimately much, much more.

MAKING A CONSCIOUS DECISION AND STARTING OUT

Although the path back to union with Narayana offered by Ganesha-Ganapathi is made easy by mantras that focus our efforts and remove obstacles, we must first choose to begin the process. Then we must understand that the path back may take more than an afternoon, a day, or even a month. The return journey to the state of unity called cosmic consciousness may even take several lifetimes because we have forgotten who we really are.

The doctrine of reincarnation or rebirth is based upon multiple and sequential incarnations that are determined by our karma. At its core, the doctrine of reincarnation assumes the goal of minimizing the number of lives it will take for us to re-achieve the sublime state from which we started. And achievement of that goal is entirely dependant upon the decisions we make after assuming a human form. If we have been particularly recalcitrant and coldly self-serving, more lives may be required. If we have been relatively "good" in the sense that negative conduct has not predominated, the journey back may take fewer lifetimes to accomplish. Freedom of choice and ensuing consequences are factors we cannot escape. However, by the Grace of the feminine, Ganesha-Ganapathi was created to ensure our eventual success.

Just as Jesus has said, "I am the Way, the Truth and the Life," the Ganesha principle, illustrated by Ganesha sitting astride the ego, clearly holds forth a "way" for spiritual advancement and leads one on a path in life to achieve the highest spiritual ends.

Is activation of the phantom Ganapathi-Ganesha chakra the only route to regaining our divine state? Not at all. Quite to the contrary, any path followed with effort and sincerity will achieve that sublime goal and receive grace along the way. But the story of Ganesha-Ganapathi is a vivid portrayal of both the route and the end goal of our common journey. Sanskrit mantras that belong to the way of Ganesha-Ganapathi can greatly aid in the progress of the journey and allow us to fulfill some of our most cherished desires in the process. Using mantras to consciously link the Ganesha-Ganapathi phantom chakra to our operational Ego-Mind-Personality assures us that both our higher consciousness (Shiva) and the power of the universe (Parvati) will guide us toward our highest spiritual objectives.

Before you embark upon a structured mantra discipline, you might chant mantra number two below for five minutes or so to begin the process of inner unification so that your discipline will be successful.

MANTRAS OF GANESHA-GANAPATHI

These mantras will be useful at any stage of your spiritual journey, regardless of which path you choose.

> 1. Om Sri Ganeshaya Namaha
> [Om Shree Guh-ney-shah-ya Nah-mah-ha]

This is a mantra of conscious contact with the auspicious and giving nature of the Ganesha-Ganapathi phantom chakra. Use this mantra to begin to weave a positive "can do" spirit into your everyday ego.

> 2. Om Gum Ganapatayei Namaha
> [Om Guhm Guh-nuh-puh-tuh-yei Nah-mah-ha]

The eighty-ninth Upanishad gives this mantra the designation as the remover of obstacles. Obstacles here refer to the blockages to true inner unity. Once obstacles are removed, we can accomplish inner unification of the various and diverse I's that comprise our ego. Prolonged use of this mantra, or an intense spiritual discipline for forty days using this mantra will begin to break down negative and artificial barriers among the various I's that compose our multifaceted ego. The outward effect of this beginning step of inner unification is the disappearance or dissolution of obstacles that previously stood in our way.

It may be that we want a better job and chant *Om Gum Ganapatayei Namaha* for that purpose. Suddenly, a shift in events begins to take place. A new opportunity appears on the horizon, or a familiar situation is perceived in a new way. A new or better job appears, springing from the chaotic conditions just as a splendid lotus blooms from a murky pond. However, even though you are saying the mantra for a specific reason, your entire spiritual journey is also enhanced. As through the Ganesha-Ganapathi mantra you have begun the process of unifying the various I's within. In fact, I have conducted experiments with this mantra (described in my book *Healing Mantras*) with extraordinary success.

In the journey to become a divine ego resting in cosmic consciousness, the unification of various I's is mandatory. Using Ganesha-Ganapathi mantras, compassion and grace can become attendant elements of the journey.

3. Maha Ganapathi Step Mantra

There is a long Ganesha Mantra called the Maha Ganapathi Step Mantra, so named because each "step" to constructing the whole mantra is also a complete mantra in itself. Maha has a dual meaning. In one context it means "great." But in a subtle context, it also means the heart center. Therefore, this mantra can be helpful in centering tangible spiritual power on a foundation of heartfelt impulses. This is an important idea in our development because not all of our raw impulses are either heartfelt or helpful.

In the following discipline, the power of the mantra is built with increasing intensity by repeating each step from three to one hundred and eight times; this is also called repeating one mala (the Hindu rosary), which consists of 108 beads. Over the course of working with each longer and longer mantra, you are, with perfect precision, building the entire mantra within yourself. This technique can be especially useful in learning long mantras with which you are unfamiliar. At the same time, it is also a wonderful way to increase the power within of the various *bija* or seed mantras contained in the final mantra.

If you are planning to perform this mantra discipline in the classical way, saying each step 108 times, allow yourself at least an hour each day for the practice. Ninety minutes is probably closer to the time you will need when starting out, unless you are very familiar with the mantras and can repeat them quickly.

The complete Maha Ganapathi Step Mantra progression looks like this:

Om Swaha	(repeat 3-108 times)
Om Srim Swaha	(repeat 3-108 times)
Om Srim Hrim Swaha	(repeat 3-108 times)
Om Srim Hrim Klim Swaha	(repeat 3-108 times)
Om Srim Hrim Klim Glaum Swaha	(repeat 3-108 times)
Om Srim Hrim Klim Glaum Gam Swaha	(repeat 3-108 times)
Om Srim Hrim Klim Glaum Gam Ganapatayei Swaha	(repeat 3-108 times)
Om Srim Hrim Klim Glaum Gam Ganapatayei Vara	
Varada Swaha	(repeat 3-108 times)
Om Srim Hrim Klim Glaum Gam Ganapatayei Vara	
Varada Sarva Janam Me Vasham Swaha	(repeat 3-108 times)

COMPLETE MANTRA

Om Srim Hrim Klim Glaum Gum Ganapatayei
Vara Varada Sarva Janam Me
Vasha-manaya Swaha   (repeat 3-108 times)
[Om Shreem Hreem Kleem Glowm Guhm Guh-nuh-puh-tuh-yei
Vah-rah Vah-rah-dah Sahr-vah Jah-nahm Mei
Vah-sha-mah-nah-yah Swah-ha]

Rough Translation: "Om. May the abundance-producing Great Remover of Obstacles that transcends this apparent reality bring all things that concern me under my control."

The Ganesha-Ganapathi phantom chakra operates by both rewarding and occasionally obstructing the progress of the ratlike ego, "reminding" the ego of its true task of spiritual evolution. If one strays too far in conduct or goals, a limiting force may temporarily appear. However, such a timely reminder is actually a compassionate expression of our highest good. Once we have understood the message, the things and conditions we desired that had been temporarily forestalled flow to us unimpeded once again.

SPIRITUAL PROGRESS WHILE SMELLING THE FLOWERS

Once the journey has begun, Ganesha-Ganapathi positively reinforces mantra work with quick (and sometimes lavish) rewards and tangible spiritual progress. But the journey will take longer than the ego believes in the beginning stages. So surprises and wonders will be revealed at places along the way, similar to scattering candy along a long and winding path to reward the traveler and ensure continued effort. Native Americans might call the Ganesha-Ganapathi phantom chakra an ally. At every step in the unification of multiple I's, he is with us, and is available to help and bless us as he moves with the Ego-Mind-Personality and shepherds it toward its divine destiny.

PART III

THE CHAKRAS

CHAPTER 12

SEPARATION WHILE STILL JOINED

TILLNESS. VOID. Nonbeing. Yet still existent.

In some incomprehensible reality a drama begins. In a place the mind cannot find, our senses cannot penetrate, and our intellect cannot fathom, a Being exists. The infinite unknown, in a form of its own creation, lies dormant, unmoving, yet containing consciousness and power with abilities to operate that human understanding simply cannot contain. Without preamble, a flash of an unknown spiritual substance enters a space we can only liken to a womb. There, an incipient universe, ours, and others, is conceived.

Opening from within itself to a newly created "somewhere," a fluid of some sort flows forth; a mixture of energy and light, of consciousness and activity, of blossoming mind, purpose, and the means to accomplish.

It is completely still, yet contains an infinite dynamism. It stretches forth like a brilliant shining sea upon which no wind moves nor waves appear.

Suddenly, a dimple appears on the surface of the many-dimensioned sea. Quickly it draws the sea down from a dimple to a whirlpool, to a surging wormhole leading to a new reality that it, itself, is creating second by second. Yet the deepening wormhole is still a part of the sea above. There is still unity. Only one thing exists in a state of pure Being.

Then, like a tail, the plunging whirlpool separates ever so slightly from the surface of the sea, like a bubble sucked below the surface of a vast ocean. The bubble, on the top of a still plunging whirlpool, is now separate from the surface of the sea. The clinging surface tension of the cosmic ocean has been breached and something separate now exists within it. For its part, the ocean has not been diminished, even as something new is created and contained as separate from it yet part of it. It is still one thing in the throws of gigantic process.

The bubble contains all the ingredients of the sea. It contains light, brilliance, consciousness, might, will, a form of insurmountable sovereignty, and something new: self-awareness.

The bubble understands in some sublime manner that it is a "thing." It perceives itself as something separate from the shining, shimmering, conscious sea. It understands that it is one with that sea, yet separate. With that understanding comes the beginning of a cosmic ego. To even generate and cognize that there is something of which it is a part automatically means that there is a new sense of self which contains that observation and reflects upon it. The perception of its separation is a function of cosmic mind. The reflection upon the meaning of that separation is a function of cosmic intellect. Both are housed and contained in a blossoming cosmic ego.

That part of the bubble that can now perceive casts its attention downward to the deepening tail of itself that still spins down into newly created places that appear simply through the act of deepening itself. The cosmic ego beholds the process and watches as other and new things also begin to appear within itself, as its tail plunges ever downward.

Brilliant designs, shapes, colors, and potencies come into existence. The cosmic mind observes and the cosmic intellect considers. The designs are mandalas of new levels of consciousness, manipulative ability, avenues of activity, fields of endeavor, vistas of speculation. Each complex design of color, pattern, and design is a chakra, a processing vortex of consciousness and energy functioning on its own plane according to its own frequency. Cosmic Laws and Cosmic Limits operate within each chakra, defining its field of play.

Down, down, down the tail of the bubble descends. After establishing several points that are sublime chakras, it pauses. At a new point it creates and establishes a realm in which it places a blueprint of itself in complete detail—both its individual existence, and its essence as part of the great sea. Then it continues diving downward until it reaches a dividing point between what will be called the realms of light and the realms of darkness. Of course this is a misnomer, because even the realms of darkness have light. But the light of the darker centers are of a completely different composition and character. At the dividing point, the descent stops briefly.

At the dividing point between the realms of light and darkness, a new separation appears inside the bubble. A portion of itself sits at the division, seemingly as a guardian at the gateway between the two realms. At this place, a new internal energy point is also established. Then the newly created guardian of the gateway moves and places itself on the Energy Point. The tail of the bubble descends downward until a mirrored structure of the upper levels is created. There are fourteen design stations or mandalas in all. Seven of the stations are in realms that we would call light, and seven in what we would call darkness.

Now the bubble ceases its activity. It observes, considers, and reflects. Sending a tendril out from within itself, it establishes a contact of consciousness with both the guardian and the Energy Point at the division within the realms of light and darkness. Just as the bubble considers itself as separate from the sea, even while still connected, the guardian considers itself separate, even as it knows it is connected with both the bubble and the sea. The Energy Point is inscrutable and seems to have its own consciousness, energy, will, and purpose. It is both part of the bubble yet separate from it in some mystical way.

There are no questions, no "what ifs," no "maybes." There is only the unending joy of existence flowing in, between, and among different levels of existence, all floating on and in a sea of consciousness that permeates everything. It is still but not static. It is full of energy but quiescent. It is purposeful but not active. The stage has been set but the drama not yet begun.

Let's pause, now, and define the characters in the unfolding drama.

1. The bubble is each one of us, individually, in our complete cosmic character. The closest character in Hindu Mysticism is Subramanya. In *Hindu Gods and Goddesses*, Swami Harshananda states, "Subramanya consciousness is the highest state that any individual entity can attain or maintain. Beyond it lies only the great ocean in which everything eventually merges."

2. The tail is our spine, called the peacock or Subramanya's vehicle. Individual consciousness and ego, from the most humble to the most sublime, has something that carries it. In the beginning decent from its very high state, the still divine ego rides in and is contained by the body. This is the Subramanya state of consciousness carried by a peacock.

   As an early representation of individual existence, the Subramanya principle with its peacock vehicle is a most beautiful, yet carefully hidden map of how that piece of Narayana, of Shiva, that is our soul moves "down" into a physical existence from a place of consciousness united with all creation. An examination of the peacock begins to reveal the deeper meaning of Subramanya, who is most often referred to as the god of war.

3. The blueprint of itself, Narayana is the soul, self, *atman*, *jiva*. It is both part of and separate from the great Ocean of Consciousness and Energy. As Spock says in *Star Trek* (in the episode, "The Amok Time") "Separate but never parted."

   The soul, *atman*, moves down from the surface of the Great Ocean of Consciousness, down from crown chakra at the top of the head, into the rest of the brain. Later it will move into the body. In the brain the soul or *atman*, understanding itself is a separate conscious entity, creates a new form. When our individual *atman* was totally immersed in Shiva, it was in a state of consciousness in unity with the consciousness of the entire universe: We were a cup poured into the ocean. Although the cup of our individual existence stood ready, the contents of our being was immersed in the great water of the ocean, and also part of it.

When the cup dips into the ocean and brings up a portion of the water, separation occurs—the water in the cup is now separate from the water of the ocean.

4. The energy patterns are the chakras, seven upper luminous *Lokas* and seven nether spheres. The chakras are energy processing vortexes, each containing a collection of energy potentials, frequencies, and capacities for operation.

When we are held within and part of the shimmering sea, all potencies are infinitely available. There is no separation. There is only Shiva and the bliss of absorption. Then the center of our being dips downward into the rest of the brain, and we become aware of our individual existence because we experience separation from the ocean of Shiva-Shakti. We understand the potential offered by individual existence. A divine ego forms and we become self-aware and cognizant of others who are also self-aware.

From the Subramanya state in the head just below the crown chakra, where our highest individual superconscious awareness operates, we descend with our sublime and divine ego still part of our cosmic soul, into the successive dimensions of familiar reality represented by the chakras and the elements that predominate or rule them. From the head, we dip into the spine and spy all the principles of matter yet to come.

First stop is the Ajna Chakra at the brow center where overall unity is established insuring that all levels of subsequent creation will be integrated into this place of consciousness. From here spring the pairs of complementary opposites: male and female, hot and cold, yin and yang, and so on. Forms of spiritual electrical currents come into being and vehicles for containing and directing them are created: the masculine current *ida;* the feminine current *pinagala;* and the *shushumna* or spine. The latter will hold centers called chakras that correspond to the great levels or spheres of the manifest universe. Then the cosmic ego and the still connected *atman* slip into the newly created spine and begin their descent down toward materiality.

The next stop is the Vishuddha or throat chakra where time-transcending ether is born. Here the construct of time appears, and will play itself out for billions of years.

Then the soul and cosmic ego descends with perfect consciousness into the Anahata Chakra or heart center. The soul or *atman* pauses here and constructs a resting place. Called the Hrit Padma in both Hinduism and Buddhism, we might call it the "sacred heart." It is a small eight-petaled chakra where the *atman* waits and observes. The Hrit Padma is formed just below the Anahata Chakra or heart center into which the soul settles as it continues to create the rest of its spiritual vehicle, the human subtle and physical bodies.

Now the individual ego is still exalted, but no longer divine in the sense that it was before its separation from the *atman*. It continues to descend into the realms of matter to experience and learn. This is our own personal Ego with its cousins, the Individual Mind and the Personality.

One by one, the lower chakras come into existence: the Manipura Chakra at the solar plexus and the Swadhisthana Chakra at the sacral plexus. Finally, the earth is reached at the bottom of the spine with the creation of the Muladhara Chakra at the coccygeal plexus. Here, the creative power of the very universe itself rests in each human individual, sliding into a semi-sleep mode.

Now, the soul has completed the first phase of its directive from Narayana. It has "involved" into a state of individual existence in a material universe. Involution is complete. The divine essence, shimmering like a flame, rests in the sacred heart. Here this light—"not of this world"—always shines. Through our human incarnations, Narayana, as the soul or *atman*, our divine essence, will begin to learn the lessons of "materiality."

At once completely detached, and yet totally involved, the soul watches in perfect serenity as this new thing, the human body with its subtle energy body and dormant feminine power, functions in the world.

The soul has followed the original impetus of Shiva or Narayana and begun a quest via a journey of involution to learn about
materiality. The initial part of the journey has finally come to an
end at the base of our spine. Here individual evolution commences with all of its experiences, choices, consequences, and
distractions, toward that state which we left so long ago.

5. The guardian at the place between the realms of light and darkness is what the Hindus call Ganesha. He is the symbol of unity,
of consciously directed movement and evolution, and an ally of
growth. In the broadest of terms, one could call this point a "son
of God," leading and helping individual souls back to their divine
heritage.

6. This point is the kundalini shakti: She who powers everything in
the drama. She is the light and the power of movement in the tail
of the bubble. She is one with the shimmering sea from which all
has come. Yet she also creates a character for herself in the cosmic drama.

We cannot take one breath of air nor think one thought without the power of shakti. She of infinite compassion and power
without limits is the very energy of Shiva. She of limitless, yet
conscious and dynamic energy and power, takes an active role,
like any mother does, in the growth of her children. She establishes herself at the base of our spine, links subtly with the *atman*,
and waits. Yet while waiting, she supplies all the power necessary
to the evolutionary journey we have decided to undertake.

Our wondrous soul also contains the essence of compassion.
Since the evolving Ego-consciousness will experience both pain
and enjoyment while occupying a physical form, the soul-*atman*
empowers that consciousness with two gifts. The first is free will
or choice. The second gift is a "device" that allows the individual
consciousness to operate in the relative world of materiality. This
is called the *ahamkara* in Sanskrit — the sense of individual self —
which I will refer to as the Ego. This includes the Individual Mind
and Personality or The Ego-Mind-Personality.

It is the Ego-Mind-Personality that can choose *how* and *whether* to grow and evolve while in the physical universe. The lowly Ego-Mind-Personality is even offered the priceless gift of becoming divine, should it choose to consciously evolve. Through spiritual growth, the human Ego-Mind-Personality can attain immortality. This is a staggering idea in itself. Think about it, if the Ego-Mind-Personality is really divine and created for the soul or *atman* to experience a drama of growth, then it is already divine. It is already joined with everything. It needs nothing to complete it. Yet, there is a cosmic decision to experience something. So the soul creates it to do just that. Our Ego-Mind-Personality is part of a divine mechanism that the soul devises to experience itself in new ways.

So it separates itself into its essential blueprint of everything cosmic — the soul or *atman*. And it creates within itself something that will carry an understanding of the unity of everything, along with a strong sense of separation expressed through the Ego-Mind-Personality. It also creates deep within the Ego-Mind-Personality the knowledge that it can eventually reunite with the soul—with the divine essence from which it was hatched. It can also, of course, choose not to reunite and eventually perish through sheer obsolescence.

There will come a time when it will no longer be needed in the process of experience. Of course, it will still have a sense of its own existence. So from the standpoint of the soul, the Ego-Mind-Personality must eventually choose between continued life, or expungement. And it must choose which course it will take long before the moment of obsolescence appears. By the time the consequences of the choice really dawns upon the Ego-Mind-Personality, it will be too late to change its mind. The choices will have long since been made. The Ego will be either on the path of light or darkness. It will evolve or be moved. It will choose good or evil.

Miraculously, even those Egos that chose evil will have paths to redemption open to them, because divinity is inherently compassionate. If the Ego-Mind-Personality has made a choice for continued self-gratification while the whole mechanism of the earth is ready to enter a new and higher vibratory state, the Ego-Mind-Personality's vehicle, the physical body, will not be able to transition to the new, higher vibration. If no work has been done by the Ego-Mind-Personality to make the transition, the *atman* and the Ego-Mind-Personality will have no choice but to take incarnation on another planet that is just entering the vibratory state that the earth is leaving. The chances for choices to evolve are unending. They just may not all be on planet earth.

Choice to evolve brings a form of Grace with it. By moving up the spine, unifying its various I's and eventually joining with the *atman* to become something new at the heart center, the Ego-Mind-Personality becomes something it could never have anticipated. The mechanism for the ego to accomplish this journey is called Ganesha, which I have dubbed the Ganesha-Ganapathi phantom chakra.

7. The cosmic ego that first comes to its awareness as separate from the surface of the sea is Subramanya. We have briefly discussed his vehicle, the peacock. Later I will discuss Subramanya himself in more detail.

8. The Sea is a fusion of Shiva, Primordial Consciousness, and Shakti, Primordial Energy.

9. The void of nonBeing where it all begins is either Narayana, or Maha Kali, or Parama Shiva, depending upon the way one chooses to relate to things (or Beings) beyond our ability to understand.

10. The pregnant something that lets the flow come forth is Brahma or Hiranya Garbha, the egg containing the seed of the universe.

11. The Being of Infinite Ability and Infinite Consciousness established in a form of its own making can be called Satya Narayana or Sada Shiva, according to one's inclination.

THE STAGE IS SET: "PLACES EVERYONE!"

The ancient Indian game of Lila is the forerunner to the child's game of Chutes and Ladders. In this game, one makes decisions that lead up a ladder, advancing to victory at the top. However, if one makes a bad decision, the consequence will not lead up, but shove one back down a level or two. If the decision is a particularly bad, one may slide back several layers that have taken a long time to ascend. It can be disheartening.

The game is a good model for the consequence of decisions. Everything has a consequence. As the old adage says, "even not to decide can be to decide." If one endlessly considers whether or not to evacuate before some natural disaster, the nondecision will eventually become a decision.

CHAPTER 13

THE FIRST CHAKRA:
MULADHARA CHAKRA

Ruling Principle: Earth
Issues: Survival and Security
Seed Sound: Lam [Lahm]
Location: Base of the spine

ANY OF US HAVE a nodding acquaintance with Maslow's Hierarchy of Needs. Taught through the use of a pyramid, Maslow points out that we have to have "the basics" to survive. The basics are symbolized by the bottom of the pyramid. If we don't have food and shelter, we won't or can't really be concerned about much else. Survival is the first order of conscious existence. If you can't breathe, air is what you need. So the first level is physiological in scope. The same kind of foundation, with exceptions, is established in the Muladhara or first chakra.

Once survival is assured, security comes next in Maslow's model. Freedom from constant anxiety connected to issues of physiological need is the first level of security. The second level has to do with pleasure and sexual identity.

After these two sets of needs are satisfied to the extent that the mind feels free enough to consider other things, exercise of personal will and power, the need for love, and a sense of belonging appears. We develop a sense of relationship with friends and lovers, family, and others stemming from social needs of human being's social character. Within a social dynamic of any kind comes the need for recognition, in the form of esteem. We need or desire to have good standing within the group. We long for a sense of competency, achievement, some kind of mastery with its corresponding status or fame. We desire to receive appreciation by the group, city, nation, or career group—recognition that is deserved, as opposed to squeezed through inappropriate pressure by threat of harm, giving of money under the table, and similar kinds of fraud. The last stage in Maslow's Hierarchy of Needs is self-actualization, where a person comes to do that for which they are the most suited by nature and constitution. Musicians must play music; athletes must compete while they are able; mathematicians must figure in those areas that delight them. You get the idea.

Spiritually speaking, these steps may be altered and shuffled a bit. A person with humble physiological resources who is intensely interested in the mysteries of existence may join a monastery or become a wandering mendicant. In India, this means becoming a swami, in Tibet, a Lama. In the monastery, physical needs are taken care of. Survival is not an issue.[12]

Since the customary purpose of the monastery is self-actualization, conducted on a predetermined path with specific ends in mind, other areas of Maslow's formula may be squeezed in anywhere. At some place along the monastic path, one may become diverted into monastic politics, and desire to become a manager or supervisor. Then the route to self-actualization can become displaced or suborned to another more secular desire.

Now we have arrived at something Maslow discusses peripherally: The function, strength, and appropriateness of desires. These areas we will look at from a spiritual standpoint throughout the discussion of the chakras.

MULADHARA CHAKRA

The chakra at the base of the spine is where we will begin. From birth to the age of four, we develop an inner sense of who we are and what our relationship is to the world. Basic communication skills can become quite good, while certain pieces of analytical cognition are completely missing.

Once when I was playing with my goddaughter, Ariana, the television was right beside us on the floor. She was about five at the time. We were playing Speak and Spell, and would occasionally stop and watch television. A *Columbo* mystery was on at the time. After about a half hour of alternately playing Speak and Spell and watching television, I realized that I had no idea what was happening in the TV program. I casually asked Ari, "What's going on in the story on TV?" She replied, "I don't know . . . I never know."

I just about fell over. The absolute honesty wowed me. But the message was equally interesting. I concluded that, in my own way, I had entered her five-year old consciousness. I had wanted to be with her, so I adapted by matching my conscious state to hers. I adjusted so that we could literally "hang out" together. The result was that my consciousness was in a place where what was going on "right now" was the overriding wave of the moment. The past-event—two minutes ago—was long over. The future was a nonexistent concept, except in the theoretical way, "If you put away your toys, you can have ice cream." Ice cream in this sense is part of the present, not the future.

I understood, for the first time, that there are stages of consciousness where everyday continuity, such as watching television, play no part at all. Sure, I could watch television, but I would only understand the activity at the moment I was watching. The past events in the program and potential future had no relevance for me at all. I had entered Ariana's world. It was wonderful and magical in its own way, but it had no correlation to the way I lived my life. That consciousness is a pure expression stemming from the ego's place in the Muladhara Chakra.

If we are truly curious, anything can teach us. That experience with Ari was a piece of a mystical puzzle. For, in that specific moment, concentration is very high. But analysis of the experience is very low. When one meditates as an adult, we seek to regain that natural concentration but from a different point of view, using different mental tools. The poet Walt Whitman wrote about "sermons in flowers, stones, and babbling brooks." I understood those words in a classical Eastern mystical way now. It is well understood in the East that when you are able to concentrate deeply on something, it will reveal its secrets to you.

At the Muladhara Chakra, we have a stream of developing consciousness that at first is based entirely upon perceptions. Later, cognition appears, the analytical faculties start to develop around the age of seven or eight. It's no accident that the first initiation a child receives in orthodox Hinduism is at age eight, when the Gayatri Mantra is imparted.

CHAKRAS AND INITIATIONS

Mystical writers such as H.P. Blavatsky and Alice Bailey are part of what I call modern esotericists. They lived in the last 125 years, not two or five thousand years ago or more. These two mystics clearly state that each chakra has seven stages of development within it, so in total there are forty-nine steps in our spiritual development. What they call Major Initiations occur when one's predominant center of consciousness, the Ego-Mind-Personality, moves from one chakra to the next above. Within each chakra are seven lesser initiations.

MANTRAS AND DESIRES FOR SURVIVAL

The first chakra is "ruled" by the earth principle. That is to say its primary field of activity involves the earth and materiality. The seed sound for the Muladhara Chakra is Lam [Lahm]. By saying this seed sound, out loud or silently, one begins to draw in energies that will clear this chakra and start the process to insure basic survival. Some schools of spiritual practice in India teach meditations that concentrate solely on the seed sounds that rule the chakras. Their thinking is that if they clear all the chakras, the potentialities of each will be easier to attain. This idea is controversial, and different schools have different ideas of how to clear the chakras and what kind of energy should be drawn in.

The Siddha lineage and practitioners, for instance, use a mantra that works directly on the elements themselves, rather than on the chakras. They reason that mastery of the elements that rule the chakras will accomplish the goal achieved by saying the seed sound of the chakras and much more besides. The Siddha lineage uses this basic mantra:

Om Namah Shivaya
[Om Nah-Mah Shee-Vah-Yah]

The syllables of the mantra begin to bring the elements that rule or predominate in each chakra under conscious control.

Om	Mind
Na	Earth
Ma	Water
Shi	Fire
Va	Air
Ya	Ether

Through this mantra, all the elements are eventually brought under control of the conscious mind. It might take one person ten lifetimes to accomplish this. For another, it might take one hundred lifetimes. Or for another, only fifty years in a single lifetime. It depends on the state of our instrument, on the agreement between Shiva (consciousness) and Parvati (shakti) within, and on our karma. But no matter how long it takes, eventually mastery will come. Our devotion to Truth will make it come faster. Our dedication to spiritual progress will make it come faster. Our spirit of service to others will make it come faster. The grace flowing to us from those who have already attained will make it come faster. Killing a saint or great sage can make it take longer. Malicious intent toward sentient beings can make it take longer. Unrepentant violence can make it take longer. So you see, even if our karma seems to be inexorable, still many things can greatly affect it.

Earth Plane Desires

Since our survival, emotional as well as physical, is often tied to desires, here are some mantras that will help us navigate the storms created by some basic desires. There will be other mantras later in this work that also relate to desires.

Abundance

This Lakshmi Mantra that will help you achieve abundance:

> Om Shrim Maha Lakshmiyei Namaha
> [Om Shreem Mah-hah-Lahk-shmee-yea Nah-mah-hah]

This Ganesha Mantra will help remove obstacles to abundance:

> Om Lakshmi Ganapatayei Namaha
> [Om Lahk-shmee Guh-nuh-puh-tuh-yeh Nah-mah-hah]

This Lakshmi Mantra will provide energy that leads to the accumulation of positive attributes in life:

> Om Bhakta Saubhagya Dayinyei Namaha
> [Om Bhahk-tah Sauw-bhahg-yah Dah-yeen-yei Nah-mah-hah]

Fear

One of great enemies of peace is fear. Fortunately, there is a mantra that is very helpful in removing fear. It asks that the energy pattern of fear be released back into universal mind and energy so that the energy may be returned to the chanter in a way that it can be used productively.

Shante Prashante Sarva Bhaya Upashamani Swaha
Shahn-teh Prah-shahn-the Sahr-vah Bhah-yah Oo-pah-shah-mah-nee
  Swah-hah

Once the basic security needs in life have been taken care of, the mind starts to think about other things.

CHAPTER 14

THE SECOND CHAKRA:
SWADHISTHANA CHAKRA

Ruling Principle: Water
Issues: Pleasure, Sexual Identity
Seed Sound: Vam [Vahm]
Location: Genital center

THERE ARE THOSE who take great pleasure in music. For others, there is nothing like the throb of a well-tuned motor at the beginning of a race. Painters paint and writers write because they must. What all of these have in common is the expression of creative pleasure. These are activities pertinent to the second chakra, where pleasure is defined according to our karma.

Sexual identity is also established through the energy of this chakra, similarly dictated by karma. And yet there are choices to be made every day. Sexual preference, by all evidence, is not a choice but a biological imperative, but how we exercise that preference is our choice. Relationships are karmic. How we behave in them is by choice.

Another aspect to the second chakra that is not often discussed: occult abilities. The Ego-Mind-Personality can access the fifth or Vishuddha Chakra and draw in information available through that chakra. This process enables psychics to get information. Just as not everyone is an Olympic athlete, not everyone has innate psychic abilities of an advanced nature. Using the same analogy, anyone can get in good physical condition. Similarly, anyone can develop intuition beyond what is available to them through karma. Again, developing this ability is a matter of choice. The same is true of healing abilities that we discuss in a subsequent chapter.

The energy of the second chakra is extremely powerful. It can be harnessed and developed for extraordinary healing capabilities. Or it can be used to inflict insidious psychic damage to others. It's similar to fire in that respect. Fire can be used to cook your lunch or burn down the forest. It is all in the application. In the choice.

The sign of Scorpio, which is my astrological sign, can be ruthless in the application of energy for its own advantage. In most Scorpios, there is an innate desire to manifest that energy. Of course, that energy can propel one to spiritual heights or lead one on the path to ruin if used indiscriminately. Realizing this, and schooled by an outstanding set of teachers and a guru, I have come to understand that only applications of power based in love have any value at all. Such applications are also the most karmically freeing.

My guru, Sadguru Sant Keshavadas, used to publicly warn everyone about the pitfalls of power. Compounding matters is the realization that when one has what I will call "spiritual abilities," they are accompanied by a very strong desire to use them. That is why many gurus will tell their students to be very, very careful when such abilities appear. If it serves in some way, it is probably all right to use it. If not, it might be best to oppose the natural inner desire to use it.

Addiction is another problem that has its genesis in this chakra. We all want pleasure. Sometimes we find paths of pleasure that are downright destructive. Drug and alcohol abuse. Sexual addiction. Even smoking. In our search for pleasure, we must be judicious.

MANTRA TOOLS

Here are some mantra tools related to issues occurring at the second chakra. Here are mantras in combination that can be used to help address various kinds of behavior. You can do what I call "stacking." This simply means that you can select several mantras that have the same general objective and construct a discipline using the mantras that will lead in the same direction. The guide in stacking is the purpose for which you are doing the discipline.

Addiction

Use the two mantras below in combination to help you quit smoking.

This mantra helps conquer desire. It invokes energy that can be used to conquer a specific, nonhelpful desire that you identify.

> *Om Jita Kamaya Namaha*
> *[Om Jee-tah Kah-mah-yah Nah-mah-hah]*

Here, the quality of great effort combined with determination is invoked. You want to be successful in your efforts leading to self-mastery.

> *Om Vyava Sayaya Namaha*
> *[Om Vyah-vah Sah-yah-yah Nah-mah-hah]*

Weight Loss

Here are two mantras that can help. Feel free to stack them if it feels right to you.

This mantra praises the divine feminine who manifests a slender waist. It is a Lalitha mantra: She of a thousand powers:

> *Om Sato Datyei Namaha*
> *[Om Sah-toh Daht-yeh Nah-mah-hah]*

Lalitha is also said to have powerful yet delicate and pleasing limbs. This mantra invokes those qualities:

Om Koma Langyei Namaha
[Om Koh-mah Lahng-yea Nah-mah-hah]

Depression or Anxiety

Anyone can have periods in life where depression seems to come out of nowhere. These mantras help powerfully. There are more helpful mantras . related to healing in a subsequent chapter.

Outside conditions can overwhelm us a times. This mantra acts as a positive energy attractor, relieving outer, misery-causing conditions:

Om Shrun-kala Bandha Mochakaya Namaha
[Om Shroon-kah-kah Bahn-dhah Moh-chah-kah-yah Nah-
mah-hah]

This mantra invokes the quality of cheerfulness in the midst of any and all difficulties:

Om Prasannatmane Namaha
[Om Prah-sahn-aht-mah-neh Nah-mah-hah]

This mantra is an antidote to sadness and misery, automatically invoking the kind of positive energy that will counter the inner condition:

Om Sarva Dukha Haraya Namaha
[Om Sahr-vah Dook-hah-rah-yah Nah-mah-hah]

CHAPTER 15

THE CATCH

HE FOREGOING DISCUSSION of the chakras deals mainly with the smaller initiations within the First Great Initiation and up to the second level of the Second Great Initiation. After that, the rules change and things get murky. Why should this be so?

By the second level of the Second Great Initiation, the Ego-Mind-Personality has chosen either the path of spiritual development through one of the paths of light, or it has chosen the path of self-gratification. When the latter choice has been made, the Ego-Mind-Personality may muck about for many lifetimes until the choice to move to the path of light takes place. The path of gratification has its own teachers and role models, its own temporal rewards.

I was once complaining to my guru about the state of the world. With a serious look, he turned to me and said, "The other side has their gurus, too." I was stunned. But as I thought about it I realized that I had assumed that people with what I call negative goals, primarily for control of other people, are stupid. It's obvious that this is not true. Those on the side of negativity can be just as intelligent and organized as those on the side of the good. Students are recruited. Adherents are trained and set to work. We might immediately think of organized crime as an example, but I suspect that crime is only one of the lower levels. Higher ups might look quite respectable and have respectable occupations. When you think about it, it explains a lot about the way the world works these days.

A LOOK AT THE SECOND CHAKRA, THE SECOND GREAT INITIATION

In his book, *Kundalini Yoga,* Swami Sivananda describes second chakra attributes that correspond to the Second Great initiation. "He who concentrates and meditates on the Devata [Brahma and Rakini] has no fear of water. He has perfect control over the water element. He gets many psychic powers, intuitional knowledge, and perfect control over his senses. He has full knowledge of the astral entities. Carnal desire, anger, jealousy, attachment, and other inpure qualities are completely annihilated. The Yogi becomes the conqueror of death."

Clearly this is an exalted state. But it is when one has become pure only up to the second chakra, with all of its subdivisions. Most of the discussions in this book are to lead us to the point summarized by Swami Sivananda. However, since our evolutionary journey is not commonly thought of in terms of the Great Initiations, but in terms of the smaller ones within the first and second chakras, I am trying to make things clear here.

So we are left with advanced beings who have progessed through the first two great initiations and beyond. They have walked among us, had students, and have written and taught about routes to true spiritual advancement. Unless we can identify, unerringly, those who are in such an advanced state who are now among us, we are left with two of the classical methods of proof of any body of spiritual knowledge.

1. Legitimate scripture received through revelation.
2. Testimony from reliable authority.
3. Direct perception and/or experience of that which we all hope to achieve.

The remainder of this book will deal with items that pertain to all first level and partial second level great initiations. We will cover those concepts, methods, and goals from scripture, teachings, and reports from direct experience that apply to our topics. This does not make what is contained here any less important. If anything, it opens the possibilities even more than you might have previously considered.

CHAPTER 16

THE THIRD CHAKRA:
MANIPURA CHAKRA

Ruling Principle : Fire
Issues: Applications of Personal Power; Change in Karmic Circumstance.
Seed Sound: Ram [Rahm]
Location: Solar Plexus

ROUND THE AGE of twenty-eight or twenty-nine an energy shift takes place in all of us as the Ego-Mind-Personality shifts its locus from the second to the third chakra. There is a significant body of evidence of various kinds to support this idea.

Western astrology notes that at age 28.8 the planet Saturn returns to the exact sign and degree it occupied at the time of our birth. Western astrology calls this period of time the Saturn Cycle. When it comes back around, it is referred to as the Saturn Return. It marks the beginning of a new learning cycle, where new issues are brought into one's life. Sometimes new sets of desires can appear or older ones that we have kept on the back burner come rushing to the forefront. Even sociological observations note this phenomenon.

Sociologists have noted that between the ages of twenty-eight and thirty-five (the seven year period at the start of the new learning cycle in astrology), a number of things pertaining to young adults can be seen. This period marks the greatest incidence of significant career changes in young adults. The assumption is that in this age period we begin to measure our achievement with the goals we set earlier in life. Career can become much more important than it was in our early twenties. Also during this time there is interesting statistical information on marital status. If you were single during this time, the chances are higher than at any other time in your life you will be married at the end of the seven year period. If you are married, there is the highest statistical chance in your life that you will be divorced at the end of the seven-year period. This time period is also a time when adults have the highest incidence of emotional problems. For women, the biological clock goes off very loudly during this period.

Issues of power also begin to manifest from the age of twenty-eight onward. In the mystical view of things, it is natural because the energy emphasis shifts from the second to the third or power chakra. If one has not been a spiritual seeker before this age, but the latent interest is there, it will probably begin to manifest after the age of twenty-eight. Power struggles related to career advancement are the norm for this period.

SECULAR ADEPTS

The first part of the name of this chakra, *mani*, means mind. The mind begins to examine and explore routes to power, secular or spiritual. Sometimes occult abilities appear that are controlled by the mind, as it explores abilities developed in previous lifetimes. If you think this sounds "out there" I have two examples for you. The first concerns T.V. Learson, a man who ran IBM in the early 1960s. The following is taken from the book *THINK*, a biography of the Watsons and IBM.

"His skills encompass every conceivable attribute of the compleat corporate executive save in the subjective area of sentimentality, the appearance of kindness, or an inherent willingness to give a man a second chance . . . He has scared grown men in a way and to a depth that no Watson [founder of IBM] ever quite managed . . . Men outside the IBM corral marvel at him with some of the admiration they hold for nuclear power or the unexplained phenomena of the universe . . . Learson's mind and searchlight eyes focus on subordinates and associates like a laser beam that transmits back to him all the millions of bits of data the questioned man possesses, leaving him momentarily stripped of knowledge or will, his memory core deprived of both a program and capacity for storage."[13]

The second example concerns a man I met in 1969 and later in 1973. He was the chairman of Post Newsweek television stations.

I had been trained as an Army officer to evaluate large scale operations and then write reports on what I found. At the time I was in the Army this report was called a Staff Study, but it was primarily the responsibility of one individual who gathered data from various sources.

When I went to work in the Training Program of WTOP-TV in Washington, DC, I moved from running a sixteen-state operation for the First US Army Recruiting District, to being a floor director who also helped produce sixty visuals per day for the three daily news broadcasts. The Training Program was a mess. I was aghast at the lack of organization that permeated it everywhere, but there was nothing I could do about it.

After just a few weeks at WTOP-TV, a new chairman of the television station group, Larry Israel, was hired from the executive ranks of Westinghouse Broadcasting. This was my chance.

Doing what I had been trained to do, I wrote up an analysis of the Training Program, complete with nine recommendations and took it to his office. When I dropped if off, I asked for an appointment. A day later Mr. Israel's secretary called me to give me the time of an appointment a few days later.

When I entered his office, he greeted me most cordially and he quickly got to the point. "When I read this, it seemed like you were privy to my innermost thoughts." I was brash and ignorant and tossed his comment away with, "Maybe I am. Now I can tell you I want to be your assistant." I had missed his opening gambit entirely.

The interview lasted another five minutes or so during which he could see that I was just another ambitious young man. That I was not really "a fit" for him. You see, I had not had my spiritual "opening" yet. I had no idea that there were other dimensions to life. I lasted another few weeks at the company during which time about seventy people were terminated in a mass housecleaning. All of my recommendations were adopted. I was not one of those let go. In fact, Larry Israel would see me from time to time and was both gracious and solicitous of my future. He told me that if I went into sales I could probably move quickly. I demurred since I wanted management not sales. I didn't know that sales was then a path to upper management. And I was much more concerned with broadcast content than what it cost and how much we made in sales of airtime for commercial products.

Soon after I left WTOP-TV I had my "opening." Sitting on my couch reviewing notes for a business project, a golden light appeared in a circle on the middle the page I was looking at. In it was a three word personal message. I thought, "What in the world is that?" Then I started to lift out of my body. I remember seeing two identical scenes of my living room. One was staying in place and the other was rising. Then a tunnel opened up in my chest and a third part of me started to descend down the tunnel toward my heart. I realized I was going to die. Obviously I didn't die, but that incident started a chain of events that has led me to where I am now.

Within a few months of the experience I got rid of most of my possessions and went around the country looking for a spiritual teacher. I eventually found one, but not while I was looking. I settled in as a priest in the new Washington, D.C., organization and went to work for a public TV station in Northern Virginia. When they lost their state funding, I pitched the children's program for which I had been associate producer to my old TV station, and they bought it.

A couple of weeks after I returned to WTOP-TV in a different capacity, I ran into Larry Israel in the lobby. He greeted me with a huge smile and said, "Well look who's back!" He stuck out his hand. I grabbed his hand and a burst of energy came out of his hand and up my arm. He looked at me impishly and said, "Interesting, isn't it?" Then he turned and strode away.

By this time, I had experienced spiritual energy from several different people, all spiritual teachers, and had some idea of what had happened.

I concluded that he was a genuine adept, working in the world. From that and other incidents it became clear to me that the determining ingredient to running any large company was simple power. The most powerful person who is ambitious, wins. You can hire experts to do anything. Running the empire has nothing to do with knowledge, and everything to do with power.

FACE TO FACE

At the third chakra, we begin to face our power issues, our dominance issues. Mental processing can become fascinating, as we understand things that eluded us before. Mind and power unite as the karma stored at the third chakra is released when the energy rises from the second chakra. How we handle all of this is, again, a matter of choice. And these choices will, in their turn, create another wave of karma we will navigate at sometime in the future.

MANTRAS

There is a Hanuman Mantra that greatly infused the *prana* with positive and eventually divine abilities and vibration. Hanuman is a character in the Indian epic, *The Ramayana,* who is a symbol for the consciously awakened and divine *prana,* or life energy.

> *Om Hum Hanumate Namaha*
> *[Om Hoom Hah-noo-mah-teh Nah-mah-hah]*

The great *Taraka Mantra* of Rama also helps transmute all negative tendencies that may be stored here, into positive energy. This is also a liberation mantra, meaning that it will eventually free one from the necessity for rebirth to work out karma. Mahatma Gandhi practiced this mantra from the time he was a boy.

Om Sri Rama Jaya Rama Jaya Jaya Rama
[Om Shree Rah-mah Jah-yah Rah-mah Jah-yah Jah-yah Ra-mah]

Next, a shakti mantra that moves the energy to the crown chakra. It uses the *Swaha* ending which helps it relieve difficulties held at the third chakra. This is a Tantric Mantra that asks the shakti move to the head, making one Shiva, a being with infinite consciousness. It starts with the seed syllable *Hrim*, which is the seed sound for the Hrit Padma, an esoteric chakra that is the true seat of the soul.

Hrim Shrim Klim Param Eshwari Swaha
[Hreem Shreem Kleem Pah-rahm Esh-wah-ree Swah-hah]

SUN MANTRAS

There are twelve spiritual gifts of the sun that can be obtained through the chanting of mantras that invoke the desired qualities. These mantras "rule" (as they say in astrology) each of the planets. Although there are at least a hundred mantras for each planet, the mantras below are considered foundation mantras. You will see that each of the planets have strong influence on certain parts of the body. So if you have a problem in a certain area, you can reduce the karmic difficulties for that part of the body by working with its corresponding planetary mantra.

Sun

Material Result: Sun (Surya) mantras are chanted to increase courage and fame. There are twelve sun mantras that produce the fruits indicated when the mantras are chanted over time.

Esoteric Result: Illumination. Healing abilities. Spiritual magnetism.

Physiological Associations: Heart and Circulatory System (centripetal circulation), Thymus Gland, Upper portion of the back.

Sun Mantras:

Om Hram Hrim Hraum Sau Suryaya Namaha
[Om Hrahm Hreem Hrowm Saw Soor-yah-yah Nah-mah-hah]

Om Suryaya Namaha
[Om Soor-yah-yah Nah-mah-hah]

Below are the twelve gifts of the sun and the mantras which produce their respective fruit.

MANTRA	FRUIT
Om Hram Mitraya Namaha [Om Hrahm Mee-trah-yah Nah-mah-hah]	Universal Friendship
Om Hrim Ravaye Namaha [Om Hreem Rah-vah-yea Nah-mah-hah]	Radiance
Om Hroom Suryaya Namaha [Om Hroom Soor-yah-yah Nah-mah-hah]	Dispeller of Darkness
Om Hraim Bhanave Namaha [Om Hr-eyem Bhah-nah-vey Nah-mah-hah]	Brilliant, Shining Principle
Om Hraum Khagaya Namaha [Om Harown Kha-gah-yah Nah-mah-hah]	All-Pervading Through the Sky
Om Hrah Pooshne Namaha [Om Hrah Poosh-ney Nah-mah-hah]	Mystic Fire which Gives Strength
Om Hram Hiranyagarbhaya Namaha [Om Hram Hee-rah-yah-ghahr-bah-yah Nah-mah-hah]	Golden Colored One (Healing Gold)
Om Hrim Marichaye Namaha [Om Hreem Mah-ree-chah-yea Nah-mah-hah]	The Pure Light of Dawn, at the Crack Between the Worlds

Om Hroom Adityaya Namaha
[Om Hroom Ah-deet-yah-yah Nah-mah-hah]

Light of the Sage:
An Aspect of Vishnu

Om Hraim Savitre Namaha
[Om Hra-eyem Sah-vee-trey Nah-mah-hah]

Light of Enlightenment

Om Hraum Arkaya Namaha
[Om Hrowm Ahr-kah-yah Nah-mah-hah]

Remover of Afflictions, Giver
of Energy

Om Hrah Bhaskaraya Namaha
[Om Hrah Bhahs-kah-rah-yah Nah-mah-hah]

Brilliant Light of Intelligence

Moon

Material Result: Moon (Chandra) mantras are chanted to increase mental health and peace of mind.

Esoteric Result: Intuition. Spiritual acuity. Understanding of weather phenomena. Understanding of dreams.

Physiological Associations: Fluids and secreting functions, Digestive System, Pancreas, Female Reproductive System, Breasts, Sympathetic Nervous System (dealing with elimination, assimilation of nutrition, protection of the organism).

Moon Mantra:

Om Shram Shrim Shraum Sau Chandraya Namaha
[Om Shrahm Shreem Shrowm Saw Chahn-drah-yah Nah-mah-hah]

Om Chandraya Namaha
[Om Chahn-drah-yah Nah-mah-hah]

Mars

Material Result: Mars (Angaraka) mantras are chanted to increase determination and drive, and protect one from violence.

Esoteric Result: Spiritual force and penetrating energy. Understanding the true nature of conflict.

Physiological Associations: Muscular System, Urogenital System, Gonads, Adrenals, Sympathetic Nervous System (in conjunction with the sun), Red Blood Cells, Kidneys.

Mars Mantra:

Om Kram Krim Kraum Sau Bhaumaya Namaha
[Om Krahm Kreem Krawm Saw Bhow-mah-yah Nah-mah-hah]

Om Angara-kaya Namaha
[Om Ahn-gah-rah-kah-yah Nah-mah-hah]

Jupiter

Material Result: Jupiter (Guru or Brihaspati) mantras are chanted to increase satisfaction in and facilitation of marriage and childbirth.

Esoteric Result: Spiritual gifts of various kinds. Divine Grace.

Physiological Associations: The Liver, Gall Bladder, Posterior Lobe of the Pituitary Gland.

Jupiter Mantras:

Om Gram Grim Graum Sau Gurave Namaha
[Om Grahm Greem Grawm Saw Goo-rah-vey Nah-mah-hah]

Om Gurave Namaha
[Om Goo-rah-vey Nah-mah-hah]

Om Brihaspatayei Namaha
[Om Bree-hahs-pah-tah-yea Nah-mah-hah]

Venus

Material Result: Venus (Shukra) mantras are chanted to increase riches and conjugal bliss.

Esoteric Result: Scriptural understanding. Real knowledge, as distinct from simple information.

Physiological Associations: Venous Circulation (centrifugal circulation), Parathyroid Glands, Kidneys (with Mars), Throat, Genital area (with Mars), Chin, Cheeks, Eustachian Tubes, Lips, Navel, Neck, Olfactory Nerve, Seminal Vesicles, Thymus Gland (with the Sun).

Venus Mantras:

Om Dram Drim Draum Sau Shukraya Namaha
[Om Drahm Dreem Drawm Saw Shoo-krah-yah Nah-mah-hah]

Om Shukraya Namaha
[Om Shoo-krah-yah Nah-mah-hah]

Mercury

Material Result: Mercury (Budha) mantras are chanted to facilitate health and increase intelligence.

Esoteric Result: Communion with beings in higher realms.

Physiological Associations: Central Nervous System, Sensory System, Thyroid Gland, Respiratory System, Arms, Gall Bladder (with Jupiter), Sight, Tongue, Vocal cords.

Mercury Mantras:

Om Bram Brim Braum Sau Budhaya Namaha
[Om Brahm Breem Brawm Saw Bood-hah-yah Nah-mah-hah]

Om Budhaya Namaha
[Om Bood-hah-yah Nah-mah-hah]

Saturn

Material Result: Saturn (Shani) mantras are chanted to facilitate victory in quarrels, overcoming chronic pain, and bringing success to those engaged in the iron or steel trade.

Esoteric Result: When lessons are mastered, admission into the higher realms. *siddhis* (magical abilities) accompanied by proper understanding. Spiritual gifts of all kinds.

Physiological Associations: Skeletal System, Skin, Anterior Lobe of the Pituitary System, Ears, Calves of the Legs, Cartilage, Blood Circulation in tissues, Ligaments, Peripheral Sympathetic Nervous System, Spleen, Teeth, Tendons.

Saturn Mantras:

> Om Pram Prim Praum Sau Shanaishcharaya Namaha
> [Om Prahm Preem Prawm Saw Shahn-esh-cha-rah-yah Nah-mah-hah]

> Om Shanaish-charaya Namaha
> [Om Shahn-esh-chah-rah-yah Nah-mah-hah]

> Om Sri Shanaish-waraya Swaha
> [Om Shree Shahn-esh-wah-rah-yah Swah-hah]

Moon's North Node

Material Result: Moon North Node (Rahu) mantras are chanted to gain dominance over enemies, favor from the king (or queen) or government (or corporation), and reduction in conditions caused by Rahu.

Esoteric Result: Barriers lifted. Tensions eased. Endeavors become favored.

Rahu Mantras:

Om Bhram Bhrim Bhraum Sau Rahuve Namaha
[Om Brahm Breem Brawm Saw Rah-hoo-vey Nah-mah-hah]

Om Rahuve Namaha
[Om Rah-hoo-vey Nah-mah-hah]

Moon's South Node

Material Result: Moon South Node (Ketu) mantras are chanted to gain
dominance over enemies, favor from the king (or queen) or government (or corporation), and reduction in conditions caused by Ketu.
Esoteric Result: Barriers lifted. Tensions eased. Endeavors become favored.

Ketu Mantras:

Om Shram Shrim Shraum Sau Ketave Namaha
[Om Shrahm Shreem Shrawm Saw Keh-too-vey Nah-mah-hah]

Om Ketuve Namaha
[Om Keh-too-vey Nah-mah-hah]

CHAPTER 17

THE FOURTH CHAKRA:
ANAHATA CHAKRA & HRIT PADMA

Hrit Padma

Ruling Principle: Divinity
Issues: Soul Destiny (determined at the point of Great Decision)
and determination of the form (or nonform) of the Divine Beloved
Seed Sound: Hrim [Hreem]
Location: Two Fingers below the heart

WHEN NARAYANA PIERCES the expanding bubble of this universe with a ball of his essence, he is peopling the creation brought forth by Brahma. The ball of that substance explodes into millions of pieces and the souls that will inhabit the new universe are created. All of us are brought into instantaneous existence.

In the subsequent creation of our bodies, first in the nonphysical dimensions, and later in the physical dimensions, the soul or *atman* will carve out its own location from which to view the unfolding drama. That place is the Hrit Padma or Sacred Heart.

The involution of our spiritual mechanism, our body, continues. Chakra by chakra our vehicle construction continues until we reach the earth plane. Now the Ego-Mind-Personality is anchored into its place at the base of the spine, Ganesha-Ganpathi is created and the drama begins.

INSPIRATION AND CONFUSION

The bit of divinity called the soul, self, or *atman* can be meaningfully contacted by our Ego-Mind-Personality through a combination of heartfelt devotion and concentrated mental intention. There is even a ceremony in Hinduism designed specifically for the purpose of contact, called the Satya Narayana Puja. But contact also can be with only concentrated devotion and no ceremony at all. When meaningful contact is made, there is sometimes a dazzling experience or profound encounter with whatever we regard as God or Divinity. In the *Bhagavad Gita*, Krishna tries to explain this phenomenon with the phrase, "However one approaches me in Love, in that way I appear and respond to the devotee." Although wonderful, it can also create fanaticism.

If someone of sincere intent and devotion has a genuine experience through contact with their own sacred heart, there is a tendency to say (at least to oneself) I GOT IT! Now the person understands God or Truth. Usually, this understanding is so powerful that the person thinks their revelation is the true, one and only. If this person is at all evangelical, the trouble begins. Anything that does not conform to that person's vision and conclusion about God and Divinity is labeled as false. Intolerance sprouts almost immediately.

WHAT COLOR IS GOD?

There is a classical story from India about a group of people who entered a very large house with many bedrooms. They gathered in one section of the house and reverently brought forth a blue light bulb respectfully resting on a satin pillow. With great outpourings of prayer and chanting, they screwed in the light bulb. It lit up! Now they knew without any doubt that GOD IS BLUE!

But in another section of the house there was another group going through a similar routine with a green bulb. They prayed and meditated and sang and screwed in their green bulb and it lit up! They now knew without any doubt whatsoever that GOD IS GREEN!

Throughout other portions of the mansion, other groups were working with red bulbs and yellow bulbs and so forth. Eventually, these groups met in the hall. Naturally, they were ready to put each other to death. Each group had an indisputable corner on the truth about God.

What they had neglected to observe was that God was the current that gave power and light to all the bulbs. They had confused the electrical current with the light bulb. Similarly, we find ourselves in a world where various religious factions want to do war with one another. They are also confusing the current with the light bulb. God is the animating force behind the world's great religions. At the very core of those religions are ideas, ideals, prescriptions for life, and goals for spiritual attainment that are remarkably similar.

In the Sacred Heart, the Hrit Padma, God is the essence of our own eternal being. God is the source of all the religions always leading us closer to divine truth. External conditions are always subject to variables. No one has a corner on absolute Truth. Or if they do, they don't speak about it, since they know we will only see it through the lens of our own limited minds.

DIVINE EGO-MIND-PERSONALITY

Riding the Ego-Mind-Personality up the spine through all the great initiations and levels leading to each one, Ganesha-Ganapathi, as the principle of unity, finally sees the Ego-Mind-Personality reach the Hrit Padma. Here the first great transformation takes place. The Ego-Mind-Personality is rewarded for it choice and subsequent effort by merging with the soul, self, *atman*. It becomes immortal.

Now transparent, devoid of negative qualities, tranquil, and serene, the Ego-Mind-Personality intuits a glimpse of what is to come and experiences profound joy. The rest of the journey up the spine is much easier. There are experiences to undergo and things to understand. But the hard part is over. The next significant choice will be the point of great decision, a bit down the road.

The Anahata Chakra

Ruling Principle: Air
Issues: Correct manifestation of Divine Love
Seed sound: Yam [Yahm]
Location: The Heart

The Anahata Chakra is where humanity is united spiritually and where it will ultimately be united in everyday life. This is the place where we are one. This is where love manifests. If we operated from here as a species, there would be no hunger, no want, no deprivation, no withholding what is needed for some economic or selfish reasoning.

Internally, this is the place of what is called the *Vishnu Granthi* (knot). Located at three places along the spine are barriers that the kundalini will not pass unless it is safe for the subtle and physical body. A great energy like the kundalini, has its own intelligence that tell her when it is safe to move forward. By analogy, it does no good to place 500 watts of current in a 100 watt bulb. It will only blow up the light bulb. Similarly, the kundalini should not rise to levels within before our capacity to handle and use the energy exists. To aid in this process, three knots are placed along the spine. Eventually the kundalini will pierce each knot at the proper time and the Ego-Mind-Personality will continue its evolution.

The knot at this location is called the knot of Vishnu or *Vishnu Granthi*. Passing this location, one can be in contact with the great beings and spirits who tend the evolution of the human species and sentient beings in other places. It is Vishnu who is the spirit and principle of preservation of sentience everywhere. Vishnu incarnates as savior, teachers, avatars of various classes, and true gurus. Most of them revere Shiva as the pinnacle of consciousness both individually and in the aggregate.

Now that the Ego-Mind Personality has reached the Anahata Chakra, the aspect of shakti know as Lakshmi begins to show her higher aspects. In the lower levels she was the fulfiller of all kinds of abundance, materially and sometimes spiritually. Here she reveals herself as the power of love itself, and the journey continues under her command in concert with Ganesha.

SHAKTI — HIGHEST TEACHINGS

In every Eastern tradition I have studied, or teacher from whom I have had the opportunity to take instruction, the mysteries of Shakti, the Great Feminine, are reserved for higher levels of initiation and teaching. Whether it is the towering student of Tantra, Agasyta, asking his guru Hayagriva about the higher initiation, or the incomparable Sadguru Dattatreya instructing the Avatar Parasurama, the same idea occurs again and again. One of the highest initiations is the imparting of the knowledge concerning the very power of the universe and our power within, shakti. Even when the great Brahmarishi Vasistha is ready to make the struggling Vishwamitra into a Brahmarishi—a sage with the very highest spiritual realization—it is Arundhati, Vasistha's spouse, who finally melts the heart of Vishwamitra. The signs, portents, scriptures, and hidden teachings proclaiming the mysteries of shakti can be found scattered throughout the branches of Hinduism in Indian lore.

SHAKTI MANTRAS

The first mantra entreats the kundalini shakti to come all the way up the spine.

> Hrim Shrim Klim Param Eshwari Swaha
> [Heem Shreem Kleem Pah-rahm Esh-wah-ree Swah-hah]

The next mantra invokes protection against the seemingly unconquerable. It may be invoked when any outside difficulty threatens. A fringe benefit from repeating it that has been reported to me over the last few years is an increase in self-confidence.

> Om Eim Hrim Klim Chamundayei Vichhe Namaha
> [Om I'm Hreem Kleem Chah-moon-dah-yeh Vee-cheh Nah-mah-hah]

The third mantra calls upon the most powerful and compassionate mother in the Tibetan tradition, Tara. There are several variations of this mantra given for specific purposes. But this is her universal foundation mantra that brings incalculable blessings.

Om Tare Tuttate Ture Swaha
[Om Tah-reh Too-tah-teh Too-reh Swah-hah]

Lastly, Lakshmi gives a number of mantras for attainment of her in the Lakshmi Tantra. But one of the simplest yet most powerful ones invokes the power and consciousness of the crown chakra down onto the earth plane.

Sahasrara Im
[Sah-has-rah-rah Eem]

While some knowledge and power related to kundalini is given at various stages of our development, it is at the Hrit Padma and the Heart Center of the Anahata Chakra that the teachings begin in earnest. It stands to reason. Great power must be governed by great love. One of the first things that love will try to do is heal us of our difficulties and afflictions.

CHAPTER 18

CHAKRAS IN THE HANDS AND FEET

ENERGY OF HEALING AND TRANSFORMATION

S THE EGO-MIND-PERSONALITY continues its journey up the spine, the place on the spine near the heart where energy spins out to the hands is reached. For some, this marks the beginning of a new chapter in their lives where they discover they have a talent for healing.

There are chakras in the hands that in most people are dormant. In genuine healers who work with the body, they are active and open. Shakti, either in the form of *prana* or in tangible electrical energy, can come out of those chakras in the hand producing remarkable effects in the recipient.

TWO HEALERS

My friend Peggy Rodriguez is a holistic health practitioner with a health massage business where she works on a variety of clients with wide-ranging complaints. She has worked diligently to learn every kind of healing massage available. Through our discussions, years ago, she came to know that the planets have a subtle but far-reaching effect on many aspects of our life, including health. A mantra practitioner for many years, she concluded that there must be a mantra for each of the planets, and that they could benefit her clients. So she learned the basic mantras that invoke energy from each planet, and conducted a rigorous chanting practice with the goal of unwrapping the power of each mantra within herself for the benefit of her clients.

Classical astrology describes how each part of our body is strongly affected by one or more of the planets. By chanting mantras for planets that have effects on specific body parts, problems with those body parts can be softened or even solved. I have conducted my own experiments over the years, so I know this to be true. Peggy understood this and concluded that the more she could unwrap the power of the mantra within, the more she could chant and attune herself with each of the planetary mantras, the better effect she would have with her clients. She had a plan in mind.

When she felt she was ready, she would silently chant the mantra for the part of the body she was working on: Jupiter—liver; Saturn—spleen and knees, and so forth. She worked each body part while chanting the positive energy of the planets into the organ, gland, or limb. Because she had done her homework by working with the mantras extensively before she applied them to her clients, she had developed great facility for bringing in healing, beneficial energy of the planets into her clients. Peggy is a great healer who has my respect for her diligence and integrity, in addition to her healing skill. Peggy's hand chakras are open and she knows how to use them for the benefit of anyone who desires her help.

Marilyn Shaw is one of the healers with whom Peggy has studied. Marilyn had a dramatic opening she shared with me several years ago. Essentially, she had an experience during meditation where shining in a inner blue sky, a group of stars clustered together and formed a tornado of light that tunneled into her chest. She saw light pouring into her whole body. The torrential inflow of light energy left a sore red mark that lasted for two months. She was instructed what to do and how to do it. Her life changed in an instant. Many people over the years have credited her with various healings. Marilyn is humble, however, and always gives credit to the divine, operating through the celestial forces that blessed her.

Because she is an educator, Marilyn Shaw saw healing abilities in the context of part of the range of human abilities. If she had been given this gift, she reasoned, then other cultures and societies must have its equivalent. So she began to travel the world: the Far East, Africa, South America, Australia, and the Southwest United States, visiting shamans and healers and learning as much as she could from them. She has amassed more knowledge and information in the field of healing than anyone I know. It is my hope that she will write a book, one day, sharing with us some of what she has learned. It would benefit many.

My wife, Margalo, is also a gifted healer although healing is not her profession. In mid 2004, I awoke in the middle of the night with a throbbing pain in my right lower abdomen. I had had my appendix taken out as a youngster so I knew it couldn't be that. I woke Margalo up and told her that I might have to go to the emergency room because of the intense pain. She said, "Let me see what I can do." She put her hands on the place that hurt and closed her eyes. Fifteen seconds later the pain simply disappeared. I was flabbergasted. I asked what she did, but she just shrugged and said, "I brought in the golden light and got out of the way."

Margalo studied healing in 1979-80 at the Healing Light Center Church in Glendale, California, founded by Rosalyn Bruyere. While a student there, her teacher, a healer by the name of Rayla-Billie, took people through an exercise and then quizzed the students. She came around to Margalo who said simply that she just let the golden light work. Rayla-Billie told her that she was a master healer as they are the ones who work with that color.

All of these healers use the chakras in their hands. There are also chakras in the feet. In fact, the ones in the feet are reputed to be the largest chakras in the subtle body. There are hints of this in mystical literature and cultural tradition.

In most of the East, but particularly in India, there is a tradition going back thousands of years where one shows respect to a spiritual teacher by bowing down and touching their feet. You've probably seen it somewhere. What many people who practice this custom do not know is that there is a specific reason one would do this.

In most of us the chakras in the feet perform the function of drawing in energy from the earth. The spiritual magnetic energy of the earth is health giving. This is why it is so healthy to go barefoot sometimes or walk on sandy beaches in our bare feet. The chakras in the feet are completely unobstructed when we do this and can draw in large amounts of this beneficial energy. The natural function of these chakras is to draw in energy.

In the advanced adept, these chakras have an entirely different function. They can send out energy in the form of light and *prana*, just as the hand chakras do. But the amounts and intensity is greater. These chakras can also transmit a powerful spiritual electricity that is palpable to the touch. This electricity can heal, and it can transform. Huge leaps in spiritual evolution can take place if the adept who is transmitting so wills it.

EXAMPLES OF SPIRITUAL ELECTRICITY

Paramahansa Ramakrishna is reported to have pulled the leg of the unsuspecting Vivekananda onto his foot and transmitted energy so powerful that the young lad thought he was going to die. Instead, he became spiritually transformed and began the spiritual career that included laying the foundation for the Vedanta Centers that are still scattered all over the world, long after his death.

When I was a very new priest in my guru's organization in 1974, the director of the local branch came breathlessly out of his room declaring, "There is electricity coming out of his feet!" I thought she had completely lost it. But when I bent down and placed my head on his feet, I was jolted by a powerful current. When I raised my head a sweet smile was waiting for me. Since that day, I have experienced the same electricity from spiritual adepts in three of the world's great religions. To me, this means that it is certainly operating through adepts in all the religions. It is part of the human potential, and not the province of any one religion.

There is a hint of this electricity in the New Testament where Jesus prepares to wash the feet of his disciples. They object, and he replies,

"I must do this." Then later he states, "What I do now, you do not understand, but you will when I send the Holy Spirit." It is my conclusion that in washing the feet, Jesus is preparing their feet chakras to be able to transmit the powerful electrical energy. I interpret the Holy Spirit to be that electricity. It seems a poetic way to communicate something for which there was no ready corollary, such as the electricity we have all around us today.

The Human Potential

The activation of higher abilities of the chakras in the hands and feet will happen to many serious seekers sooner or later. It offers the opportunity to eradicate karma from past lives by rendering great service in this one. It also provides a vehicle for displaying what we do with more abilities. How will one use the new abilities? How does money in large amounts figure in? What about fame and reputation as achievable goals now that new abilities have manifested? The answers to these questions and inner motivations that appear once one has new abilities can determine our eligibility to safely progress to higher states of consciousness without creating problems for ourselves. There are no right or wrong answers. There are only those answers that resonate with the truth of our own inner being.

Mantras for Healing

There is a mantra that invokes the energy and some say the conscious aid of the celestial healer who is known in India as Dhanvantari. His mantra is chanted to find the right path to healing under the care of the proper and appropriate practitioner, either traditional or nontraditional. Alternately, his mantra is chanted to help ensure that one's healer has the best insight into treatment of our condition.

Om Sri Dhanvantre Namaha
[Om Shree Dhahn-vahn-treh Nah-mah-hah]

There are two sun mantras that invoke powerful healing energies. The first calls in healing for afflictions.

Om Arkaya Namaha
[Om Ahr-kah-yah Nah-mah-hah]

This next mantra calls in the golden colored healing light.

Om Bhaskaraya Namaha
[Om Bhahs-kah-rah-yah Nah-mah-hah]

There is another sun mantra that is used for healing afflictions of the eyes. It is best to chant this mantra while spending a little time in the sun, even if it is just in the sunlight in front of a window.

Om Grinihi Suryaya Adityom
[Om Gree-nee-hee Soor-yah-yah Ah-deet yohm]

GENERAL PURPOSE HEALING MANTRAS

There are two traditional, very powerful general purpose healing mantras, which I call "freight train" mantras because they are somewhat long.

The first is the Maha Mrityunjaya Mantra of Sage Markandeya. The name of the mantra translates into the "great mantra which defeats death and disease."

Om Trayum-bakam Yajamahe Sughan-dhim Pushti Vardanam
Urvar-ukamiva Bandhanan Mrityor Mukshiya Mamritat
[Om Trah-yum-bah-kum Yah-jahm-mah-heh Soo-gahn-dim Poosh-tee-
vahr-dah-nahm
Oor-vahr Oo-kuh-mee-vah Bahn-dahn-ahn Mrit-your Mook-shee-yah
Mahm-ree-that]

The second great healing mantra is the Apadamapa of the Avatar Rama. It asks that healing energy be sent right here "to the earth, to the earth" ("bhuyo, bhuyo") in the spot or for the purpose for which chanted.

> Om Apa-damapa Hartaram Dataram
> Sarva Sampadam
> Loka Bhi Ramam Sri Ramam
> Bhuyo Bhuyo Namam-yaham
> [Ohm Ah-pah-dah-mah-pah Hahr-tah-rahm Dah-tah-rahm
> Sahr-vah Sahm-pah dahm
> Loh-kah Bee Rah-mahm Shree Rah-mahm
> Boo-yoh Boo-yoh Nah-mahm-yah-hahm]

One final note about the use of mantra for healing. Mantras work on the karma that is standing in the way of healing. They may or may not produce healing directly. The classical way that mantra chanting for healing works is for some previously unknown or untried path to healing presents itself for your consideration or use. You may not have even heard of it before. Your karma did not permit its presence in your life, even if it may have worked had you known about it. When a healing discipline is concluded, one or more paths or remedies may seemingly suddenly appear. Follow up every lead, every new possibility. Do not sit around "waiting for your miracle." The miracle might well be the herbologist across town that you just learned about after finishing a forty day healing discipline.

FORTY-DAY DISCIPLINE

The Forty-Day Discipline is a staple in India. The discipline must be done every day, without fail, for the full forty days. If a day is missed, the discipline must begin again. Personally, I define a day as the time you get up until the time you go to sleep at night, even if it is after midnight and technically into the next calendar day. Naps do not count as sleep times between days.

You can go to bed at night, be still awake and think, "My god, I haven't done my discipline yet today!" You are still fine, you have not gone to sleep yet. You can still get up and do your discipline. But if you fall asleep for even a few minutes . . . sorry. You have to start all over again. You have lost a battle but not the war.

I have done dozens of Forty-Day Disciplines and been consulted about dozens of others. Typically between day thirty and thirty-eight, there is one tumultuous day. Car breakdowns, family crises, upheavals at work . . . something. These events usually shake things up so much that the discipline may be entirely forgotten. It's a classical scenario.

Although the events have no real-world correlation that can be traced, they are always connected in my mind. Our habits and practices that we are trying to overcome seem to defend themselves. As I discuss in the chapters on Ganesha and the Ego-Mind-Personality, we are not unified internally. There are places that seem to operate on their own. If you are overweight and trying to lose weight, you immediately understand what I am saying. There is a place that wants to lose weight and another place that wants to eat whatever it wants, whenever it wants. The two places are in conflict. There is no inner unity about eating.

Our inner habits can defend themselves so tenaciously that tumultuous outer events can be created to divert our attention from the ongoing (and threatening to be successful) struggle. We are much more powerful than most of us have seriously considered. So once you have decided to conduct a formal mantra discipline, do not waiver, do not give up.

Lastly, results vary widely due to the karmic differences among us. One person may have to do a discipline several times to get good results, while another might get results right in the middle of the first attempt. Karmically, we are all working on the basis of insufficient data. We just don't know what our karmic predicament is. But we must persevere. We will overcome.

CHAPTER 19

THE FIFTH CHAKRA:
VISHUDDHA CHAKRA

Ruling Principle: Ether
Issues: Will and Spiritual Authority
Seed sound: Hum [Hoom]
Location: Throat

S STATED EARLIER, in the Old Testament, it is reported that God creates by speaking, "Let there be light." In the New Testament, the Gospel of John starts, "In the beginning was the Word." Since we are "made in the image of God," it should come as no surprise that the chakra at the throat is a center of the will in us as well. Speaking a thing and making it so is directly tied to this chakra.

We are taught as children that "sticks and stones will break our bones, but words will never hurt us." Not so. Words spoken in anger can destroy friendships and relationships. A word of encouragement at just the right time can change a life for the better in profound ways.

In the spiritual approach to things, the power of words becomes immensely strong the further along one goes. The higher the stage of development, the more powerful the words. In fact, in the higher chakras, one needs only say a thing or think a thing and it will manifest.

KAUSTUBHA GEM

In the mythic stories of the avatars of Vishnu, they are endowed with a magical gem just above the heart and below the throat chakra. This place, called the Kaustubha Gem, is powered by the shakti of Lakshmi. It will make whatever is spoken aloud or silently come into existence. Significantly advanced adepts may also be given this power by an authorized spiritual source such as a Sadguru, Jagad Guru, or Maha Siddha. This usually takes place if the adept is carrying on the work of his or her teacher. The student who has become an advanced adept has shown him or herself to be reliable enough so that they may carry this power without misuse. It is a gift for everyone when it is given to a student-adept. He or she will use it for the advancement of those who come into contact with them. And the wielder of this power will learn much that can be used in the next stage of evolution and the next position of service. There is not a mantra that will directly activate this center that exists in all of us, but you should know that even the avatars use the contents inherent in the subtle human form. If you are sincerely on the path of service, you may find yourself the recipient of this responsibility one day. We all will be benefited when you are given this gift that operates in conjunction with the Vishuddha Chakra.

TUNING IN

Psychic gifts are also connected with this chakra. When Edgar Cayce would get information useful to a person for their health or other parts of their lives, he would go into an unconscious state, and then begin to speak. Upon awakening, he would remember nothing of what was said. In his unconscious state, his Ego-Mind-Personality would temporarily tap into the *akasha*.

Ruled by its element, the ether principle, this chakra is the gateway to the Akashic Records. Everything is stored here, yet time in the normal sense does not exist. Time is like a rolled up canvas on which all the events of a particular cycle of creation are written. In the Book of

Revelations in the New Testament, the "end of days" and other prophe-
cies are recorded. Some are sealed and expressly told to be withheld.
We know that they were given, but we are also told that they would not
be revealed. This kind of information can be obtained through the
Akashic Records, where everything is available.

Like every other field of endeavor, there are varying levels of achievement of mastery of this chakra. Simple psychics have a rudimentary
access to this information, but they can only get certain frequencies of
it. More advanced spiritual people can get more and higher frequencies
of information. And almost any truly spiritual practice will open the
doors leading to this chakra and the clairvoyant ability.

When I first began my spiritual disciplines in 1973, I had no idea what
psychic even meant. Over time, I noticed that my intuition kept getting better and better. Finally, my wife began to ask me specific questions about things I had no knowledge of whatsoever. I just sort of tuned
in and began saying things that occurred to me. Then I would stop and
ask if it made any sense. Margalo, who was writing as fast as she could,
said, "Absolutely!" and continued writing. Who knew?

A good friend of mine, Rena Elliott Chiu, is a very fine professional
psychic. In fact, she is the best psychic I have ever met and I have met
many. She is humble about her ability and says quite sincerely that anyone can do what she does. That's true up to a point. But while anyone
can run the hundred-meter dash, only the very talented can break ten
seconds flat. Rena is very talented.

But she is also correct, anyone can increase their sensitivity and anyone can eventually tap into the Akashic Records. At the very highest
level, one can tune into and understand the Vedas, which are the foundation scriptures of Hinduism.

Here are some mantras that employ the seed sound of the Vishuddha
Chakra (throat), *Hum*. They will help you develop an attunement with
this chakra even as you progress spiritually. The first two mantras relate
to the figure of Hanuman in the Hindu classic, *The Ramayana*. Hanuman
is the conscious *prana* that is the foremost servant of the divine self
and the evolving Ego-Mind-Personality. This mantra salutes the
conscious *prana*.

Om Hum Hanumate Namaha
[Om Hoom Hah-noo-mah-teh Nah-mah-hah]

The next Hanuman Mantra proclaims that the *prana* will be victorious over all impediments to advance.

Om Hum Hanumate Vijayam
[Om Hoom Hah-noo-mah-teh Vee-jay-yam]

The Great Mani from the Tibetan tradition also opens the way to the abilities of the Vishuddha Chakra.

Om Mani Padme Hum
[Om Mah-nee-pahd-meh Hoom]

Many Tibetan teachers pronounce the mantra "Om Mah-nee Pay-may Hoong." They have attained spiritual heights using this pronunciation. But classical Sanskrit pronunciation is what I have given above. I was initiated into this mantra by the XVIth Gyalwa Karmapa, a great Tibetan master. He gave me the pronunciation in classical Sanskrit so that is what I practice and teach.

The great Gayatri Mantra will also develop an attunement with this chakra.

CHAPTER 20

THE GAYATRI MANTRA:
A MASTER MANTRA

MONG ALL THE MANTRAS, the Gayatri is called the essence of all mantras. All spiritual powers and potencies are contained hidden within it. The Gayatri is meditation on spiritual light. In all the teachings and scriptures, Gayatri is called supreme in bestowing enlightenment. It is practiced by Hindus and Buddhists alike. For pure spiritual potency in the accumulating of the highest spiritual light, there is nothing to compare with the Gayatri Mantra. While other mantras are great for their purpose, this one is specifically for the purpose of enlightening the intellect. Once the intellect is flooded with the energy of enlightenment, it "informs" the mind with transcendent ideas. The relationship of intellect to the translucent mind, operating through the activity of the Manas Chakra, is taken up a bit later. The Gayatri Mantra appears in three of the four Vedas.

The Gayatri Mantra contains sounds that summarize the vibrations of the upper seven luminous *Lokas*, which are spheres of consciousness or planes of existence. Only the first three planes are physical. The rest are nonphysical and contain dwelling places for celestial beings, sages, saints, masters, Maha Siddhas, Rimpoches, and other classes of highly evolved sentient beings. By unwrapping the power of this mantra, one can sit in meditation and commune with beings in these realms. In deep sleep one may travel in a spiritual body to these realms. Some of you reading this have had what I call super dreams. These are dreams that are so colorful, dynamic, and different from regular dreams that they demand their own category.

Because of its ability to bring into the subtle body keys to tuning one's consciousness to the higher realms, the Gayatri is called a Master Mantra.

Pictures and murtis (consecrated statues or images) of Gayatri show her with five heads, Lakshmi, Saraswati, Durga, Radha, and Bhu Devi. The heads represent, respectively, the primordial power of manifestation, the power of knowledge and divinely empowered speech, the power of protection, the power of ecstatic bliss, and the power of the Earth.

AUTHOR'S PERSONAL NOTE

I have practiced the Gayatri Mantra since 1974. It one of the foundations for my spiritual practices, and I cannot recommend it highly enough. The *prana* becomes energized. There is a beneficial energy that comes through you which is helpful to everyone in the nearby vicinity. Your attunement to the masters who have gone before who have practiced this mantra grows. An ineffable quiet begins to permeate the mind. I will leave off my praise, but not before I tell you two small incidents that happened early in my practice of the great mantra. I learned something of value about it very early.

I had been practicing the Gayatri Mantra for only a very short period of time. Certainly not enough to develop a spiritual proficiency. On a trip to Philadelphia from Washington, D.C., I stayed at an urban ashram of spiritual people who also practiced this mantra. The first night after dinner, the director of the household was preparing to wash the dinner dishes and she passed by me very closely on her way to the sink. As she passed, I heard "Om Bhu . . . Om Bhu . . . Om Bhuvaha . . . Om Bhuvaha. . . ." It was strange beyond my ability to communicate. I was "hearing" her spiritual discipline, or so I concluded. I have never forgotten that brief moment. It is still vividly in my mind all these years later.

The second incident happened while I was a priest in residence for my guru's organization called Sanatana Vishwa Dharma or the Temple of Cosmic Religion. During my tenure at the Temple, I practiced the Gayatri Mantra intensely. My minimum number of repetitions was 1,000 per day. Most of the time I would do many more. The mantra sat well with me, just as one knows when one is eating good food.

One day after I had been there for four years, a visitor rang the bell. This was not an unusual occurrence. But the person ringing the bell was not usual. It was a young Buddhist monk from the Buddhist Vihara up the street. He was no more than thirty-five years old and had a flashing and infectious grin.

I invited him in and asked him if he would like a cup of tea. He agreed and I put the water on and took him on a tour of the quarters we occupied. After a few minutes, he looked at me intently and remarked, "I see you also do the mystic formula." I had no idea of what he was talking about and I said so. He smiled and began to chant the Gayatri Mantra. When my eyebrows went up about a foot, he laughed in a friendly fashion. He indicated that he also did the mantra. After a cup of tea and pleasant conversation on spiritual matters he went on his way.

Years later I learned that people with spiritual sight can see the various qualities of spiritual light invoked by certain mantras. He was able to tell what mantra I was doing by the amount and quality of light in my aura.

The Gayatri Mantra is for enlightenment of the intellect.

Long Form

Om Bhur Om Bhuvaha Om Swaha
Om Maha Om Janaha Om Tapaha Om Satyam
Om Tat Savitur Varenyam
Bhargo Devasya Dhimahi
Dhiyo Yonaha Prachodayat
[Om Bhoor Om Bhoo-vah-hah Om Swah-hah
Om Mah-hah Om Jah-nah-hah Om Tah-pah-hah Om Saht-yahm
Om Taht Sah-vee-toor Vah-rehn-yahm
Bhahr-goh Deh-vahs-yah Dee-mah-hee
Dhee-yoh Yoh-nah-hah Prah-choh-dah-yaht]

O Self-Effulgent light that has given birth to all the *Lokas* (spheres of consciousness), who is worthy of worship and appears through the orbit of the Sun, illumine our intellect.

Rough Breakdown of the Individual Phrases

Om Bhur	Om and Salutations to the Earth Plane (first chakra)
Om Bhuvaha	Om and Salutations to the Atmospheric Plane (second chakra)
Om Swaha	Om and Salutations to the Solar Region (third chakra)
Om Maha	Om and Salutations to the First Spiritual Region Beyond the Sun (fourth chakra)
Om Janaha	Om and Salutations to the Second Spiritual Region Beyond the Sun (fifth chakra)
Om Tapaha	Om and Salutations to the Third Spiritual Region Beyond the Sun, Sphere of the Progenitors (sixth chakra)
Om Satyam	Om and Salutations to the Abode of Supreme Truth (seventh chakra)
Om Tat Savitur Varenyam	Om and Salutations to that Realm Which is Beyond Human Comprehension
Bhargo Devasya Dhimahi	In that place where all the celestials of all the spheres have
Dhiyo Yonaha Prachodayat	Received enlightenment, kindly enlighten our intellect

Short Form

Om Bhur Bhuvaha Swaha
Om Tat Savitur Varenyam
Bhargo Devasya Dhimahi
Dhiyo Yonaha Prachodayat

The short form is much more commonly practiced than the long form. The only organization or teacher that I know of that teaches the long form, other than my guru who initiated me into it, is the Arya Samaj organization in India.

For building attunement with the realms of light, for preparing the intellect to have capacity to receive enlightenment, for wiring your intellectual-mental equipment for the receipt and processing of spiritual knowledge, the Gayatri Mantra reigns supreme.

CHAPTER 21

THE AJNA CHAKRA AND OTHER CHAKRAS IN THE HEAD

Ajna Chakra

Ruling Principle: Mind
Issues: Appropriate individual instrumentality of Divine Will
Seed sound: Om
Location: Between the eyebrows

THE AJNA CHAKRA between the eyebrows has two petals. The seed sound for the chakra is the sound "Om" which has almost become part of our pop culture. This sound is the seed sound for the place of cosmic unified mind, the sounds of creation of the universe. When Paramahansa Yogananda described a meditation in *Autobiography of a Yogi* in which he had 360 degree vision, his consciousness was established at this chakra. It is here that the Ego-Mind-Personality ends its relationship with Ganesha-Ganapathi, whose job is now finished. The Ego-Mind-Personality is introduced to Subramanya who now takes the translucent and divine Ego-Mind-Personality through the centers in the head. When it reaches the Guru Chakra at the underside of the Sahasrara Chakra, it will have arrived at the point of great decision.

Mantra: *Om*

MANAS CHAKRA

In the back of the head, this chakra, the seat of higher functions of the mind, can be found. This is the place where enlightenment is actually applied. The Manas Chakra receives the light coming from the illumined intellect and operates in a divine way.

The mind is the analyzer. It weighs and thinks, compares and contrasts, looks at, measures and conducts mental processes that lead to conclusions. But it is not the originator of ideas. That task is a function of the intellect that feeds the mind. When the intellect becomes enlightened, it automatically sends higher classes of ideas to the mind, which must be capable of receiving them. There is a mantra that transforms the mind into such a powerful divine instrument that its vibrations can change the very planet we inhabit. It is the Great Mani.

> Om Mani Padme Hum
> [O Mah-nee Pahd-meh Hoom]

The next mantra is said to develop *bodhicitta*, the mental desire and state of readiness to receive higher knowledge and enlightenment. I have worked with it regularly for years and can tell you that it produces great, dynamic calm. The mind is sharp but tranquil.

> Gate Gate Para Gate Para Sam-gate Bodhi Swaha
> [Gah-teh Gah-teh Pah-rah Gah-teh Pah-rah Sahm Gah-teh
>   Boh-dee Swah-hah]

The Manjushri Mantra can produce feelings of joy, even as it sharpens the concentration and intuition. In the Tibetan tradition, Manjushri's spouse, or shakti is Saraswati. In Hinduism, Saraswati is paired with Brahma the creator.

Manjushri is the iconographic figure shown holding a sword. This does not mean he uses it as a weapon. Rather, the sword is called the "sword of discrimination," which cuts away obfuscation of the mind, enabling it to distinguish the real from the unreal.

Om Ah Ra Pat Sa Na Dhi Dhi Dhi
[Om Ah Rah Paht Sah Nah Dhee Dhee Dhee]

SOMA CHAKRA

The Soma Chakra is higher in the head than the Ajna Chakra, located just above the roof of the mouth. Looking like a full moon when completely active, this chakra has the function of speeding our journey back toward that place from which we have come. It is a major player in the achievement of immortality by the Ego-Mind-Personality.

This chakra contains an etheric liquid called the *amrita* or nectar of immortality. In its active state, the chakra drips liquid down into the spine where it then is carried into the *nadi* system, the subtle body equivalent of veins and arteries. There are 72,000 separate *nadis* or astral nerve tubes in the subtle body. Wherever the liquid from the Soma Chakra drips, that *nadi* or portion thereof will never again accumulate karma. The liquid acts as a cosmic Teflon that does not allow any karma to stick. This is the proverbial mind-boggling idea. Karma is stored in the body as patterns of vibrations and energy that can be triggered by external circumstance. Thoughts, emotions, actions, and predispositions are all karmically influenced, with traits and tendencies developed over many lives. But there are other circumstances such as the country and family we are born into, the kind of wealth we are inclined to have, the education, relationships, and living conditions. All of this is stored in the subtle body because it pertains to the very life we are living now.

Imagine a force that enters your life that says, "From now on, in this particular circumstance, you will not accumulate karma, no matter what you do." This is what this liquid can do. Because this force is powerful, only small amounts are released at any given time. And it becomes active only through grace, usually because an advanced being who knows how, has activated it by initiation. This activation can take place in a dream or through a living teacher in the flesh.

Pictures of the emblem of consciousness, Shiva, show him with a crescent moon on his forehead. This moon is the Soma Chakra. But in Shiva's case, it is no longer active. Shiva has long since achieved immortality and has no need for it's functioning. So it is shown in a deflated condition, the full moon now reduced to a crescent, its function fulfilled. The same scenario will happen to us when we reach the immortal state. There will be no need for this chakra to function so it will cease to operate.

Certain practitioners of Hatha Yoga in the Himalayas strive to increase the flow of this nectar of immortality through specific practices that most people in the West would view as grotesque, if they knew about them. These Yogis will use their hands to milk the tongue, elongating it over time so that it can be rolled up into a ball and pushed against the roof of the mouth. This activity stimulates the production of the etheric fluid and hastens its flow into the *nadis*. To aid the tongue in this practice, the *frenum lingui*, the little slip of tissue under the center part of the tongue, is cut, bit by bit over a period of weeks. When the tissue is completely gone, the tongue can roll up farther back and do a better job of simulating the Soma Chakra. This rolling of the tongue is called the *Kechari Mudra*.

This practice is supervised by a yogi who knows how to go about the practice, who acts as a teacher for those learning the process. Disgusting as this whole process may seem, it works. These yogis know what they are doing and achieve much faster results than just allowing the liquid to work on its own schedule.

For most aspirants, the work of the Soma Chakra can continue over more than one lifetime. But continue it will, until all the *nadis* have received the nectar.

Many of you reading this possess an active Soma Chakra, even if you are unaware of it. Here is how you can tell. When the etheric liquid drips into the *nadis*, you can feel it as a wet coolness that travels three to six inches somewhere inside. For instance, you may feel that you have spilled something on your leg because it feels wet, but when you check, it is dry. This is because the dripping is on the inside rather than the outside.

The process of dripping will go on wherever the *nadis* are open and not clogged. Almost all of us have clogged *nadis* at some place. There are a variety of ways of unclogging the *nadis*: Hatha Yoga, *pranayama*, Self

Realizations Fellowship's energization exercises, some Pilates movements, and chanting all work to clear blockages in the *nadis*. By chanting, I mean *puja* (ritual worship conducted in Sanskrit), *kirtan* (devotional singing, usually in Sanskrit), and mantra practice. You will be interested to know that there is a mantra that can stimulate the activity of this chakra. This means you will not have to cut your tongue and roll it up. What a relief.

The mantra to stimulate the chakra, called the Kechari Mantra, has seven seed syllables.

> *Hrim Bham Sam Pam Pham Sam Ksham*
> *[Hreem Bhahm Sahm Pahm P-ham Sahm Kshahm]*

In *Kundalini Yoga*, Swami Sivananda says that by repeating this mantra 500,000 times grey hair and wrinkles will disappear.

KALA CHAKRA (KALACHAKRA)

The Tibetans refer to this chakra as the Kalachakra. In Hinduism it is more often called the Lalani Chakra. Whatever you call it, its function is the same. *Kala* means "time" and *"chakra"* means wheel in Sanskrit. Therefore, one might well call this chakra the Wheel of Time within.

The disciplines pertaining to this chakra are the final ones taught by the Buddha. There were only a dozen or so people with the Buddha as he lay in a coma near death. All present thought they were attending what would become his wake. Instead, he roused out of the coma and gave his final teaching: the Kalachakra Tantra.

Most of those with him were from northern and central India, with only King Suchandra of Tibet as the lone foreign representative. All took as complete records as they were able of the teachings. After the Buddha passed, those who were there returned to their home. Soon after, one of the periodic invasions from the West took place, with its accompanying destruction. All of the notes containing information about the Kalachakra Tantra were destroyed except one: the notes of

King Suchandra from Tibet. Today, the only place you can get the final teachings of the Buddha is from the Tibetans. The book, *The Kalachakra Tantra*, by the Dalai Lama and Jeffery Hopkins is the most complete source of information with which I am familiar.

The practices of the Kalachakra Tantra are very complex and some time after the Buddha's death consideration was given to stop teaching about it altogether. Instead, it was decided that some simplification would take place and the teaching of the techniques and philosophy would continue.

My wife and spiritual son, Marc Bennett, and I received formal initiation into the Kalachakra Tantra from Kalu Rimpoche of the Karma Kagyu lineage in 1982. I have practiced the mantra, given on page 169, vigorously for years. My friend Peggy Rodriguez, the Holistic Health Practitioner I spoke of earlier in this book, has also practiced it in a very dedicated way. After several years of intense work she told me that it was starting to work in an interesting way. Traveling around the Los Angeles basin to give massage treatments meant that she was often in terrible traffic. The freeways are crowded most of the time. She began chanting the Kalachakra Mantra one day when she observed that she was going to be somewhat late for an appointment. She immediately noticed that time seemed to slow down. She got to her appointment on time. Thereafter, whenever she was late, she would chant the mantra. Since then, she is rarely late.

I confess that since I had done the mantra for over twice as many years and at least as intensely, and had had a formal initiation, I was mildly envious of her results. Nothing like that had happened for me. Then one day when I was doing a ritual called the *Satya Narayana Puja* (Universal Truth worship in the Hindu Tradition) it happened.

I was just beginning to chant the Purusha Suktam. I got about two stanzas chanted when a hole opened up somehow in my mind. I was transported to a time and place just after the creation of the universe. Sages and Maha Siddhas were conducting a mental fire ceremony to propitiate the source of this universe and invoke the presence of that great Being whose reality this is. All of a sudden, there I was. They looked over at me vacantly, probably wondering who this guy was. For my part, I was in a state of astonished rapture. I watched the proceedings for a few minutes, and then the hole in my mind closed and I returned to where I was chanting. No time had passed. I had merely taken a breath between stanzas and was ready to chant the next verse.

> Om Ha Ksa Ma La Va Ra Yam Swaha
> [Om Hah Ksah Mah Lha Vah Rah Yahm Swah-hah]

The syllables break out in this way. *Om* is the seed sound for the Ajna Chakra. *Ha* and *Ksa* activate energy in the petals of the Ajna Chakra. *Ma* takes the energy down the left side of the body. The next three syllables, *La Va Ra* are seed sounds for the first three chakras starting from the bottom (the Muladhara, Swadhisthana, and Manipura) with the "m" left off. The "m" sound adds the principle of manifestation on the earth plane to sounds. So this mantra invokes the energy of the chakras without including the appearance of the energies on the earth plane. Then *Yam* is chanted which is the seed sound for the heart chakra with its "m" intact. The mantra intends that the energy of the heart's lotus reach the earth plane in a manifest way.

GURU CHAKRA

On the under side of the Sahasrara Chakra the top of the head is a small, relatively new chakra, evolutionarily speaking. It is the Guru Chakra. If there was ever an argument to be made that the guru exists in each and every one of us, this chakra is the proof of that idea.

It is a common idea in modern esoteric spirituality as well as ancient mysticism that there are seasons of consciousness just as there are seasons of the year. In spiritual summer (*Satya Yuga*), over 90% of the population of the planet is enlightened. Earth is a nice place to be. At the current time, we are over 5,000 years into spiritual winter (*Kali Yuga*) where the earth is not such a nice place to be. But there are trade offs.

In spiritual summer, spiritual progress is difficult to make. Disciplines undertaken to advance take a long time to produce noticeable results. However, in spiritual winter just the opposite is true. Even a little effort brings immediate and substantial spiritual advancement. The analogy often used is that if you try to row a boat in air, you will not get very far very quickly, no matter how much effort you put forth. But if you lower the oars into water, progress is rapid. It is the very resistance, the very density of the water that provides the medium for advance. Spiritually, disciplines are the oars. Because spiritual winter is so dense, disciplines have a good effect right away and progress is fairly rapid. Winter will last another 427,000 years before we get back to spiritual summer (*Satya Yuga*) again.

As we approached the current spiritual winter, over 100,000 years ago or longer, we evolved a small chakra on the underside of the Sahasrara Chakra (probably with the assistance of some divine being or agency). The purpose of this chakra was to send energy down the spine to where the Ego-Mind-Personality was taking residence. Since in spiritual winter so few people choose to become seekers or even have the impetus to think about spiritual matters, the Guru Chakra is a remedy for that condition.

Energy from the Guru Chakra has a stringent effect upon the Ego-Mind-Personality. It wakes it up, to a degree, and begins to send important questions to the Ego-Mind-Personality, the answers for which will propel it onto the path of spiritual development. What is my relationship to this planet? To other people? Is there something more to life than I am aware of? If so, what is it? Why do some people seem to get everything they want or need, while others struggle hard? Is there a reason people are born in a particular country? If there is a God, what is it—really? And if there is, why is the world in such a mess?

Very advanced spiritual teachers in the Sadguru, Jagad Guru, and Maha Siddha classes of beings can activate the guru chakras in groups of people or individuals at will. They do this for their own reasons at times they alone understand.

Still, there are mantras that can directly or indirectly stimulate and activate this chakra. Chant the first mantra if you want to become a genuine spiritual teacher with both knowledge and wisdom—knowledge being of the mind and wisdom of the heart. Also chant this mantra to increase your attunement with the guru principle in general.

Guru Om
[Goo-roo-Om]

If you want to become more attuned to a specific guru you can chant the previous mantra or this one. There are two more guru-related mantras at the end of the Chapter 26.

Om Sri Gurubhyo Namaha
[Om Shree Goo-roo-Byoh Nah-mah-hah]

When the Ego-Mind-Personality reaches this place, it will now have to make a choice. Will it continue on by going into the Sahasrara Chakra or will it delay that decision? I call it the place of Great Decision, discussed in the next chapter.

Sahasrara Chakra

Technically, the Sahasrara Chakra—the thousand-petaled lotus at the crown of the head—does not have a specific mantra. It contains all mantras. Here one becomes *Paramashiva*. There are no more levels to be accomplished. Nothing to do or know. Another state of existence is reached that cannot be comprehended by individuals who are still identified by the solitary "I".

However, there is a mantra that Lakshmi teaches in the *Lakshmi Tantra* that brings energy from this chakra directly to the earth plane. I have conducted a Forty-Day Discipline with this mantra and can report to you that the energy it brought in was indescribably wonderful. It is short but powerful and very uplifting.

Sahasrara Im
[Sah-has-rah-rah Eem]

CHAPTER 22

THE GREAT DECISION

VENTUALLY, the journey will reach a critical point. The Ego-Mind-Personality achieved divinity when it reached the Hrit Padma. It continued to accumulate knowledge and see how applications of power, founded in divine love, work in the grand scheme of things. At the Guru Chakra, a new choice begins to emerge. It is a choice for which there is no right or wrong. It is simply a decision.

When the time comes, if we choose to move into the Sahasrara Chakra, our individual existence as we have known it will cease. The Ego-Mind-Personality will have served the purpose of bringing knowledge and experience into the soul. While the soul itself will not have changed in its nature one iota, still something has been added. That which has been added was the purpose of the descent of the soul into matter and evolution in the first place. Since the Ego-Mind-Personality worked hard to achieve this state, something of it also advances with the soul into the final merging in the Sahasrara Chakra. But making the decision to merge will ensure that any sense of individuality will be gone. Then there will only be everything, existing in an eternal cosmic moment where past, present, and future all coexist simultaneously. This state exists beyond time and, in a way, time has emerged from it by an act of cosmic will.

Some individuals choose to postpone the final mergence into the Cosmic All. They choose, instead, to retain the state they have achieved and go back down the spine, the tree of life and evolution, and work for the redemption of other conscious beings. We see this idea embodied by various persons in several of the world's great religions.

In Hinduism there is the title that stands for extraordinary spiritual attainment combined with the spirit of service and directed by divine love. It is the *Dasa*, the accepted servant of God. Accepted means that the evolutionary status attained is so high that it is as if God becomes the servant of the servant. This is said to be so because the *Dasa* has no personal agenda at all. The upliftment of humanity is their only agenda. Purity of purpose shines so brightly that no other motives ever appear as shadows in consciousness. This is primarily a Vaishnavite (pertaining to Vishnu) title. So those whom you see who have *Dasa* or *Das* after their name are on the path of service to all of us. Not all of those who have *Das* have achieved the rank of "accepted" servant. But they are telling us that this is their goal. They are now and will be a blessing to us all.

Shaivites (followers of Shiva, many of whom teach and follow the path to expansion of consciousness) can also become dedicated to service. The great Jagad Gurus of the Shankaracharya tradition and Maha Siddhas (great adepts) are extraordinarily divine personages who have chosen to take human embodiment to serve. They also train and prepare many other teachers as true gurus who, in turn, serve humanity.

In Christianity, the concept of the shepherd expresses this idea. The person who achieves cosmic consciousness and comes back to help us also achieve it is likened to a shepherd, and we are likened to their sheep. The shepherds operate in several modes, depending on their nature. One type of shepherd embodies divine leadership by going first through the gate to higher states of consciousness, telling us to follow him or her. This is leadership by example, sometimes called the kingly shepherd. Another type will herd all the sheep through and then go last. This type of protective leadership ensures that no sheep fail to make it through the doorway into higher consciousness. This is known as the good shepherd.

A most moving description of the vow of service appears in Buddhism. It is called the Bodhisattva Vow. The story of Avilokiteshwara conveys the Herculean efforts of a great being who finally reaches a high level of spiritual attainment. The efforts it takes is often compared to climbing to the top of a very tall hill. Upon reaching the top of the hill, Avilokiteshwara saw a high stone wall that he could not see over. Piling up stones, Avilokiteshwara finally was able to mount the pile and see over the top of the wall. He was astounded. Preparing to jump to the other side, he leaped up on top of the fence. He had decided he would jump over, after which he would enter a new stage of being altogether and pass forever from humankind.

At that moment, he heard a great moan from behind him. Turning around, he beheld the collective unconscious of humanity beginning to grieve for the loss of him from among them. Overcome with compassion, he decided to put off this final stage of enlightenment, his final beatification, for the sake of sentient beings everywhere. That decision became known as the Bodhisattva Vow, the vow of service to conscious life everywhere.

Many serious Buddhists today take that vow. The depth of seriousness of those who take the vow varies, but if you think about it, every great spiritual teacher of mankind must have taken a vow or made a decision similar to this, why else would they have come back to help us?

I took the Bodhisattva Vow from the XVIth Gyalwa Karmapa, one of the most amazing beings I have ever had the good fortune to meet. Following the lead of my guru, Sadguru Sant Keshavadas, I will return (with Sant Keshavadas and Guru Mata, his wife) to serve as long as there is work to do, as long as they want my help.

There will come a time when you, too, will arrive at the moment of great decision. You may choose to complete your journey and merge into the Sahasrara Chakra, into the formless all-inclusive Truth. Or you may decide to stay in this realm as a free and enlightened being to serve others in their journey. Be at peace, there is no right or wrong decision. There is only that decision that is consistent with your nature.

PART IV

DIVINE BEINGS
AND DIVINE US

CHAPTER 23

THE EGO-MIND-PERSONALITY

EOPLE HAVE BEEN GETTING more and more into their bodies since the 1980s. A great many people are jogging, going to health spas, taking aerobics classes, and working out in a variety of ways. Starting with Hatha Yoga, Qi Gong, and Tai Chi Chuan, we can see that along with the physical fitness movement there has also been a spiritual dimension to these patterns of movement as well. Besides these obvious examples, there are other examples such as the mystical movements taught by the Gurdjieff organization, Yogananda's spiritual energization exercises, and physical work-as-meditation taught by some of the Buddhist organizations. Clearly there has been an increasing flow of conscious awareness being expressed in and throughout the body for at least the last two decades.

Spiritually, this trend has been going on much longer. Even movements going back nearly a hundred years show methods for elevating consciousness by using the physical body and understanding its relationship to the ego. But as was discussed in Chapter 11, the Ego-Mind-Personality is a moving center. As it inhabits various places within, it may not agree with what it felt or decided while it is in another location. While psychologists might speak of the fractured self, Ouspensky in his book *The Fourth Way* says the ego moves around and manifests in different ways depending upon where it is residing at the moment.

For instance, the digestive system composed of the liver, stomach, colon, and other organs has quite a different set of priorities from the reproductive system and its organs—testicles or ovaries, fallopian tubes, penis, and so forth. Using Gurdjieff's idea of the ego moving around inside us, it is quite possible for the ego to express one idea as "I" while in the vicinity of the colon, which is quite contradictory to another idea expressed when that same "I" is in the vicinity of the pleasure nerve centers of the reproductive area. Can't you see one sexual partner saying to the other, "Sex will be even better when I lose a few more pounds. And I'm really going to do it this time." Of course this may change when the ego moves out of this area. The colon might not go along, and decide that it wants two pieces of chocolate cake. While the ego is in the vicinity of the colon, the colon is king.

Internal conflicts develop on the basis of where this center of consciousness (ego) resides, and how much the desires of any one part conflict with the desires of another part. Order is maintained according to how well an overriding sense of overall total organism need, or supersystemic need, can be made to manifest all or most of the time.

The desire for alcohol, for instance, is an expression of the desire of the lower organs in the body for a release of tension. Alcohol causes the *prana* to be redistributed in such a way that energy concentrations in the reproductive area and viscera are redistributed higher in the body into the solar plexus, the arms, and sometimes the neck. As the *prana* moves into these areas, the sexual area experiences relief. Excessive consumption of alcohol causes energy to leave the lower centers altogether. This produces a loss of grounding, and unconsciousness ensues. At this time, the desire for the release of tension by certain organs within the body has superceded the needs of the total body, and it ceases to function normally.

Never mind that there may be other ways to release the tension. Never mind that the organs desiring tension release may be completely ignorant of tension releasing alternatives. For the moment we can see that one desire has overrun all balancing mechanisms and caused harm to the total organism. If the desire for alcohol is an uncontrollable and recurring one, the balancing mechanisms become damaged, perhaps permanently, and all other activity of the organism become subservient to this one desire.

Alcohol is but one example. There are all kinds of desires. Many of the subtler ones that are more easily disguised have become socially acceptable, just as alcohol has become acceptable within certain consumption levels. Cravings for power, for instance, cause men to eschew nurturing needs essential to a healthy psychological makeup. These cravings result in permanent imbalances that may endure for the lifespan of the organism. Desires for sex, left uncontrolled, can so distort the energy distribution systems within the body that normal and balanced development of other internal systems is impossible.

The important thing to remember is that we are talking about ego manifestations (desires) that have taken over the decision-making functions of the organism. Keeping in mind that the ego is a false center, we are left with the idea of a false center expressing needs, that are sometimes real, as in tension release, that take over the organism entirely.

We know that the ego has a necessary and vital function. In fact, without an ego, the soul could not remain in the body at all. But it must be tamed; brought under control and taught to serve the higher needs of the spirit. Its reward can be evolution into an immortal state.

Whenever the soul incarnates, the Ego-Mind-Personality is the expression of consciousness until such time that it is of such purity and evolutionary development that it can express soul qualities directly without harm to the body. Purity here is defined as the ability to hold power, spiritual charge, without burning up, blowing up or becoming an egomaniac.

So the Ego-Mind-Personality is a necessary and natural part of the evolutionary process that is directly involved with the physical body. But to develop properly, balance among needs and desires is requisite. It helps to keep in mind that the Ego-Mind-Personality is a moving center expressing itself relative to the initiation level of the evolving consciousness.

That development process, embodied in the basic precepts of spiritual growth of various paths and schools, includes precepts for behavior among traditional religions, and aspirants on various branches of the spiritual evolutionary path. All paths and all disciplines ultimately lead to inner unity, which results in two important attributes of Mind:

1. **Clear thinking:** Since the needs and desires are balanced and subordinated to the overall purposes of the organism, distortions are at a minimum, allowing consciousness expressed through the ego to see causes, effects, implications, relationships of things in greater clarity and detail.

2. **Tangible will power:** With this, we are able to make a balanced decision that is good for the entire organism. We can even create a certain kind of internal agreement causing that decision to have great effect.

Inherent in the unification and thus growth of the Ego-Mind-Personality is the idea of integration of personality via true willpower founded in spirituality. This is the Ganesha-Ganapathi principle in action that was discussed previously

INITIATIONS

Each chakra represents a great initiation along the path of evolution. The whole idea of initiations is widely and deeply discussed in the works of modern esoteric writers such as Alice Bailey, H.P. Blavatsky, Rudolph Steiner, Earlene and Robert Chaney of Astara, and others.

A person who has taken the first great initiation operates in an entirely different manner from a person who has taken the second great initiation, or the third. But the same parallels of moving "I" hold true. While the shifting "I" may revolve around different issues, the phenomenon is the same, particularly so long as the physical body is involved. For instance, a first initiation person may have a strong sexual nature fueled by a desire to bring sexual activity into balance with other parts of their body. The issue here is sex as a physical phenomenon and the control of occult abilities that naturally appear at this level of development.

A person who has taken the second great initiation and is approaching the third chakra may have needs for the expression of personal power. This can result in a display of mastery as an expression of power, rather than love. Expressions of power are all right, but they must spring from love and understanding, and not the raw power urge that often masquerades as love in the form of "your own good" or "you don't know who I am." A third initiation person must learn that the true power is in love and not in the exercise of will that can alter many external circumstances. Understanding this concept will prepare them for the fourth great initiation at the Anahata Chakra.

Let us say that the first initiation person has a central location in the first chakra. They have mastered the survival issues and successfully established their energies there. They have come to realize that there is more to life than eating, sleeping, mating, and fulfilling desires. They have a hunger to understand and become more than they are. Their intuition has already told them that there is much more to life than they currently know. They seek, experimenting with various paths, until they find one with which they resonate. After taking up some discipline, they qualify for and receive initiation at the second chakra.

Now they begin to understand, study, and explore the full range of the uses, potentialities, and enjoyments of sex: Sexual energy as power, as ecstatic lovemaking, as healing energy, as aspirational zeal, etc. Picture an imaginary line extending upwards from home base in the first chakra through the second chakra to the colon where you place a small dotted circle. Further picture that this dotted circle moves freely throughout the body, always connected to home base in the first chakra. The "energy" of the level of initiation then expresses through the ego location of that dotted circle. It is the dotted circle that identifies itself as "I". This false identification occurs up through the fourth initiation, even though the false ego *knows better* from the time of the second initiation forward. Once the fourth initiation is reached, the soul energy becomes anchored in the sacred heart, merging with the evolving Ego-Mind-Personality, the center of consciousness which has gone though the initiations. The false ego "dies" forever.

There have been other deaths at each of the great initiations, but after the center of ego consciousness makes its passage to the next level, the ego reasserts itself and again begins the process of identification as "I". "I" have just had a great experience. "I" have moved on to my next level. "I have been chosen by God to . . . fill in the blank. You get the idea.

At each level, the Ego-Mind-Personality must learn and assimilate new lessons. When it reaches the sacred heart just below the Anahata Chakra, and merges with the luminous self, false identification of the "I" ceases. There is now only the divine "I" that ascends up the spine increasing in divine joy and understanding. When the self and its vehicle, the Ego-Mind-Personality or Ganesha's rat, which is now golden and divine, reach the Ajna Chakra, the brow center, Ganesha-Ganapathi's job is finished. The translucent and immortal Ego-Mind-Personality is "introduced" to Subramanya, the higher state of consciousness from which the journey down the spine started so long ago. The Subramanya state of consciousness beckons to the Ego-Mind-Personality as it makes its way through the centers in the head, to the place of great decision.

CHAPTER 24

SUBRAMANYA: THE ELDEST SON OF SHIVA AND PARVATI

T WAS COLD, VERY COLD, and the wind was sharp as an icicle. But Shiva and Parvati didn't notice. Once their marriage ceremony was completed they had headed back to Kailas Mountain and shared a cup of tea that Parvati delighted in brewing. So satisfying was her tea that celestials would often devise some crisis or problem demanding Shiva's attention just so they had an excuse to travel to Kailas to see him. They knew that Parvati would automatically serve them tea, a fact that swept through the ranks of celestials.

Of course Parvati, ever at one with Shiva, one with consciousness everywhere in the universe, knew all this. She is the very power of consciousness and thought itself, as well as the power of everything else in the cosmos. So she was never surprised when a delegation would appear at their doorstep with some difficulty for which they sought Shiva's counsel.

But today, their first day back from the wedding ceremony, Parvati had other things on her mind. The joint meditations of Shiva and Parvati were wondrous beyond all measure. Before the wedding ceremony, Parvati had joined in Shiva's solitary meditations and changed his interesting but static contemplations into palettes of shifting colors and forms. Dynamic, ever-new and full of wonder, even Shiva had not been prepared for the differences Parvati made in their now joint meditations. He had marveled and delighted in the difference her presence made. So now that the formal wedding had been duly completed according to the prevailing rituals and customs of the time, Shiva thought they might return to their glorious meditation practices. Thus he was mildly surprised at the reply he received when he casually said to Parvati, "We'll, let's get back into meditation for some time before we have tea or supper."

"We are married now. I have in mind a meditation of a somewhat different sort." She shyly glanced at him from the corners of her eyes, and he got her meaning immediately.

"Oh, well, yes. It is proper that we consummate our glorious union," he said.

"Umm." Parvati replied.

Soon their meditation of a different sort commenced. In ecstatic embrace they began to explore the dimensions of their love, their union. The dance of Shiva and Shakti began to warm the cosmos. In a very short time, the wind calmed and the ice began to melt, and this was just at Kailas Mountain. In other parts of the universe where most of the celestial were now residing, the heat quickly became unbearable. But Shiva and Parvati were completely unconcerned. The celestials, however, were very concerned—and for more than one reason.

Prior to the incident involving Kama, the celestial whose mantra arrows awakened Shiva from his deep solitary introspection, the *asuras*, demon enemies of the *devas*, had been completely defeated by the celestial forces. One of the defeated *asura* kings, Akhirsen, had a lovely daughter named Maya who was born with powerful gifts as a sorceress. As the king was speaking with her one day, he shook his head and complained that the *devas* always seemed to win and he was tired of it. Having compassion for her father, Maya became inspired and swore to her father that she would be a vehicle for revenge against the celestial forces. In her mind, she conceived a plan that bore better fruit than she had imagined.

Her idea was a simple one. She would find a great sage, bear him a son whom she would then train as a warrior and magician. The combination of her magic and the great power of the sage would produce a powerful offspring who would exact revenge on the *devas*.

Entering into meditation, she searched for the appropriate candidate. Her consciousness traveled across the spiritual dimensions of the cosmos and after some time, she saw the great Sage Kashyapa sitting in deep meditation, which he had been engaged in for a long time.

Sage Kashyapa is one of the Prajapati beings born from the very mind of Brahma. Possessing and wielding unimaginable power as easily as we don a favorite pair of sandals, Kashyapa also has a history of fathering great races of beings—an activity he must have enjoyed because he was so prolific. Celestial musicians, races of heroes, as well as demon warriors, and nonhuman sentient races were created through his interaction with a variety of comely celestial maidens from camps of both positive and negative forces. To him, beauty and charm combined with high intelligence, a spirit of service, and proficiency in spiritual arts were much more important than whether or not they followed a positive or negative path. He was unbiased, one might say.

To Maya, Kashyapa was the perfect candidate for her designs. Assuming a most beautiful and exotic form, she went to the hidden place where Kashyapa sat in deepest meditation. Sitting down in front of him, she fanned herself so that the magical perfume she had dabbed on herself would waft his way. Seeing an infinitesimal stir in him, she rose and began to dance and sing softly to herself. The soft tones and nuances of her exquisite voice caressed his immovable form. After a few minutes, the great sage opened his eyes and beheld her beauty. He heard the soft and captivating song she sang so effortlessly, and saw the graceful movements she composed to go with her song. When she had finished, she sat before him with humbly bowed head.

"You are an exquisite cosmic beauty of great talent and charm, young maiden, but why do you carry on so, here, before me, a sage of nominal interest in sensual things?" He asked her.

"I desire to serve you, O great One, and be your wife. What could be more meaningful in life that serving one such as you? The scriptures all declare it. Is it not so?" Maya still held her head low, not looking into his eyes.

"What you say is true, O charming One, but why would you be interested in one who is starting to wrinkle, as I am?" Kashyapa was testing her now.

"Given the spiritual power you possess, those wrinkles could disappear instantly, or last 10,000 years according to your desires. But I crave to mother the children our union would produce. Is this not a noble and true thing for me to desire?" Maya spoke only the truth that she knew he would perceive.

"Young beauty your boldness is matched only by the clear truth of your speech. I accept you in every way." Kashyapa reached out to hold her hand, and the next act in a huge drama of the unfolding universe was set into motion.

Maya and Sage Kashyapa lived happily together in the forest, and in due course of time a baby she named Surapadman was born to them. After a little more time, two more sons named Simhamukha and Taraka were also born. When the boys came of age, Sage Kashyapa felt the call of solitary meditation once more. He saw that his duty to all of them had been completed and he now yearned to return to his forest retreat. So, addressing his now mature sons he spoke. "I am going away my sons. Take care of your lovely mother, Maya, and lead a good and true life with proper devotion to God." With those instructions to his sons, he saluted them with joined palms and strode into the woods.

Maya was pleased at this turn of events. In her eyes, this was an omen. It meant that now was the time to act, that her plan was due to come to fruition. Knowing that Lord Shiva, the emblem of consciousness everywhere is easily pleased through devotion and supplication, she instructed the young lads to make repeated meditative obeisance to Lord Shiva. Maya wanted them to propitiate Shiva until he appeared to them, asked them what they desired, and then granted them the boon of invincibility.

The three young men were completely obedient to their mother. They had been told her plan as young boys, and it agreed with their inner nature. So now that they had heard that the time for the next phase had come, Surapadman and his brothers took refuge in the forest, found a proper secluded place, and laying a deer skin on the ground under cover of a large tree, they entered into deepest meditation. For a long time they stayed in a deep meditative state praising the greatness of the Lord of Consciousness everywhere. Yet Shiva made no appearance to them.

Perhaps he was otherwise engaged. But if so, why did he not come when he concluded with whatever he was doing? They prayed and supplicated, meditated, and concentrated. Still he did not come. Finally, they emerged in exhaustion from the efforts put forth in their inner state and made a huge fire. When it was roaring in full blaze, Surapadman decided to make the supreme sacrifice to Shiva. With a mental salute to his mother and brothers, he leaped into the flames.

Instantly Shiva appeared and saved Surapadman from the flames. Then Shiva asked, "Why are you sacrificing yourself?"

Surapadman immediately replied, "Lord of Consciousness everywhere, I tried the best way I know how to please you through prayer, meditation, and austerity. I have heard you are easy to please through such activities. When you did not respond, I sought to destroy my imperfection in those flames. But now that you have appeared I feel bold enough to ask you for a boon. I ask that I be given a body that will not perish under any conditions. I want to be master of this creation."

Shiva chucked and noted, "No one can have an immortal body in such a form as you now request, but I can help you in other ways. I hereby grant you the boon of invincibility. You shall not be defeated by any power in this universe other than mine. Tatastu. So Be It."

Surapadman called out to his brothers. Coming immediately from a short distance away, the three boys saluted Lord Shiva and then returned home to tell their mother the news. Her plan had borne the right fruit.

Now the boys recruited and formed an army with Surapadman at its head as supreme commander. Taraka and Simhamukha were generals in his army. Very quickly after formation, their army moved into territories controlled by the *devas*.

One by one the celestials and their aides were defeated and their tasks taken over by the *asuras*, Surapadman, his brothers, and their armies. They even captured the home of the celestials, *devaloka*, and installed a throne for Surapadman there. Once installed in his new luxurious surroundings, Surapadman was as derisive as he was evil. Capturing Indra, chief of the celestials, Surapadman had Indra brought before him where he ridiculed him and laughed. He also had Vayu, the Wind god, brought before him and caustically said that he looked like he had no wind in him at all, that he actually looked deflated. Then he ordered Vayu to continuously provide gentle breezes for his troops. Capturing the sun *deva*, Surya, he commanded him to have only moderately warm days where his troops and he were stationed. But where the captured celestials were held, the sun should provide a scorching heat. Even Vishwakarma, the divine architect who later would build a celestial city for Kubera in Sri Lanka, was captured. Surapadman ordered him to build a stupendous city which, when completed, was called Mahendra Puri and became Surapadman's headquarters.

A few of the celestials evaded capture. But not Jayanta, son of Indra. However, Jayanta was able to whisper to another escaping celestial that someone should go and tell Shiva about the state of affairs. This was a controversial request among the celestials.

Jayanta, as well as the rest of the celestials, knew about the time that the celestial Kama had gone to Kailas and disturbed Shiva's meditation. Shiva had turned Kama into a pile of ashes for interrupting his breathless state, immersed as he was in primordial consciousness. Even though Kama had done so at the request of Parvati, Shiva's future destined wife, Shiva had been unrelenting. But others noted that Shiva brought Kama back to life, also at Parvati's request. So after discussing everything back and forth, a delegation was sent to Shiva's home, Kailas Mountain.

The celestials arrived but were not greeted with tea by Parvati. Nor did Shiva hail them. They arrived to find Shiva and Parvati busily involved in conjugal embrace. The celestials shifted from foot to foot. What should they do? Finally they decided to take action. A member of the delegation was selected to act as spokesperson. He reluctantly moved forward until he was just a few feet from the couple and cleared his throat loudly. This was just the kind of disturbance that would momentarily halt the thunderous embrace of Shiva and Shakti.

Pausing briefly in their ecstasy, a drop of masculine and feminine fluids escaped their union and fell through a crack in the space-time continuum. The spirit of the earth-to-be quickly spoke up and stated most emphatically that she was not yet formed and could not contain the potent drop, lest she be destroyed. Agni, the spirit-god of fire said that he could hold the drop only for a bit lest he be consumed by it, even as he usually consumed most things. The drop was just too spiritually powerful even for him. One by one various celestial and sublime spirits came forth saying that they could not contain the essence of the drop.

It seemed that no spirit or element could contain the power of the drop. But the spirit of the holy Ganges River stepped forward and spoke. "I shall receive millions and millions of prayers from pious seekers. Their power will be enough to allow me to contain the drop, so I shall carry him." With that, the drop settled into the Ganges where he was carried to the Sharavana forest and placed in a grove of arrow-shaped reeds. Then the spirit of the Ganges departed.

The drop cooled just enough to reveal itself as seven sparks of divine fire that spoke as one. "Although the power of our fire is Parvati, our essence is of Shiva. We will slay the arrogant Surapadman and the other *asuras* when we have matured but a little." Then the sparks turned into seven babies floating joyously on lotus flowers.

At that time, seven celestial maidens happened by and spotted the babies. Immediately attracted to them, they each took an infant to their breast, fed them, and loved them. They played with them and sang to them as the seven boys grew. Each of the maidens spent loving hours with the boys until they reached teenage years. Then Parvati, who had seen all these events from afar, came to where they dallied along the Ganges River-to-be and called her sons unto her. "We must go to your father. There is a task he has for you." At that, the boys merged into a single form and waved goodbye to the seven maidens.

Professing their affection for those who seek truth, he was called Subramanya (he who is fond of Brahmins). For being taken care of by the Krittika, the seven maidens, he was called Karttikeya. Also known as Skanda, Mahasena, Guha, and a host of other names, the eldest son of Shiva and Parvati returned to Kailas with his mother for the task he knew was coming.

Some have speculated that the seven maidens were from the heavenly star system called the Pleiades, sent to help nurture a divine being who would intercede for the protection of sentient life, first in the celestial realms and then on the earth plane.

When Parvati and Subramanya were just heading up the slope of foothills leading to Kailas, Shiva came down to greet them. Pointing to a lake , Shiva spoke. "Behold, my son, here are your servants, your *ganas* (powers), the chief of which I now present: Subramanya meet Virabahu."

Thereupon, Virabahu and one hundred other *ganas* led by Virabahu offered praise and worship to Subramanya. When they were finished. Shiva called them all to him and spoke. "Some time ago, the young man Surapadman received my blessing. He has since become bloated with arrogance and self-importance. You have my very own energy as well as the transcendental power of your mother, Parvati. Therefore, I charge you and your *ganas* to now defeat Surapadman, his brothers, and his army of demons. The celestials are no more to be kept under his iron hand. With my blessing and with the power of your mother Parvati at your disposal, you cannot fail. Go now, and return when you are finished so that we and the celestial *devas* may all celebrate your victory." He then gave Subramanya a spear that could not be stopped, defeated, or altered in any way once launched.

Subramanya and his party immediately set out to find and destroy Surapadman. On the way, they encountered a large mountain that was in reality a demon that had assumed that form. Blocking their way, he spoke, "You many not pass. This road leads to the abode of Surapadman. You may not enter except by his invitation."

Subramanya answered, "Here is my invitation." He hurled his spear and the mountain was cleft in two. The *asura* who had manifested as its form was destroyed. The pass between the two halfs of the divided mountain subsequently became known as Krauncha Pass, after the name of the *asura* who had blocked the way.

The news of Subramanya's defeat of Krauncha quickly spread back to the headquarters of the *asura* demon horde. On the way to Surapadman's city and throne, Taraka, the youngest son of Maya, came to meet Subramanya. After ritualistic greeting, the two met alone on the field of battle. Subramanya, full of respect for his foe, spoke. "You need not die. Release your weapons, repent, and you will be spared."

Taraka just laughed and drew an arrow back from his bow. "This bow was given to me by Shiva himself, I dispatch you now." He fired.

Subramanya just shook his head and threw his spear. It struck the arrow fired by Taraka and split it uselessly. "You cannot stand before me. Since you persist in hostilities, I now send you to your next abode." He again threw his spear which had returned to him of it own accord, and, hugely surprised, Taraka died.

All of the *ganas* rejoiced, and Subramanya now spoke to his chief *gana*, Virabahu. "The death of Taraka may have restored logic and sensibility to his brothers. I now charge you as my representative to go to Surapadman's capital city of Mahendra Puri and meet with him. If he agrees to stop persecuting the *devas* and restore their rightful duties to them, he may live."

Virabahu saluted his lord and sped to the city of Mahendra Puri. Entering the city, he knew that official duties would soon consume his time, and he desired to see how Indra's son, Jayanta who was incarcerated, was fairing. Taking the form of a tiny insect he flew unobserved to the prison where the young man was held. Once inside he found the cell and buzzed close to Jayanta's ear. "Noble Jayanta," Virabahu, as the tiny insect said, "You shall soon be rescued by Subramanya, the son of Shiva and Parvati." Jayanta was filled with joy at the thought of seeing his family again.

Then Virabahu, still in the form of the insect, flew to the court of Surapadman to secretly see what was going on. As soon as he arrived, an opulent empty throne appeared right next to the throne of the Surapadman, the *asura* ruler. This amazed Virabahu until his intuition began to work, and he realized that Subramanya was already at work. Resuming his normal appearance, Virabahu casually sat upon the throne and spoke to the astonished Surapadman. "I am the messenger of Subramanya."

Surapadman became greatly agitated and spoke, "The same one who slew my brother?"

"Yes," replied Virabahu simply, then continued. "He desires that you cease hostilities against the *devas* and return their spheres of activity to them. If you comply, you will live. Otherwise . . . " his voice trailed off.

"A mere child threatens me?" Surapadman grew enraged. Seeing his firm resolve to continue his ways, Virabahu hid himself with magical abilities and left the city.

Watching everything, Surapadman's brother Simhamukha spoke. "I think this is no ordinary fellow, this boy who sends a representative to us. Remember what happened to Krauncha? I think we might consider Subramanya's offer."

"SIMHAMUKHA!" shouted Surapadman. "Have you become a coward?"

"My brother," replied Simhamukha, "it is unfortunate that wisdom is sometimes lost to those who consider themselves powerful. Speaking thus and suggesting a reasonable course, I have done my duty. Now the final decision on all matters is, of course, yours."

Surapadman spoke quickly, "It is war against this pup."

During this exchange, Virabahu made his way back to where Subramanya was waiting for him and said, "It is no use. Surapadman only wanted to capture and imprison me."

"Then march to battle we must," replied Subramanya.

A day later Subramanya and his army arrived at the outskirts of Mahendra Puri where he was met by Surapadman's son Banupokan who challenged him. Virabahu slew him instantly and a demon messenger who had accompanied Banupokan immediately rode off carrying the news back to Surapadman. The bad news shook Surapadman, but he was committed, and so he sent his brother, Simhamukha, to do battle with Subramanya.

Simhamukha was wily and had tricks up his sleeve. Just as the battle was about to be joined by both sides, Simhamukha sent forth a mantra missile that unwound into a long rope completely surrounding Subramanya's army and, picking them up, soared into the sky. Many miles away, it came to earth and the *gana* army of Subramanya was held motionless. Seeing this action, Subramanya sent forth his own mantras and loosened the bound army as soon as it hit the earth. Confronting Simhamukha, Subramanya chastised him, "You should not use the powers you have accumulated for such tiresome acts." But Simhamukha merely charged him. So Subramanya loosed a *vajra* (thunder) bolt given him by Indra, and felled him on the spot.

As he lay dying, Simhamukha spoke, "O great One, I live with the negative ego with which I have been bound. I now see your divine glory and praise both you and your parents."

Seeing the repentance of Simhamukha, Subramanya smiled and blessed him. "Your repentance and your devotion to your mother are pure and great. Therefore, I bless you now to become the vehicle of Mother Kali and serve her endlessly."

Simhamukha died in a state of great joy at such a blessing.

Seeing that there was no other way, and infuriated at the deathbed confessions of his brother revealed to him in meditation, Surapadman himself came to face Subramanya in battle. As they met on the field, Surapadman noticed that the way the boy conducted himself was not the way of a novice but that of a seasoned warrior. Battle alone would not be enough to defeat Subramanya, so Surapadman decided to use magic just as his brother had done.

Chanting the Sanjivani Mantra that restores life to those departed, he brought all of his dead soldiers back to life and taunted Subramanya. "You cannot kill my army, young one. See? They are all still alive." Then he launched into the sky in his chariot. Seeing this, Subramanya loosed his spear and plucked *asurva* Surapadman right out of his chariot. As he fell to earth, Surapadman saw that his chariot was flying to Subramanya, where it slowed and allowed the young boy to enter.

"Hey, this is a nice chariot you used to have," shouted Subramanya. "Thanks!"

But Surapadman was not easily defeated. He changed himself into a gigantic bird of prey and began to attack the *ganas*. But he had miscalculated the power of Virabahu and the *ganas*. As they rushed him, the slash of the young *ganas* swords damaged his wings and he began to plummet toward the earth. Using magic once again, he transformed himself into a gigantic tree.

Subramanya was not fooled nor would he be stopped. He slashed with the pointed edge of his spear and chopped at the tree with a mighty blow. The tree split in two. Now Surapadman assumed his normal form and raised his fists to threaten Subramanya.

That was as far as he got. Subramanya hurled his spear at Surapadman and caught him full in the chest. As he lay dying, Surapadman could see the supernal light that surrounded Subramanya and the innate compassion on his face. His ego melted and he perceived the innate divinity of the son of Shiva and Parvati. Filling with repentance he heaped praise on Subramanya, "O great One, please forgive my evil ways. In this demon body I was unable to see your glorious divine nature, with justice filling your limbs and compassion that is infinite and soaring in its nature. I confess and repent all my evils ways and pray for your blessing at the moment of my dying. Please show me that compassion that shines in your countenance."

The sincere humility of Surapadman even in his moment of dying moved Subramanya, and he gave his blessing. "Surapadman, true repentance washes away the sins of even the most evil of beings. I now select you to become my vehicle. In two parts I now divide you. The larger part shall be a divine peacock upon which I shall always ride. The smaller part shall be the rooster that will adorn my banner. Tatastu. So be it."

Thus it came to pass that Subramanya rides the peacock with a rooster upon his banner.

Some Comments on the Symbolism

In Part One of this book, I describe the vehicle of Subramanya, the peacock. When the peacock spreads its multicolored fan, an entirely new and previously hidden dimension of its beauty comes into view. A realm of color and design of which we had no inkling whatsoever comes suddenly into our sight.

Similarly, a transcendental and superconscious state in us moves down from the crown chakra at the top of the head into the rest of the brain. By moving down from the Sahasrara Chakra at the top of the head, a journey from complete unity to individuality has begun. Later this consciousness will move into the body.

In our brains, consciousness understands itself as a separate conscious entity occupying a physical form. This is the individual Ego-Mind-Personality which is the peacock of Subramanya consciousness. When our individual consciousness was totally immersed in a state of consciousness in unity with the consciousness of the entire universe, we were like a cup poured into the ocean. The moving down of consciousness from the ocean of existence at the crown chakra has filled the cup of our individual consciousness. We are in a sublime state, but now have a divine ego that perceives itself as separate from the vast ocean of consciousness, even as it participates in it.

When the consciousness of our individual self is resting in the crown chakra, we know nothing of self and other. There is only consciousness and the bliss of total absorption in it. We are Shiva. When a portion of universal consciousness dips downwards into the rest of the brain, we become aware of our individual existence. We then become aware of and understand the new potential offered by an individual existence. As a natural part of the process, the new divine ego forms, and we are now in Subramanya consciousness. Soon we become cognizant of others who are also self-aware.

As consciousness descends further moving from the head into the spine, the full potential of the chakras comes into full view. The capabilities of our chakras become self-evident. Mastery of the vast spiritual capabilities that exist in each chakra becomes accessible through the elements that rule the chakras: earth, water, fire, air, and ether or *akasha*.

The brilliant powers of the chakras light up the incipient spine so that it becomes like the marvelous designs on the open fan of the peacock's tail. The peacock of consciousness has spread its fan and that which was hidden becomes apparent. The rooster is eternal vigilance, always announcing the dawn of divine understanding at the highest level the Ego-Mind-Personality can comprehend.

As a representation, Subramanya is the first divine child of Shiva and Parvati. Shiva as consciousness unites with Parvati as power, and a state of mind is created that is individual, self-aware, powerful but not yet physical.

Subramanya's spouse is Valli, the goddess of nature. Of course, all the elements—earth, water, fire, air, and ether—are found in nature. So Valli represents the conscious power of the phenomenal universe in its diversity among the elements.

As consciousness descends down the spine, the arms are reached where Vishnu reigns as the great protective principle for individual consciousness. He and Lakshmi, the abundance of creation, spread their consciousness out to the other realms with endless patience, as they teach and lead individual souls back toward union with the realms above. Descending further, the level of the sun at the solar plexus appears, and the physical universe makes its appearance now. Physicality is made manifest. Then, quickly, consciousness continues to descend down the spine until the Earth plane is reached. Here our Ego-Mind-Personality takes up residence because it is here we have chosen to learn our lessons.

At the foundation of it all is shakti, the primordial feminine principle that becomes anchored in us at the base of the spine. That energy powers us as individual beings and provides energy for the entire universe as well. We know from physics that the further down we go seeking the source of matter, we arrive at increasingly subtle forms of energy. Molecule, atom, electron, neutrino, meson . . . there is only energy. No matter ever really appears. Everything is illusion—*maya*. It exists seemingly to confound the mind, because all we ever find is vast reaches of subatomic space and highly charged patterns of energy. There is no fundamental substance of "matter" to be found anywhere. But there is still reality, even in the illusion. This must be so, or we would have no existence every day. No family, spouse, job, enjoyment, pain, joy, or despair.

But as individual beings we have all of these things because we have descended into individual consciousness, into individual existence.

Subramanya consciousness is the highest state one can attain while still identified as an individual. The peacock is the spine with its brightly colored chakras with all their abilities and powers.

Surapadman and his brothers are negative qualities with modes of behavior and patterns of action that occur to the Ego-Mind-Personality as it descends farther from the state of divine union. There are many powers and abilities that come to us on the journey. These were listed in Chapter 11. The active, intelligent kundalini shakti, in collusion with the divine self, appears as delusion, Maya, Surapadman's mother.

You may recall that the Sanskrit language is referred to as the Matrika. She who binds and She who sets free. She binds, according to the Shiva Sutras and the Lakshmi Tantra, if we do not understand her ways. But when we do, she is a vehicle of Grace and a path to spiritual freedom. In our story, Maya interacts with the great sage Kashyapa, who understands the Matrika thoroughly. But their offspring do not, not having been properly instructed by either one of them.

To provide indelible instruction to the evolving Ego-Mind-Personality, the shakti may provide both power and fantastic, if limited, knowledge. Understanding the limitations of ego-based development is one of the foremost lessons we must learn on the evolutionary path. Maya, delusion, is one of our very greatest teachers.

Eventually, the Ego-Mind-Personality understands the folly of its ways and submits to the divine. The Subramanya state of consciousness does not disappear, but simply waits in the higher regions of our being until Ganesha, his younger brother, brings the Ego-Mind-Personality back to him.

Once our consciousness has reached the earth plane, Parvati and Shiva complete the drama by creating Ganesha-Ganapathi. Another offspring of consciousness and power, this being will use the Ego-Mind-Personality as his vehicle, discussed earlier as the rat, and ascend back up the spine until the brow center is reached. Here, a form of unity we call cosmic consciousness is reached. At this point, Ganesha's job is finished. He introduces the now completely translucent ego to his elder brother, Subramanya, who leads the Ego-Mind-Personality through the centers in the head to the great jumping-off place back to universal consciousness where we will once again not be identified as individual beings. We will return to the beginning of things. Of course, nothing will be quite the same. By the time the Ego-Mind-Personality has been created and gone on its wondrous journey, the divine Self now returns with a range of experiences it did not have before.

This is the drama of our existence as divine beings living in the ocean of consciousness powered by the Great Feminine. This is our lives—all of them. However long we take to descend and ascend is an individual and mystical affair, known only to the soul and the great Self to which we all belong.

The paths of the journey are varied, but there are tools of mantra and *pranayama* (spiritually scientific breathing) that any of us can use.

SUBRAMANYA MANTRAS

In 2004, a woman came to me with a problem of horrifically violent dreams that had plagued her for years. I meditated on her problem and discovered that the dreams were manifesting from the masculine part of her spiritual anatomy. She needed to clean house, as it were. I gave her the mantra below to chant. Within a few weeks our paths crossed again, and she tearfully reported that that dreams had subsided. Here is the mantra I gave her. It is very useful in purifying our masculine side. As spiritual androgynous beings, we all have both a masculine and a feminine side.

This mantra gives salutation to Subramanya, that great one who was raised in the reeds along the river shore, quaintly referred to as "arrow shaped grass."

Om Shara Vana Bhavaya Namaha
[Om Shah-rah Vah-nah Bha-vah-yah Nah-mah-hah]

Another Subramanya Mantra merely states his name, invoking his vibration. You can use this mantra by combining it with some specific objective in the mental realm or for resolution of some external conflict that seems inappropriate to you. Be warned that you may discover that the source of the external conflict lies in you, and that you may be ultimately responsible and required to undertake some action to correct an inner issue you had not seen before. More on this in the next chapter.

Om Subramanyaya Namaha
[Om Soo-brah-mahn-yah-yah Nah-mah-hah]

CHAPTER 25

TOOLS OF THE
EGO-MIND-PERSONALITY

LEAR THINKING has already been presented as a tool that emerges from our spiritual practices. Combined with study of scriptures and texts by those who have gone before and charted the catacombs of the evolving mind and emotions, certain ideas begin to have a real existence for us, even if we have encountered them before in a casual way. They become useful tools for our advancement.

CAUSE AND EFFECT

The whole idea of karma is based on the Law of Cause and Effect. What we have done before, will come back to haunt us, unless seemingly causeless divine grace comes our way and blows it away like the fluff of a dandelion. What we have created will have to be worked out somehow. Everything is related to karma: our relationships, jobs, children, ease or difficulty in life, financial status—everything. From the first part of this book, you will recall that four different types of karma were described. One of those, Kriyamana Karma, is the present action we are taking now that will produce a future result. With this knowledge, we can view certain religious tenets and proscriptions for behavior in a different light.

The Four Noble Truths taught by the Buddha, and the Eightfold Path that springs therefrom are really components of a future karma optimization kit.

FOUR NOBLE TRUTHS

1. All existence as we know it is suffering.
2. Misery is rooted in ignorant craving or desire.
3. Misery can be abolished by eliminating ignorant craving or desire.
4. This elimination can be accomplished by following the prescription offered by the Eightfold Path.

THE EIGHTFOLD PATH

1. Right Understanding
2. Right Mindfulness
3. Right Speech
4. Right Action
5. Right Livelihood
6. Right Effort
7. Right Meditation
8. Right Emancipation

I will leave it to a qualified teacher of Buddhism to explain the ins and outs of these, but I will state that if you follow them, you will be creating good karma that will come to fruition at some future time. However, at some time we have to give up even good karma. The object is to become free of all karma, as they say in Hinduism and Buddhism, "Karma is like a chain, and a golden chain will bind you just as securely as an iron one."

Similar to the Eightfold Path, the same idea can be found in the Golden Rule, "As ye sow so shall ye reap." This is a pure and simple statement of karma. There are other more modern statements that reflect the same idea. "Actions return to their source," and, "What goes around comes around," express the idea of karma in different ways.

With this idea as a platform, it can be said that, in general, we all get what we deserve. This is a harsh idea on its face. There has been so much suffering in the world that to dismiss it as some kind of justice seems thick-skinned, to say the least. Yet how will the karma accumulated by

Genghis Kahn, Attila the Hun, their barbarian hordes that swept through Europe in the Dark Ages, the Inquisition conducted by authorities in the Roman Catholic Church, the evil of Hitler, Idi Amin, and Pol Pot be resolved? How will slaveholders resolve their karma? Probably by being slaves themselves in future lives.

Does this mean that I think the Jews killed in the Holocaust deserved their fate? Actually, I don't. I think that the karma humanity had accumulated was so horrific that it needed to be worked out somehow, and a group of people, the Jews of WWII, and others, volunteered to help work it off. Jesus was called "the lamb of God," who worked off a tremendous amount of human karma through his sacrifice. But what if more was needed to keep us from blowing ourselves up? What if a group of people volunteered to help us all out? This can't be proven, of course, but this is what I believe.

My dear, brotherlike friend Peter Bock, Professor of Electrical Engineering at George Washington University, is fond of saying, "The universe is a clean machine." To me this is an elegant expression of karma.

All of us must work out our karma, whatever it is. Thankfully, as we will see later, there are extraordinarily benevolent beings of great spiritual attainment who act as instruments of grace and help us erase huge karmic debts, once we have "seen the light" and started to work diligently on karmic course correction.

CHOICES

In most of us there are a series of inner struggles and decisions that take place every day. We use our value system to wrestle with the choices we should make. To complicate matters, there are myriad external influences attempting to influence our thoughts, emotions, and decisions. Mass media, popular music, friends and family, relationships, organizations, both secular and spiritual, all have ideas about what we should do and how we should do it.

Through all of these influences, we still retain responsibility for the choices we make. The only spiritual guideline that seems to come up again and again is to be true to our own nature. Sometimes the real task is to figure out what that is. To some extent, the barrages of events and stimuli have hypnotized us in the current age, as French philosopoher Camus once put forth.

Camus relates a story which is not literally true but which is a good analogy. There was a group of people who were imprisoned. Then they were hypnotized into thinking that they were not in prison. One day a group of rescuers, after great effort, broke into the jail to liberate the prisoners. They overpowered the guards, got the keys, and opened the cell doors crying, "There, you are free!" The prisoners looked blankly at their liberators and said, "Free from what?" They were still hypnotized into thinking that they had been free all along.

This is where most of us are. We live our lives, attempt to fulfill our desires and labor under the falsehood that our everyday existence is all there is. We have been hypnotized by this existence, making it all the more difficult to show us higher truths, even as the prisoners in Camus' story did not realize that they could live a different life than the one they experienced in prison.

To unhypnotize us, most of the great religions have at their center a leader who has appeared and pointed the way to another kind of existence altogether. Most of us behave like the hypnotized prisoners and do not know what the religious leaders are talking about. We understand that there are different kinds of behavior with different kinds of results, but most of us miss the point that proper behavior combined with correct effort is a way to begin our journey back to the consciousness from which we have long ago descended. The great ones have arrived at, or have been given by the mystery of divine grace, an understanding of who they really are and who we really are. Then they try to let us all in on it.

The words of Dante the Pilgrim in the opening lines of the *Divine Comedy* also aptly describe us, when one day we will realize that there is much more to life than eating, sleeping, mating, and fulfilling our seemingly endless desires. Dante the Pilgrim came startlingly awake one day and observed, "In the middle of the journey of our life, I found myself in a

dark wood. The true path, from whence I had strayed, was lost to me."
Dante tips us off by casually using the words "our life" instead of "my
life." He is stating the very human condition of one who has awakened,
as if from sleep, in a strange land with no knowledge of past, path, or
purpose, but with the innate understanding that all of that can be
rediscovered.

Virgil, the voice of reason and logic, comes to Dante's aid, but with
the proviso, "I can only take you so far. . . ." Of course, because ultimately reason and logic cannot, alone, complete the journey to the sublime, supreme nature of existence. Dante, the author, introduces the
concept of Divine Grace through the vehicle of Beatrice, who helps
Dante the Pilgrim over a few obstacles. Yet still, Dante must choose to
advance. At one point Dante asks Virgil, "How do I know if God will
accept me?" To which Virgil replies, "God consents when you consent."
Clearly, a form of surrender is what is called for. But even surrender of
this type needs a great deal of preparation. This is choice. This is also
where our individual effort comes into action. But the grace of the divine
feminine is introduced through the help of Beatrice.

In the Hindu way of describing things various saviors and teachers,
prophets and gurus, some from among us long ago, heard and understood the message of spiritual evolution in some hard to define way.
Those early spiritual geniuses groped their way back up the ladder of
consciousness to higher states and positions. Then these spiritual
achievers established practices and signposts for those who would come
later. Some of these people were so powerful that entire religions formed
around them. Today many of their teachings have become our spiritual
ideals. We use what we know about them to define ourselves. They help
us become unhypnotized and recognize our own divine nature.

THE EIGHT "Ds"

1. **Decision.** We wake up one day and find that we have made a choice
   to be on the path of spiritual development and evolution. We may
   move slowly or quickly, but once the decision is made, the process is
   ongoing.

2. **Discriminating Mind.** Once we make some progress, we realize—falsely—that we are superior to other humans. We feel good about ourselves based upon this conclusion that is founded in isolation from others. This is, of course, an entirely false sense of progress. This is why so many of the religions state that progress is an illusion. It is universal to human experience that self-worth becomes equated with feelings of superiority. This superiority does not exist in a vacuum. It must be superior to something. That something is "other people" with some "acceptable exceptions."

   The antidote is humility based upon discrimination. We realize, finally, that nobody is any better than anyone else. We need only look to the ones around whom world religions have formed. They did not announce their presence and say that now we could start the new religion around them. Instead, they came to serve us.

   We can learn to discern the helpful from the obstructive, the uplifting from the enslaving, and the joyful from the merely enjoyable.

3. **Dedication.** We renew the decision at regular intervals by our actions, and by our mental and emotional behavior and traditional physical or spiritual disciplines.

4. **Detachment.** We all have goals and objectives we desire to reach. The desire for enlightenment, for instance, is a good desire. We start out by replacing nonhelpful desires with helpful ones. But eventually we will detach from any expected outcome of our activities. This is called detached attachment. It seems paradoxical, but in this form of detachment, the activity itself is the important thing. Being in the moment is the only item of importance. Concentration is so complete that any thought of a goal involving the activity becomes absorbed in the process of doing the activity itself.

5. **Discipline.** Classically, this is the application of specific methods on a regular basis that we understand will lead to our spiritual goal. True discipline will encounter blockages that must be overcome. True discipline operates even when the desire to cease the practice(s) manifests. In some cases the desire to stop all practices is very strong indeed. In the case of this book, we are referring specifically to mantra

disciplines, but this idea also applies to other disciplines such as hatha yoga, *pranayama*, sitting and walking meditations, and so forth.

6. **Dispassion**. Dispassion in this case means dispersal of the great, uncontrolled emotions that sweep through the mind. These waves can be harnessed to some degree by converting them to joy and devotion. Detachment can lead to dispassion. When the mind becomes clear and tranquil, everything becomes more transparent. People and their motives start to be automatically revealed to you. The path of the planets and their impact slides into the intuitive mind.

7. **Devotion**. With the recognition of the values of a spiritual ideal, whether through principle or person, there is positive emotional response. This is the beginning of devotion. Harnessing this positive emotion, the mind can begin the process of sublimating emotion into devotion. The pitfall is, of course, fanaticism. But by keeping a universal outlook and practicing tolerance, devotion can become one of the most useful states in the mind's toolbox.

8. **Duty**. In the midst of our spiritual journey, most of us have responsibilities: spouse, children, job, or parents. In our search for the right path for spiritual advancement, we must not be fooled into thinking that abdication of duty and responsibility will lead to spiritual progress.

In ancient India, Pundalika was a man who was completely absorbed in his own desires and thoughts. He was not particularly religious. His parents, however, were very religious and desired to go on a pilgrimage to a holy place before they left their bodies. But they could not do it alone because they were too old and frail. Seeing no other way, they asked Pundalika if he would take them on the pilgrimage. He heartlessly refused, giving a paper-thin excuse. He just did not want to be bothered with looking after them. But the idea of a trip appealed to him, so he decided to go on one himself.

Since he was a bit miserly, he looked for places to stay that would not cost money. He found that the ashrams of sages would receive him and ask only a small donation for lodging and food. On his third day out, he came to the ashram of Sage Kukkuta where he could stay the night and have breakfast in the morning. In the middle of the night he was awakened by strange noises. Looking out the window, he beheld three women with very long hair sweeping the ashram grounds. He arose, dressed, and went to them. Their vibrations were so wonderful that he was almost left breathless. Finding strength within, he approached and questioned them. "Who are you?"

They responded, "We are the spirits of the holy rivers the Ganges, the Yamuna, and the Saraswati. And we sweep these grounds as a token of our respect for the great sage whose ashram this is."

"What has he done to deserve this honor? What spiritual discipline has he so arduously performed that you should honor him thusly?" asked Pundalika.

The spirit of the Ganges replied, "He has done no other discipline than serve his parents. He truly recognizes their souls, the piece of divinity within them. Knowing that they provided his opportunity for embodiment, he serves God in them by caring for them in their advanced years. Sage Kukkuta sees God in everyone, but he serves God in his aged parents."

Upon hearing this, Pundalika's Ego-Mind-Personality dissolved in divine revelation. He heard the sacred truth in the words of the spirit, and he became changed in an instant. He dissolved in tears and was gone from the activities of the world for some time. When he came back to normal waking-state consciousness, it was daylight and the sun had risen several degrees in the sky. The spirits of the rivers were gone.

Packing his knapsack, Pundalika departed from the ashram and returned home. Upon arriving, he ran to the home of his parents and asked for their forgiveness and promised to take them on the pilgrimage they desired. They immediately forgave their son and were overjoyed that God had blessed them with fulfillment of this desire before they passed on. From that day forward, Pundalika devoted himself to the welfare of his parents, serving God in them.

After several years, an aspect of the divine called Panduranga, an emanation of Krishna that is very powerful during *Kali Yuga* (the spiritual winter that is the present age) saw the true devotion of Pundalika. With his divine insight, he saw how Pundalika had received his revelation through the spirits of the holy rivers and how it had changed him completely. Panduranga was pleased.

Materializing just behind Pundalika out of his line of sight, he called out to Pundalika, "Divine one, you have pleased me. Come now and receive the blessing of Panduranga."

Pundalika was washing the sore feet of his parents at the time, and he reached absently for a brick and placed it behind him without looking. "I did not ask to see you. I am just finishing serving my parents. Wait on this brick, and I will be with you presently." Pundalika did not give the voice much thought, engaged as he was in his task.

When he had finished, Pundalika turned around to behold a large black carved stone image of the divine Panduranga. The 700-pound statue was standing on the brick he had placed behind him. Pundalika prostrated himself before the murthi (statue of the divinity) and received the light and energy that flowed out of it to him. That very statue can be seen in India at the pilgrimage spot called Pundurapur, south of Mumbai (Bombay).

One day, I was reading Swami Sivananda's translation of the *Bhagavad Gita* and came across a footnote that explained that in old India, a "brick" was a slang expression for a saint or sage. The implication of the incident involving Pundalika is that the Panduranga consciousness will manifest through the consciousness of a saint or sage. Pundalika was, himself, the brick.

Like Pundalika, we should perform our duty with spiritual integrity and divine motive, realizing that it is a holy task.

9. **Tolerance.** Each person has a different karmic predicament. This being so, priorities will be different among seekers and nonseekers. Each person is on an individual path. Some of us make more efficient choices than others. But that, too, is a value judgment that can lead to intolerance. We need only remind ourselves that the Great Ones are and have been tolerant of us. This is an important spiritual principle that should fit into our Personal Spiritual Mosaic.

10. **Study.** We can read sacred texts and/or study with a teacher who resonates with our values. We can also engage in self-study through observation and introspection.

USEFUL TOOLS IN CORRECTION OF HABITS OF THE EGO-MIND-PERSONALITY

Over the years, I have confronted mental states, habits, and leftover thought patterns from previous lifetimes, just as I am certain you have too. Tens of thousands of hours of dedicated mantra practice have dredged up all manner of refuse that needs dumping, stuff I did not want to carry around any longer. Through trial and error, I devised a strategy for dealing with this junk. If it is useful, please feel freeto use or adapt it to your needs.

a. Observe behavior and thought patterns.   (Witnessing)

b. Discover something to be corrected
   or changed.   (Diagnosis)

c. Explore the range and depth of the issue
   to be corrected.   (Research)

d. Review or search for corrective action
   that applies.   (Corrective mantra)

e. Estimate (if possible) time needed
   for correction.   (Timetable
                                              for remedy to work)

f. Set schedule or strategy for corrective
   procedures.   (Specific plan or
                                              course of Daily
                                              Action.)

g. Implement measures.   (Mantra or Discipline
                                              practice specific to
                                              the problem)

h. Monitor progress where possible.   (Appraisal)

i. Observe Results.

(Post-Completion Analysis: Have I made significant progress in the direction of correction which is observable?)

j. Periodic Revisitation of the issue.

(Post-Completion Analysis Part II: Has the problem returned like a weed springing from an old root, or has the mantra practice really worked?)

PRACTICE

Spiritual discipline, prayer, self-observation, and development of compassion: these seemingly simple things will take us a long, long way.

WHAT YOUR HEART KNOWS

The power of Love is so strong that our very destiny as a species is tied to it. And part of the unique human contribution to the community of sentient beings is similarly linked to the power of Love. Both the Christ and the Buddha said it quite plainly. "Love your neighbor as yourself" and "Compassion can transform the world."

MANTRA TOOLS

Here is a set of mantra tools that will help you on your journey of self-discovery, self-reform, and self-mastery.

1. For development of compassion, this Kuan Yin mantra can be very effective.

Namo Kuan Shi Yin Pu Sa

The great Mani mantra, discussed earlier can also be hugely helpful.

Om Mani Padme Hum

2. For elimination and reduction of anger.

Shante Prashante Sarve Krodha Upashamani Swaha

And/or

Om Sri Rama Jaya Rama Jaya Jaya Rama

3. To supercharge the process of becoming all you can be.

Om Purushotthamaya Namaha

CHAPTER 26

GURUS

O HELP US EVOLVE, great beings come to aid sincere seekers. There are several classes of these beings: Avatars,
Maha Siddhas, Rimpoches, Sadgurus, Gurus, and Jagad
Gurus, among others. There are divisions in some of these
categories as well. For instance, Hindu scriptures speak of at least five
different kinds and types of avatars, a subject for another time. For our
discussion here, focus on the guru is relevant. True gurus wield tangible
power and have far-reaching authority.

To begin, the concept of the guru is one of the most misunderstood
concepts in spirituality. For most of us the guru conjures up pictures of a
person who tells his or her students what to do, when to do it, and how
to live their lives. This person often demands absolute obedience. The
newspapers, television, and other public accounts have revealed the
problems with this kind of spiritual authority. Abuses of sex, money, and
power have been well chronicled. Do all these stories mean that gurus are
a sham? Hardly. By way of comparison, just because some Christian
preachers broke secular or moral law, does that mean that Christianity is
a sham? Hardly.

But a new look at what a guru really is and how a guru works can be
illuminating for our spiritual journey, no matter what religious tradition
we revere.

The Sanskrit word guru means "dispeller of darkness." What darkness?
The darkness of ignorance. But this darkness is replaced by actual spiritual
light. Darkness becomes not just a metaphorical reference to ignorance,

but the tangible absence of spiritual light. The opposite of darkness, spiritually speaking, is illumination. And whether it is the nimbus (halo) of Christ and the saints, the shining aura surrounding the Buddha, or the light surrounding the priests carrying the Ark of the Covenant, the concept of illumination as a spiritual attainment exists as a common thread in religious lore.

The soul, self, or *atman* is always stainless, enlightened, and self-effulgent. What, then becomes enlightened? It is the Ego-Mind-Personality. This part of us usually operates on false assumptions concerning the nature of reality. In fact, the whole pursuit of Western scientific investigation rests upon a core of finding out what the nature of reality is and how the laws that govern it operate. In like fashion, metaphysics has been seeking the same objective for many millennia before the current age.

In the Eastern tradition, those who have understood some of the laws that govern this reality and have achieved some working knowledge about "reality" and who can teach others what they know are called sages, some of whom become gurus. Gurus dispel the darkness of ignorance from the mind of their students and bring them to a point where they can receive and accept enlightenment. Because the process can obliterate certain common assumptions that the Ego-Mind-Personality uses for conducting life's affairs, the process of enlightenment often proceeds at a measured pace until proper mental and spiritual groundwork is firmly in place. This process is for the protection of the aspirant.

BLIND OBEDIENCE: A PROBLEM

In a loose sense, any teacher of spirituality who presents truth in some form that leads us further on the path toward enlightenment is a guru of sorts. This is the common sense in which the term is widely used. It is used interchangeably with "teacher," which presents no problem so long as the teacher realizes that "teacher" should not translate into "demigod" or "semigod."

Unfortunately, some Hindu spiritual teachers have looked at their own classical literature and assumed that they are qualified to behave like great gurus from classical Indian literature. They assume that they are on the same level as Brahmarishis Vasista, Vishwamitra, or the more modern ones such as the great Sivananda of the Divine Life Society, Bhagavan Nityananda, Ramana Maharshi, Paramahansa Ramakrishna, Neem Karoli Baba, and others. These great ones are depicted as having transcendental wisdom and great compassion. In the strictest sense, one is not possible without the other.

There is, however, a monumental difference between those great ones of the ancient and recent days and some modern pretenders. Those figures, as well as the class of avatars represented by Krishna, Rama, and the Buddha, whom the ancient gurus followed, were also possessed of "the highest wisdom." To follow any of those great ones meant to subjugate oneself to them entirely. In more modern times we can see the same idea with the followers of Jesus. The disciples and followers today are required to follow his lead and direction completely. Any religious organization that has lasted more than a couple of hundred years promulgates the idea of obedience as a central tenet of its monastic wing.

With some exceptions, modern spiritual teachers do not have the same spiritual standing as those great ones. For teachers from any country to demand unquestioning obedience by students and followers is almost always inappropriate for both the teacher and the student. Obedience has its problems in the West also.

The Roman Catholic Church demands obedience from its workers in all branches. The vow of obedience is basic to the Church. It preserves the hierarchy of the organization and the leadership-derived and Cardinal consensus-driven "sanctity" of the organization's teachings. All of this is an outgrowth of the concept of the guru. We should keep in mind that modern religions have borrowed heavily from the forms that preceded them. It has always been this way. The Roman Catholic Church, during its period of formation, borrowed from the preexisting Hindu and Buddhist monastic traditions and religious forms. Incense, flowers, bells, and chanting were used for thousands of years before the Roman Catholic Mass was composed. Similarly, the idea of obedience is not in any way an invention of modern religious organizations.

The Guru as a Principle, the Teacher Within

The original concept of the guru is the *upaguru*. Where the guru is usually thought of as a person, the *upaguru* is a principle. The *upaguru* exists in all of us and in all of the noumenal and phenomenal natures of things. At all times, it is really the *upaguru* that leads, instructs, enlightens, and reveals. It is the *upaguru* that acts through any teacher. It is the *upaguru* that sends us in search of divine truth. The *upaguru* is a part of our own divine self, manifesting both as the Guru Chakra near the top of the head on the underside of the brain (beneath the Sahasrara Chakra) and as a principle emanating from the *atman* or soul. The *upaguru* is a manifestation of the omnipresent God.

The guru lies within each and every one of us. When we are ready to progress spiritually, the *upaguru* leads us to a teacher who can teach and show us what we need to know, tell us where to find it, or even present us with our spiritual birthright in a single event.

Teachers and Gurus in a Body

It is important to keep in mind that we may not have the same outer teacher for an entire lifetime. We may change teachers several times in a given lifetime. If we are open and receptive, a time may well come when we have learned what we needed to learn from a given teacher, and it becomes time to move on. But if the outer teacher or guru has demanded our absolute fealty and obedience, and we go along with this, then we are prevented from following guidance from our inner teacher, from the *upaguru*. At that precise moment, the outer teacher is standing in our way and is no longer a help but an actual hindrance to our spiritual progress.

From this it must appear evident that the really advanced and knowledgeable spiritual teachers are not attached to their students. They know well that the student has his or her own spiritual blueprint, journey, and destiny. A student may, for spiritual reasons, spend an entire

life with a given teacher. It is true that some classical guru-disciple relationships are eternal and ongoing from life to life. But it is much more
common for a person to have several teachers during a lifetime. In fact,
the various Puranas are full of stories where a person's guru will actually
send them to another teacher or guru to complete their training or provide some essential missing piece for their spiritual development. If a
guru sends a student to another guru for a time, this tells me that the
sending guru is a genuine and reliable spiritual teacher. We don't see
this practice in operation much today. Mostly it is just the opposite.
The prevalent attitude I have seen again and again is, "These are my students and they are not to see any other spiritual teacher."

So far in my lifetime, I have had several teachers of significant influence. And I have a guru (now departed from the body) and a living guru,
his widow, to whom I am devoted. But in all the years I spent with him,
Sadguru Sant Keshavadas never told me not to see or spend time with
other teachers. In fact, he and I went together to see the current Dalai
Lama when he first began giving public talks in this country.

He would invite other spiritual teachers to his centers, the Temples
of Cosmic Religion, to teach and give programs. He was friends with the
other spiritual teachers of the day. He gave *satsang* (spiritual discourse
and discussion) at the 3HO Ashram in a number of cities, and Yogi
Bhajan often introduced his lecture series in London and other places.
He and Swami Vishnu Devananda would always lunch together when
they were in town at the same time. You could hear their laughter echo-
ing down the hall whenever they were together. Swami Satchidananda
was a frequent visitor when he was in town, and he and Santji were
always guest lecturing at each other's centers. Ashoka Priyadarshan, a
Buddhist teacher from India based in London would come to Washington, D.C., to start his U.S. tour. We would pick him up at the airport
and host his first few lectures while he stayed with us. Amrit Desai knew
he could stay with us whenever he was in town. We organized one of
Ram Dass's first large-scale public talks in Washington, D.C. in 1973. Pir
Vilayat Khan was always welcome at our temple because of his loving
universal teachings. And this is only a very short, partial listing.

THE UPAGURU CALLS

Like many seekers, my spiritual experiences started long before I had any spiritual teacher in the flesh at all. My drive as a seeker came from within, not from without. The impetus moving many of today's spiritual seekers also comes from within, not from a teacher who comes into their purview, impresses them, and then demands exclusive obedience.

Most of us have responded to the call of the *upaguru*. The inner teacher uses the outer world with all its contents as a school for our development. The *upaguru* may lead us to this minister or that teacher for a while. Then we may find that we change traditions altogether for a time. I have seen people who have wandered from Vedic Hinduism to Buddhism and then gone off for several years pursuing Native American wisdom. Later they appear, following a more orthodox Jewish or Christian path.

Not once, but many times I have seen students following some variation of this winding path as they harken to the urgings of the *upaguru*. To whatever form of religious orthodoxy a student of the mystical path may return, they are never the same as when they started. Almost without exception, the return to orthodoxy is cloaked in a universal kind of understanding. They know that God is in every religion, in every path. They know that just because one's own siren song leads 180 degrees from their neighbor, no one has a corner on absolute divine truth. As Jesus said, "In my Father's house are many mansions. If it were not true, I would have told you."

Sadguru Sant Keshavadas said hundreds of times in public spiritual discourses that the guru is not a person but an inner principle. Students and *chelas* of Swami Satchidananda have told me most emphatically that he taught the same concept, and that his guru, Swami Sivananda, also taught it.

YARDSTICK TO MEASURE TEACHERS

Most of the human beings who are called gurus by their followers are simply teachers with varying levels of spiritual attainment. The more a teacher has realized and integrated pieces of the vast human potential within, the greater the teacher. The great teachers, without exception, are dedicated to serving humanity. They have no personal agenda. And they are humble.

Two things quickly emerge. First, there are people we have met who would never call themselves a spiritual teacher, but from whom we have learned some of life's great lessons. Most of us have known people who had a great beneficial impact upon us, but are living seemingly ordinary lives. However, these people have manifested the classical principle of the *upaguru*. There are certain lessons that they have learned so thoroughly that they are able to show or teach us what they have learned with simple yet far-reaching power. They may even be unaware of the example they set for us.

Second, there are those who call themselves spiritual teachers who have helped us spiritually only a little. In some cases they have actually hindered spiritual progress for their followers. These are people with some spiritual attainment who have let it go to their ego to such an extent that they cloud their own judgment and get in your way as well as their own. All persons who call themselves spiritual teachers must be held to a high standard in both conduct and in their life agenda. I leave it to you to assess teachers you have met or followed.

SOME OTHER HISTORICAL FIGURES

We need not look only to the great figures prominent in the world's religions to see proper examples of gurus. There are other modern historical persons who were spiritually evolved to such an extent that they were able to help many people. In the East, I refer to figures such as Ramana Maharshi, Paramahansa Yogananda and his lineage, Paramahansa Ramakrishna and his lineage, Neem Karoli Baba and those he has annointed with higher consciousness, the succession of the Dalai Lamas, and the Karmapas, the various lineages and orders founded by Shankaracharya, Ramanujacharya, and Madvacharya. Equally important are ones such as the transcendental Padmasambhava, the lineage of Avalokiteshwara and Kwan Yin, and the lineages of Guru Nanak and Guru Ram Dass. We must include great *siddhas* such as Bhagavan Nityananda and his disciples including Paramahansa Muktananda, as well as Sivananda and his students: Swamis Krishnananda, Chidananda, Vishnu Devananda, Venkateshananda, and Satchidananda.

In the Middle East, we have the prophets of the Old Testament from Moses onward, including the personages of Isaiah, Daniel, Elijah, and others. And more recently, Mohammed and the great teachings on true brotherhood of Islam.

In the West, it is harder to define such personages because the religious traditions are much younger. Still, we do have the disciples of Christ such as St. Francis of Assisi, and who can ignore Mother Teresa?

GRATITUDE TO YOUR OWN SELF

To keep ourselves on track, it is useful to remember that it is the *upaguru* principle in each and every one of them, and in us, that teaches and leads us to our own divine destiny. This concept allows us to feel gratitude for what we gain spiritually not just to organizations and outer teachers, but also to our own inner teacher.

OTHER FORMS OF THE UPAGURU

The *upaguru* may take many venues and forms. Some of the most popular forms of the *upaguru* currently in vogue are: The Runes, Tarot Cards, and the use of the Chinese oracle-in-a-book, the *I Ching*.

Jungians may view these tools as simply expressions of the collective unconscious working its way out in an understandable form. They might be right. But if they act as yet another venue from which our inner teacher, the *upaguru*, can operate, then fortunate are we. Some spiritualists might offer that there are spirit beings who work with each of these forms. They also may be right. With regard to the workings of the *upaguru*, it makes no difference whatsoever what we believe. The *upaguru* is constantly at work in us all. After all, the Law of Gravity works, whether or not we believe in it, whether or not we understand it. Why should it be any less for the Law of Our Own Being?

KEEPING ONE'S BALANCE

Consciously working with the *upaguru* demands an open mind. It also can mean "dancing on the edge." What is the difference between hearing voices and hearing the call of the *upaguru?* It is an important question and I do not have any pat answers. I do my spiritual disciplines, try to pay attention, and test everything I can. I remain skeptical but am ready to change my worldview about things in the face of mounting contrary evidence, no matter how outlandish or extreme the new conclusion may seem. I think many tips from the *upaguru* are ignored simply because societal and cultural conventions place them so outside the mainstream of safe beliefs that we simply cannot consider them. We filter certain unacceptable but helpful perceptions out.

COGNITIVE DISSONANCE

Psychologist Leon Festinger's well-documented studies revealed that we all have conclusions about everything from which we operate on a daily basis. Some of these conclusions are merely working hypotheses and can change rapidly when presented with an acceptable form of evidence to the contrary. But other conclusions we hold are very firmly established. Even when presented with overwhelming evidence that these conclusions are wrong, we mostly do *not* change them. Overall, Festinger found that when presented with evidence which conflicts with what we believe, we do one of three things.

1. **We change our mind.** In such an instance, we are open-minded. We are not "invested" in our operational conclusions to such a degree that we cannot objectively look at the evidence, evaluate it evenmindedly, and arrive at a conclusion. We behave rather well, in fact, logically speaking.

2. **We ignore or filter the data.** When we are heavily psychologically invested in a given set of conclusions or beliefs, and when those

beliefs are strongly challenged by competent and relevant evidence to the contrary, an internal mental dissonance sets in. Then the mind does a most interesting thing. It ignores the data.

This primarily happens when the conclusions or beliefs we are used to following are based upon perceptual data. All of a sudden, for no discernable reason, perceptions or experiences that support a conclusion different from the one under which we usually operate, stop arriving at the conscious part of the brain. Knowing that these perceptions do not coincide with long held beliefs or operational constructs, the brain "filters out" the pesky and contrary perceptions. They never reach operational consciousness. There are events we simply may not see even though they may have happened right in front of us. There are sounds we do not hear, even though they are loud and we are well within earshot.

Some sort of subconscious-psychological protective mechanism of great sophistication kicks in and we filter out the offending piece of information or data. Whatever it was, it never officially happened. Consequently, there can be times when we are not living in objective reality simply because events in that objective reality do not conform to operational beliefs.

Learning to accept things consciously, as they are, is not easy. It takes unlearning some things and relearning others.

3. **We derogate the source.** Derogation of the source of the offending data running counter to our dearly held beliefs is a phenomenon we see all the time. "He doesn't know what he's talking about!" This statement is source derogation. "That study was flawed." This statement is also source derogation. "That person wouldn't know a blankety-blank if it bit them in the hand." You get the idea.

Source derogation is the court of last resort for offending data and conclusions that get through all of our filters and encounter our very strongly held beliefs or constructs. We are so intense in our opposition to the conclusion suggested by the new data that we cut it off right at the source. After all, if the person presenting the contrary data is an idiot, then the data must, by definition, be suspect. There are times when we will do anything *except* change our belief.

Oh well, this rarely happens in really important matters, right? Not exactly. Galileo faced death if he did not recant his absurd idea that the earth revolves around the sun. Many controversial religious ideas faced a similar fate. I leave it to your own good, nonfiltered judgment to make up your own mind regarding some of the ideas presented in this book.

TRUE GURUS IN THE FLESH

There are certain individuals throughout history who are extremely advanced, but not in the ways we are accustomed to thinking about them. They do not necessarily conform to our ideas about spiritual advancement. I am not talking about the leaders of any of the world's great religions but of other individuals who have great gifts to bestow upon deserving ones. I am referring to those who have walked among humanity and taught the highest truths simply, with great power and with a humility that is difficult to fathom. I am describing people who have developed within themselves so much of the human potential that they can spend time with almost any human being or class of human beings and be taken as one of them.

They have no personal agenda for us other than our spiritual progress. They may or may not have organizations. But even if they have organizations, the progress of that structure never takes precedence over an individual's spiritual progress. True teachers and gurus are humble. They realize that God or Truth is vast. They understand, at least in part, that there are always more advanced and greater ones then they themselves. So they serve as and where they are able.

There is also a bit of a hierarchy among true gurus. There are the true gurus and beings who are Sadgurus. The latter is like a guru to the tenth power. In *Discourses*, Meher Baba relates how when a Sadguru is among thieves and murderers they think, "Oh, this person is one of us.' And when the Sadguru is among saints and sages, they think "Oh, this person is one of us." No field of human activity or mindset is foreign to the true Sadguru. Although they may be openly identified as Sadgurus, still they evade our ability to understand them. They are essentially hiding in plain sight. These rare beings have come and gone for thousands of years. Meher Baba describes such beings eloquently:

"He is interested in everything but not concerned about anything. The slightest mishap may command his sympathy; the greatest tragedy will not upset him. He is beyond the alterations of pain and pleasure, desire and satisfaction, rest and struggle, life and death. To him they are equally illusions which he has transcended, but by which others are bound, and from which he has come to free them. He uses every circumstance as a means to lead others toward realization."[14]

Millions of people have read Paramahansa Yogananda's classic, *Autobiography of a Yogi*. I dare say everyone who has read it has been deeply, perhaps even profoundly touched by this work. I submit to you that no ordinary person could have written a book like this. The effect it continues to have is a clear indication that a great spiritual force is at work through a person of high spiritual attainment. Here is a true guru.

Paramahansa Ramakrishna touched his disciple, Vivekananda, when the latter was still a teenager. Ramakrishna motioned him to come near the very first time they met, and then transmitted a powerful flow of shakti into the young lad that was so intense the young fellow thought he was going to die. But he didn't. He began to write the highest wisdom, founded the Vedanta Society, and has made a great imprint on the world. Neither of these men were ordinary.

Satya Sai Baba is controversial among spiritual seekers. But what is undeniable is that quite literally millions of people have chosen to walk a spiritual path because of Sai Baba and his miraculous manifestations. No ordinary person could accomplish this. If you listen to any of his lectures on audio recordings, it is the same wisdom you will find in the Vedas and Puranas.

My gurus, Sadguru Sant Keshavadas and Guru Rama Mata, would never allow a large organization to be built around them. Sant Keshavadas was welcome in nearly all-spiritual organizations that practiced any degree of universality. Well-versed in the world's religions, he would talk one night about Rama, while the next night's topic would be a deeply mystical exploration of the Sermon on the Mount. Other topics and mystics I saw him speak upon with easy expertise were the Baal Shem Tov of Judaism, the power of Tibetan Buddhism, the *Bhagavad Gita*, Guru Nanak, and a host of themes drawn from the world's great religions.

A spirit of mutual respect and cooperation permeated our organization Sanatana Vishwa Dharma (Temple of Cosmic Religion). It came from the top. Today I see competition among many spiritual teachers, as they seem to practically vie for students. Modern Buddhism, however, seems to have avoided this trap. Many Buddhist organizations I have known cooperate very well with organizations from different religions as well as with other Buddhist sects.

After eleven years, Sant Keshavadas saw that it was time for me to leave him because I could not grow in certain ways if I was always hanging around him. He thanked me for my *seva* (service). Then he did something outrageous that would ensure that I left and did not return. After his passing in 1997, he started coming to me in dreams with teachings, blessings, and humor.

His wife, originally called Rama Mata, traveled with him for many, many years and shortly before his passing he gave her a guru initiation on the banks of the Ganges and also gave her the new name Guru Mata. Carrying the lineage, she is exquisitely compassionate and gentle by nature but also has far-reaching spiritual authority at her disposal. She resides at Vishwa Shanti Ashram, outside Bangalore, India, but she also travels to give programs on the Hindu philosophy and tradition, and sings *kirtan* in the classical manner.

The various gurus talk about detachment, but we really don't see it very often. Organizations form and have goals, objectives, and agendas. The gurus plainly see that Americans follow a leader well and work very hard when they see any good in what they are doing. So, unfortunately, many gurus have become dependant upon their American followers just as their followers have become dependent upon them. You have probably seen it just as I have.

My relationship with Sant Keshavadas was different. He plainly told all of us who lived at the Temple that although he loved us unconditionally, he was not attached. Personally, he had repeatedly told me right from the beginning of our association that I would spread the teachings of the East to the West and that I would write books, open centers, and build temples. He wrote Sanskrit mantras with his finger on my forehead and tongue. I gave it the old "Yeah, right." I assumed that I would be a priest in his organization for the rest of my life, but I never saw myself writing any books.

Within four months of his passing, I had an agent and a book contract. Then I recalled another statement he had made in 1982: "When I pass from this life, this energy that has kept me traveling and teaching for all of these years will come to those of you who have prepared for it." My traveling and giving workshops has steadily increased since his passing.

WOMEN GURUS

Since 1990, on the fringes of the Aquarian Age, we have seen women gurus again start to become famous. Historically, the great gurus were householders, with husband and wife sharing an exalted state of consciousness. Brahmarishi Vasistha and Arudhati, Sage Atri and Anasuya (one of the leading experts on Lakshmi), and Sage Agastya and Lopamudra are but a few examples.

Most of the recent gurus have been men, but that is changing. There is an energy balancing going on. There are and will continue to be men who are genuine gurus, but there are also powerful, dedicated and humble women through whom the *upaguru* is manifesting. I salute all true gurus in whatever form they present themselves.

Then there are the Jagad Gurus. These are beings with vast spiritual responsibility for the global welfare of humanity. In the West, we know very little about them. But their power and compassion are extraordinary. I have concluded that they may very well be some of those celestials I spoke of in the first part of this book who are not originally from here. Through the grace of God manifesting through my guru, I have actually met and spent a little time with three of them, the Shankara-charyas Sri Jayendra and Vijayendra Saraswati, and a Jagad Guru from the Madvacharya tradition from Pejowar Math.

FIRST SADGURU

The first Sadguru according to Hindu scriptures is a being called Dattatreya. In the Narada Purana are mantras of attunement to this entity. The first mantra is a foundation mantra for Dattatreya. The second is a foundation mantra with certain seed sounds added. If you have a burning desire to be a true guru, either one of these mantras will aid greatly in obtaining that job.

Om Dram Om Guru Dattaya Namaha
[Om Drahm Om Goo-roo Dah-tah-yah Nah-mah-hah]

Om Shrim Hrim Klim Glaum Dram Dattaya Namaha
[Om Shreem Hreem Kleem Glown Drahm Dah-tah-yah Nah-mah-hah]

CHAPTER 27

MEETING A JAGAD GURU

HERE GURUS AND SADGURUS have responsibility for the spiritual progress of individuals and groups of people, a Jagad Guru has responsibility for the spiritual energy and atmosphere in a specific geographic area. Secondarily, they have assumed an almost paternal attitude towards the entire world. They have students and disciplines as true gurus do, but their principle activity is in blessing large areas by radiating spiritual energy throughout their area of responsibility. In the process, they bless thousands and thousands of people every year because they travel a great deal through their district. At the request of my guru, I accompanied him on a tour of India during which we visited a number of pilgrimage spots, temples, holy places, and met as many holy personages as we could.

When I visited Kanchi Puram with Sadguru Sant Keshvadas in the summer of 1978, the dusty two-lane road was a decaying application of gravel spread long ago on hardening tar. For the town, it had always been the road of life leading from one village to the next. There are thousands of them all over India.

But this town, Kanchi Puram, is special. The center of all activity here is the headquarters of the local spiritual leader, a swami whose seat of spiritual authority rests inside an adobe-walled compound in the heart of the village. In India there are five religious districts that subdivide the nation. The spiritual leader of each district or *math* is the absolute spiritual authority for the area, just as the Pope is in Roman Catholicism. Still, local spiritual teachers and organizations have complete autonomy in

what they teach and how they teach it. It's paradoxical, but it has operated this way for centuries.

As the headquarters for Kanchi Math, all commerce and social life is
somehow connected with the activities going on behind the adobe walls
that surround the compound in the center of the village. Although theft
is a common problem in most places throughout India, not dissimilar to
many other countries, there were no guards here tending the gates that
stand wide open. Although the gates are closed at night, there were neither robberies nor fear of robbers.

While the area is now enclosed, in 1978 there was an open courtyard
where beggars of a high status were given a place to seek alms. Within
the gates were certain beggars who had their stations while other beggars had their places outside along the walls at the sides of the open
gates. There were no quarrels over location, because everyone knew
everyone else's status and station. In keeping with the quiet that seemed
to permeate everything in this village in those days, the alms seekers were
relatively peaceful, as well as discreet, in contrast to beggars in Delhi
and Mumbai. Even so, there were obvious afflictions that made life more
difficult for them: one had no legs, another was blind, and some spoke
not a word. So although there was poverty, want, and crushing afflic-
tion, there was also peace and a sense of order. Things are different now,
but the center of everything is still the headquarters of the Math in the
center of town.

Twenty-five of us innocently got off the bus in 1978 at the gates leading into the headquarters of Kanchi Math with no frame of reference
for what was to come. Like most Americans, we had a ready laugh and
talked too loud for our surroundings. We were completely unaware that
we were about to enter a realm for which nothing whatsoever in our
previous life had prepared us.

We Westerners on this particular spiritual journey tended to be generous. We had to be instructed in the "do's and don'ts" of almsgiving at
the very beginning of our sojourn through a dozen assorted pilgrimage
spots, learning that only small amounts should be given to any of the
beggars, or a riot could start. Mostly, we understood and complied,

although I almost started a mob incident in the pilgrimage city of Hardwar when I erroneously decided to be quite generous with one beggar.

The leader of our spiritual tour was Sadguru Sant Keshavadas who was well-known within Indian spiritual circles. Because he was famous among spiritual leaders in India, he gained entrance for our group to places and circumstances that might be unavailable to unescorted Western seekers. Our coming audience with a Jagad Guru was a testament to his fame.

As it turned out, the Shankaracharya, Chandrashekharendra Saraswati, spiritual leader of this *math* was on a trip to another province. He had left two months ago with his entourage, walking the 250 miles to his destination. He would return by walking as well. Because of certain vows, the leaders of the *math* walked on ceremonial wooden sandals that are awkward to use. He did not mind. Neither did he mind the endless ceremonial greetings that flowed out to him at every tiny village through which he passed. It came with the position, and he knew it, and his patience for such things was as enduring as the poverty of the people.

In his absence, the "assistant pope," Sri Jayendra Saraswati, was in charge. Because long journeys are the rule for persons in these positions, each *math* has a leader and a handpicked successor. Under this arrangement, one of them always stays at the headquarters and presides while the other is traveling. Thus, the district headquarters is never without the proper spiritual authority. On this day, the assistant was presiding as he had been doing for two months, and as he would continue to do for the next several months.

We entered the gates at the front of the compound and were escorted into an enclosed courtyard with a small Ganesha Temple at one end. Inside the narrow enclosed area where the marble figure of Ganesha was installed, several priests performed the *Arati*, a short ceremony called "Waving of the Light." The symbolism of the *Arati* is that the luminance of the small light of the soul is waved before the larger light of the transcendental Purusha or Great Soul, or God "of which we are a part."

After the *Arati*, we were escorted through one of countless archway doors that lead to a small courtyard some hundred feet by fifty feet. At the far end of the courtyard sat an empty chair sitting on an eighteen-inch high pedestal.

Sant Keshavadas took a moment to explain that no one should touch this man who would be coming out, because it is considered rude. He then arranged us in a semicircle and stood quietly as we waited restlessly, standing some fifteen feet back from the chair. After several minutes, we heard a soft rustling coming from the back and turned to see a dark-skinned man with finely chiseled features entering the courtyard. He was clothed in faded orange robes and wore wooden sandals that clattered ever so softly as he made his way toward the chair in an unhurried, almost casual manner. His genuine, dazzling smile was infectious.

At a signal from Sant Keshavadas, we began to sing a simple Sanskrit religious song well-known to the Swami and his attendants who silently filed in after him. The Swami nodded and gently clapped his hands in rhythm to the simple chant. At its conclusion, he spoke quietly in Hindi to Sant Keshavadas for a few seconds. Then we were asked to sing another song, after which the Swami asked Sant Keshavadas to sing "Rama, Krishna, Hari," as a solo. . . he was well-known for composing and singing spiritual songs, which are still popular throughout India.

The Swami requested this specific, well-known song that Sant Keshavadas had written years ago and he now poured it forth. The Swami beamed in an intimate way as Santji (as he was often called) prostrated himself at his feet. An intense look came over the face of the Swami as he stared intently at the back of Sant Keshavadas who remained motionless for a few seconds. Then Sant Keshavadas rose, turned to the group and asked us to stand quietly in a semicircle. Starting at one end of the group, the Swami started looking deeply into the eyes of each person for just a second, perhaps less, and then his gaze moved on.

I stood in the center of the group and watched intently. I confess I felt the beginning of a vague sense of disappointment. I had expected the blessing to be a bit different, because I was familiar with the ceremonial bowing down to touch the feet of the spiritual teacher or guru. When there was no formal receiving line for this activity, I wondered what this new procedure might hold. I was experienced enough to know that sometimes when the feet of certain teachers, priests, and swamis were touched, a surge of electrical-type energy would come through the chakras in the feet, zapping the supplicant in the process. The electrical charge, which I had experienced on several occasions, was not in the least painful but pleasant in some hard-to-define way. But when the Swami started merely looking at people, I felt slight disappointment that was quickly followed by a shrugging attitude of acceptance.

As the glance of the Swami moved to within three or four people to my right, I began to hear a sound similar to the firing of a phaser on *Star Trek* or the whoosh of something moving by very fast. Soon the sound was right next to me and very loud. Now the Swami was looking right at me and a surge of energy of some indescribably powerful sort entered my eyes. I have never experienced anything like it.

Without burning or being in the least hot, it nonetheless burned its way quickly down into my body. With no weight whatsoever, and less mass than a spring breeze, the energy bolt shot down my spine toward a specific destination, as I quickly learned.

With a painless sizzle, the beam of energy went directly down into my testicles where the energy lingered slightly. There a wad of some material that I had been carrying all of my life disappeared quietly and painlessly. The wad simply evaporated. I felt lighter. Emptier. The lump of inert gunk had seemed so much a part of me, that I had always assumed that it was just part of my anatomy. It wasn't. And now it was completely gone. But I was not completely aware yet that the gunk was gone. I only knew that some strange energy had entered my private parts and rearranged things.

The Swami's gaze moved on, and I was left just standing there wondering if I had been irrevocably injured or hurt in some way. With a sense of urgent investigation, my mind descended into the groin area where I frantically checked around mentally to see if everything was still intact. "Maybe this hadn't been such a great idea," I thought. "What if I've been permanently injured?" I reflected wryly that I might be a first class fool to come 5,000 miles around the Earth to be spiritually castrated. Maybe this trip hadn't been such a good idea after all. I was filled with a sense of dread.

All of these potentially negative ideas raced through my mind. "I will probably never be the same," I thought. Worse, I could never explain it to anyone without their thinking I was crazy. I could just see myself going to a doctor and saying "Well, this guy looked into my eyes, and this strange energy poured out of him and into me, and now I can't have sex." It was simply out of the question.

A host of swirling doubts and fears fogged my mind for several seconds. What if I really was now impotent? What if I was no longer attractive to women? After a few seconds my racing mind quieted down and I realized that I felt—well—terrific. A burden of some sort had been lifted. It was as if someone had just taken a large load of uncomfortable rocks out of my crotch.

The Swami finished looking at everyone, a task that took no more than fifteen seconds, and with a soft command Sant Keshavadas turned the group around, and everyone filed out silently, a bit dazed.

As we filed out, a young woman friend in her early twenties leaned softly toward me and asked, "Where did he get you?" She was smiling with the restraint of one who has experienced the impossible but is still irrepressible. "Right in the testicles," I replied. "Where did he get you?" I admired her spirit, and I was as curious as she was. "Right in the heart," she replied. We nodded at each other silently as a bond was somehow formed that needed no words. We realized that each of us had received the energy in the internal place of greatest need. No one else in the group said so much as a single word.

On the path leading out to the gate where the bus was parked, the beggars who somehow qualified to be inside the walls of the compound sat quietly. I reached into my pocket for a couple of coins to give, but I didn't have enough. Taking my last remaining coin and placing it into the basket of the first beggar, I then stopped at each of the other two beggars and explained that I did not have change, but that I would be back. I had no idea if they understood.

Outside the gate I got some change from one of the other visitors and walked back the forty yards to where the beggars were stationed. Once there, I placed coins in the baskets of the other two beggars, turned and walked down the path toward the gate.

All of a sudden, I felt the soft wind of a healing energy in my back. I felt observed, slightly self-conscious, but good. The warmth in my back continued as I walked back down the path. Finally, I stole a quick look at the beggars who I was sure had sent the energy, but by then they were quietly involved with the next group of people coming down the path. I am completely certain that the beggars were working with some variation of that same energy the Swami had used. Their spiritual ability to work with that energy accounted for their position inside the walls of the *math*, while the rest of the beggars were stationed outside.

Once back on the bus, no one spoke for the next forty-five minutes. Beyond that single exchange with the young woman, no one spoke of his or her experience at all over the remainder of the trip. There would be other experiences but none like this one.

The older Swami, Sri Shankaracharya Chandrashekarendra Saraswati, who had been traveling when we arrived at the Math, passed away in his nineties. His handpicked successor Sri Shankara Jayendra Saraswati, who worked us over with that amazing energy, now occupies the number one position as Jagad Guru (world enlightener) of Kanchi Math, having assumed that position at the passing of the older Shankaracharya. He has already selected his eventual successor, Sri Shankara Vijayendra Saraswati. But the great swami, to whom I gave the nickname "Laser Swami," will hold that position until his passing, just as his predecessors have.

On a recent trip to India, a group of us met the successor Jagad Guru, Shankaracharya. Sri Shankara Vijayendra Saraswati, who will one day be the number one man. The mix of power and love he emitted is difficult to describe. I consider it one of life's great blessings to have met him, a blessing beyond measure.

All I can say is that with these two Jagad Gurus working on our behalf, we are all in good hands for the foreseeable future.

Overall, meeting true gurus and Jagad Gurus can help us to accept the world as it is. I call this the first step in becoming a spiritual adult.

CHAPTER 28

THE SPIRITUAL ADULT

I T IS A HARD LESSON to learn that the world, spiritual and material, doesn't operate the way we wish it would, the way we want it to. For instance, there are beings walking around on this planet that wield enormous personal spiritual power. Some prefer to call this power occult. Letting it pass for the moment that there are subtle but far reaching differences between spiritual and occult power, let us focus on these people for a moment.

The Yoga Sutras, the classical yoga book written by Patanjali, speaks of the nine great powers that the advanced adept manifests. He describes them as *tushtis,* the nine great magical abilities. This same list is also found in *The Ramayana, The Mahabharata,* in other scriptures, and in Chapter 11 of this book.

Tushtis

Bhuta Bhavishaya Jnana	Knowledge of past, present, and future
Dura-Dristi	Clairvoyance
Dura-Shravana	Clairaudience
Parakaya Pravesha:	Entering into another's body
Kaya-Vhuha	Materializing simultaneously in many places
Jiva Dana	Bringing the dead back to life
Jiva Krana	Causing the death of anyone at will
Sarga Krana	Creating new worlds or galaxies
Arga Krana	Destroying that which has been created

But actually there are many powers, particularly if you consult a genuine shaman of nearly any authentic tradition: Native American, African, Central and South American Indian, Australian Aboriginal, and so forth. They will speak of a spiritual and occult tradition in a language that is almost foreign to the conventional spiritual practitioner. They will speak of spirit animals, healing by symbolic fetish, casting out disease, and, very grudgingly, of conflict among the factions or tribes. They will also speak of things spiritual and occult that we might well consider violent.

What's the point? How many times in your spiritual travels have you heard the conundrum "Evil only has power over you if you give it power," or "So-and-so can't hurt you unless you allow them to." Did that little patter cause you at some place inside to quietly murmur, " I don't know about that."

Much to the contrary, I think that statement reflects more wishful thinking rather than a recognition of the world the way it is. There are forces wielded by real people that can and do harm people. Further, people get harmed whether or not they give their permission. Yes, we can go a long ways toward protecting ourselves by a variety of mental states, self-control, positive affirmation, and denying the power of evil over our lives. These things all work, some quite miraculously. But there is simply more to it than that.

When someone fires a bullet at a person, the bullet will not be stopped by the belief that it can't harm. The laws of physics are inexorable. There are people, I am sorry to tell you, who do the occult equivalent of firing bullets. And sheer belief that they cannot harm is simply insufficient to ward off the damage. Unfortunately, many of us have become lulled into a false sense of spiritual security by being told a partial truth that will only work in certain types of instances.

SPIRITUAL ADULT

To be a spiritual adult is to accept the world as it is, and not see it though the rose-colored glasses of how we wish it to be. To become a grown-up spiritual person is just as difficult as becoming an adult in the real sense of the word. Most people are stuck in an emotional pattern between three and eight years of age. We learn sophisticated ways to mask it with interpersonal rituals and fashionable attire, but I present this view for your consideration: Not only are most people emotional children, but mentally most people have not attempted to rouse themselves from very simplistic concepts about the world, religion, government, and so forth.

Even those who have really looked at the world, stripping away its veneer in the process, are sometimes so horrified at what they encounter that they immediately get caught up in emotional response patterns. The most obvious example that comes to mind is the "terrorist." Yes, many of the thinkers in the terrorist camp have seen things as they are, at one level anyway. But their response patterns are based upon devising and carrying out violent reprisals.

I think there are other and more effective response patterns based upon the practice of spiritual disciplines. For the present, I merely wish to make the point that childish response patterns plague us all. With a tip of the hat to psychologist Shelley Kopp, "Yes, you too, and certainly I, myself."

I have attempted to grow enough to be willing to view as many things as I can on their own terms. I have seen holy people in the India do extraordinary things. I have learned a little bit myself about some of the esoteric potentialities available to us all. There are occult and spiritual laws just as there are physical laws. And there is the law of one's being that opens at ever increasingly powerful and mysterious levels according to our conscious consent and willingness to go there.

So if someone tells you that "So-and-so can't harm you without your permission," I recommend you do not become engaged in a debate over the merits of that state of mind. The individual is simply expressing the way they wish the world to be. One cannot learn the lessons of power until one is willing to have concepts stripped away of what we want the world to be. It is often a painful process. Painful like growing up is painful. The key is willingness to grow. Then effort is required.

Summary for Becoming a Spiritual Adult

- Accept the world as it is.
- Accept your position in life as one you created yourself, at some point, in some lifetime.
- Accept that you have the power to affect your immediate environment and the entire earth through your spiritual efforts. You have great power at your disposal simply through decision, devotion, prayer, mantra, and meditation.
- Understand that there are spiritual laws at work, just as there are physical laws.
- Be brave enough to understand that simply saying, "I will not allow such and such to happen" may not be enough. To prove this idea to yourself, take a mental position that nothing can harm you if you do not allow it. Then go to a two-story building, jump off, and discover if your "nonallowance" saved you from falling. There are laws at work, some of which we may not be aware of now.

One more thing: If you haven't figured out that without love none of your endeavors matter at all, I suggest you put this away and seek to learn all you can about Love. From where I stand, Humanity is one: united, diverse, rich, mysterious, but above all, one being with many facets. We are those facets. Letting this realization dawn on me has brought, I hope, the beginning glimmerings of love. And as Dr. Leon Wright, former Professor of Religion at Howard University in Washington D.C., used to say, "The power is in the love. Always remember, the power is in the love!"

CHAPTER 29

LOVE AND SERVICE

THE JOURNEY TO SPIRITUAL FULFILLMENT

O MATTER HOW MUCH we dedicate ourselves to improvement and being all we can be, there is always somebody smarter, funnier, prettier, more handsome, richer, faster, more artistic, more athletic, more spiritual, better dressed, wittier, a better teacher or student, and all the rest. There is almost always somebody better at almost anything we do, are, or want to become. There are almost always superlatives that apply to someone else. But there are, thankfully, other categories of comparison where such ideas do not apply. Two of them are love and service.

Even these concepts have questions appended to them. Let us start with love. First, what or whom do you love? Do you love another person? An idea? And ideal? Second, why do you love? So that you are loved in return? Or because you cannot help doing otherwise? Third, what is the nature of your love? Is it based solely on lust? Is it based on security issues in which you must have control? Is it altruistic? The answers that arise within you define the qualities and characteristics of your love. There is no right or wrong among your answers, only information that can be useful in any self-appraisal you conduct.

Most of us love family and friends. Yes, we want to be loved in return, but true parental love also has altruistic components. After all, if we do the right kind of job as parents, we will become obsolete. We won't be needed in that role any more.

If we are a good friend, there is a part of it that is altruistic. We will sacrifice for a friend, just as we will for family. There can be problems here, as with any condition in life.

The obstacles that can present themselves in love of both family and friends are self-centeredness, selfishness, prejudice of some sort, hopelessness. But if we practice self-acceptance, it is always easier to accept others. If we recognize and forgive our own faults, we can do the same with the faults of others.

In relationships of any kind, true friendship is a precious state to achieve. Our spouse should be our best friend. If we are good parents, there may come a time when our children can become friends whose company we enjoy. If friendship has somehow eluded you, then here is a mantra, invoking the energy of the sun in a certain way, to bring the gifts of being a good friend and being befriended.

Om Mitraya Namaha
[Om Mee-trah-yah Nah-mah-hah]

LOVE IN ACTION

We cannot help but express the love we feel. Hugs and kisses. Flowers and sweets. Gifts of the heart. Laughter and surprises intended to delight. The more noble love becomes, the more it cries out to express itself in ways of service. We wait upon and care for someone we love who may be ill. Somewhere in our spiritual journey, it dawns upon us that we are all part of God, Truth, Krishna, Jesus, Cosmic Mind, or whatever our concept of the Supreme may be. If it were not so, there would be many grand truths competing among us, or in our own mind, for dominance. But the various Eastern texts and religions speak with one voice that Truth is One, approached in many ways.

To awaken divine love within, there is a mantra that declares that the chanter is that divine love.

Aham Prema
[Ah-hum Pray-mah]

I am Divine Love.

LOVE IN ACTION IS SERVICE

There are seemingly endless areas for service to others. Service to family, seeing God in all. Service to organizations, including churches and nonprofit entities. Service in promotion of universal spiritual values (love, compassion, tolerance, etc.). Service to animals (as seen in the example of Tippi Hedren). Service to the plant kingdom (as embodied by Luther Burbank). As the universal aspect of your love grows, you may feel that you are serving a particular master: Moses, Jesus, the Buddha, Zoroaster, Rama, Krishna, the Great Mother, or add your personal selection here. Ultimately, service is a state of mind founded on the idea that the path and the destination are one.

Once I questioned Robert Chaney, one of the founders of Astara, a mail order mystery school with excellent publications, about the dedication I saw in him and the sacrifice it seemed to entail. First, he was a bit embarrassed by the question and its implications, but he recovered and remarked that it was no sacrifice. It was his joy. He amassed no fortune in his years at the helm. Even though now retired, he has a joint commitment to advancement of the species and himself. In the over twenty years I have known him, I have never, ever heard him complain.

Of course, Mother Teresa stands out among modern examples of service. She had told those who would follow her example to serve joyfully or not at all. No sacrifice there, she served God in everyone and inspired the world.

MANTRA TO BECOME A SERVANT OF GOD

In Hinduism, there is a Vaishnava mantra that is said to make one a servant of God. Here, servant means something quite specific. It means an *accepted* servant of God. And an accepted servant of God is said to be waited upon by the Supreme itself. A soul, an Ego-Mind-Personality, when it becomes completely steeped in devotion and dedication to the Divine Beloved, sees God everywhere. In this state, God is everywhere available for such a one. For more on this idea, please see Chapter 22.

In modern times, Mahatma Gandhi stands as a prominent example. He practiced the mantra below from the time he was a young boy. His nursemaid taught him this mantra and he chanted it his whole life. The mantra he chanted is called the *Taraka Mantra*, or that which takes one across the ocean of rebirth.

Om Sri Rama Jaya Rama, Jaya Jaya Rama
[Om Shree Rah-mah Jah-yah Rah-mah, Jah-yah Jah-yah Rah-mah]

To serve with complete peace and dedication in our mind, it helps to have a spiritual ideal. I have found that it is useful to construct a Personal Spiritual Mosaic, composed of facets of teachers and teachings that resonate with me. I have been constructing my Personal Spiritual Mosaic for many years. It changes less every year because I have been at it for so long that there are not too many missing pieces. But sometimes I don't know that a piece is missing until I encounter one I did not previously have.

CHAPTER 30

OUR SPIRITUAL IDEAL

LL OF US have been inspired by spiritual figures whether they were mythic or historical. Some of us want to become the enlightened one, like the Buddha. This state of consciousness may call to us to dig deeply within ourselves to achieve it. Then there are those who fervently want to join with Krishna. They want to dance with Krishna and Radha. Women often would like to hold him as a baby or dance amorously with him in ecstatic bliss. Men admire the way he handled both friend and foe. They feel his absolute loyalty to those he calls a friend. Admirers of Krishna instinctively know that his words ring with truth. Fervent Christians call on Jesus to forgive sins and some Christians feel the inner draw to serve the poor and needy as well as to do other charitable works. Still others among us have met a powerful spiritual teacher and were so inspired by him or her that we instantly became followers, practicing what was taught and striving to purify ourselves to experience relief from karma.

There is a saying in mystical circles: "All you ever see is yourself." It smacks of absurdity until one digs a bit deeper. There is a logic to this statement, and it is powerful. When we look out of our eyes into someone else's eyes, a form of communion takes place. It can be wonderful, heartfelt, saddening, joyous, wondrous, anger-making, fear-producing . . . you get the idea. But the question from a mystical standpoint becomes, "How do you recognize what you see in someone else's eyes? From where comes both the recognition and the measure to determine whether what was experienced was good, bad, or somewhere in between?" The answer is that it all lies within the perceiver.

The mystics will tell you that if those same qualities were not within you, you would have no way of understanding what they were. You would see something in someone's eyes and think to yourself, "What is that?" You would have no idea what you were looking at. We know that there are some among us who are so innocent that they do not understand evil. They are proof of this idea, that the very basis for understanding lies in the character, personality, ego, and karma of the perceiver. The venerable *I Ching*, states that if you see good, you should imitate it. If you see evil, eliminate it from yourself.

These concepts lead to the concept of the Spiritual Ideal. When we gaze at the living form or pictorial likeness of a spiritual great figure, something inside recognizes that the qualities of this being are also in us. We recognize ourselves by our reflection in the spiritual being we see. The innate divinity within us blazes a bit brighter for a second, and we joyously experience it as a galvanizing event. We have seen divinity. We know it when we see it. We feel it. We intuit it. We want it. Many times we zealously pursue it and ultimately declare to the world that WE HAVE FOUND IT! Hallelujah! Of course, there are others following a different path who also declare that they HAVE FOUND IT!

Both have found it, for it lies within them. But the zeal of discovery of something external becomes translated into an all-inclusive imperative that because they have found it, everyone else needs to find the same "IT." And with this translation of the personal into the universal imperative, fanaticism is born. Now, everyone needs to become Christian and be saved or disaster is at hand. There is only one God and His name is Allah. Krishna is the greatest god. Only the Buddha can teach (through certain and specific organizations) how to become the Enlightened One. When the Messiah comes (for the first time) everyone will know Jehovah at last. And it doesn't stop here. Christian sects argue among themselves. The Sunni and Shia Moslems both claim to have the pure and correct teachings. Hindus argue about which god is the best: Shiva Vishnu, Durga, Lakshmi, Saraswati. It goes on and on. One's personal revelations become a cast-iron blueprint for everyone to follow and achieve.

Of course, God or Truth is in us. It is said in various ways: "The Kingdom of Heaven is within" or "Humanity is the microcosm of the macrocosm."

PERSONAL SPIRITUAL MOSAIC

Complicating matters further is the progress made in different religious or spiritual traditions in different lifetimes. We have, over the course of several lifetimes, been native spiritual students in different cultures at different times. We also have been in more than one of the religions in different lifetimes. This inevitably leads to some confusion as we encounter truly spiritually advanced teachers from different paths. We find that we can resonate with several different traditions. What to do? The answer is in what I call the Personal Spiritual Mosaic.

I find many people traveling a traditional path in Christianity or Judaism, who then swerve suddenly and become Siddha Yogis or some type of Buddhist. Then later I find that they have also studied with a shaman from this or that native tradition. They are building their internal Personal Spiritual Mosaic. They have traveled all of these paths before in different lives, and now they are consolidating. They are constructing an internal Personal Spiritual Mosaic using pieces from all the different paths they have traveled before in other lifetimes. It is quite personal, completely individual, and invariably beautiful.

These people know that Truth or God is vast. They know that they carry a small piece of that truth within them and that there are myriad ways to getting at that truth and unlocking its power into every aspect of their lives. They honor the various ways they have tried to unlock that truth within, with a mosaic drawn from a variety of traditions. They are constructing their Personal Spiritual Mosaic.

Now it becomes easier to understand why there are so many paths from which Truth seems to emanate. Since humanity is such an unruly species, a wide variety of approaches to seeking Truth has been presented

to us. Over time we have experienced great cultural variation, techno-
logical variation, educational variation, as well as political variations and
restrictions. Yet in the midst of all of these there has existed some path
to spiritual development and personal evolution.

In this lifetime, many of us who have been serious seekers in several
lifetimes or more are fusing the work we have done before in other lifetimes into a personal and powerful framework that serves us in this
dynamic age of global travel, historical awareness, and instant communication to almost anywhere on the planet. Serious spiritual aspirants who
have been working diligently for many lifetimes are entering a phase of
maturation. They are growing up, graduating to higher states of consciousness and assumption of greater kinds of spiritual responsibility. As
you read this, you can feel the resonance of this truth within you.

Globally, the power of spirit seems to have been turned up. There
seems to be an increase in spiritual "juice," which would account for a
number of things. Have you noticed how more people became attracted
to religions and spiritual movements starting around 1970? And the
number has been increasing steadily. Attendance at Christian churches
has risen dramatically. The growth of fundamentalist Islam is at an all
time high, historically speaking. The growth of various branches of
Buddhism has placed it near the top of the increase in numbers of practitioners for decades. Judaism had solidified its population of adherents
and seen a growth in those who follow the teachings and practices of
the Kabbalah. Although the chanting of the Hari Krishnas from ISKON
at airports and in the street has disappeared, there has been a huge
increase in the number of Hindu Temples built across the country. If
one goes to one of these shrines, one will find some Western-looking
faces among the devotees. Then there is the growth among those who
are attending sweat lodges and going on vision quests centered in one
of the native traditions. Interest in Tai Chi, Qi Gong, and Hatha Yoga
is shooting up everywhere. No matter where one looks, the number of
people seeking to advance spiritually is increasing at an astonishing rate.

I view this phenomenon as the gathering for an evolutionary leap, spiritually speaking. As part of the process, the "heat" everywhere is being

turned up. Of course, heat is not light, so there is confusion side-by-side with genuine spiritual progress. A handy rule for discerning spiritual light from spiritual heat when observing this worldwide phenomenon is in the attitude of the leaders. Those with only heat will insist that you do it their way. Their understanding and viewpoint has well-defined limitations to which they demand you adhere. Those with true spiritual light are more universal. They know that God or Truth can manifest in an infinite variety of ways. Ecumenical gatherings among spiritual leaders reflect this idea wonderfully.

For those of us who feel a deep dedication to the spiritually oriented life, the task becomes one of finding the right instrument. If humanity is likened to a vast orchestra, then we are the players of the various instruments. But to play, we must know which among the instruments is best suited for us. The spiritual quest is much like seeking such an instrument. Then, having found it, we must practice diligently. But since we are also building our Personal Spiritual Mosaic, the instruments look a bit strange. One might say they play a clarinet but also sometimes sing while beating a large drum.

As we tune and practice, we may have profound spiritual experiences. Some of them may be so overwhelming that we feel we have FOUND IT. By all means be grateful. Gratitude is a powerful spiritual state in which to be. But please resist the temptation to extrapolate your personal experience into an immutable universal imperative. Truth has many roads and byways leading to and from it.

For all the differences among the paths leading to spiritual evolution, among the various religions, spiritual organizations, prayer techniques, and spiritual disciplines, there is one constant. It all takes place inside of us. And amazingly, our spiritual anatomy is the same. We have the same number of chakras. The spiritual abilities of which we are capable are the same in number and attribute, even if there is variation in our karma.

Our Holy Task

Returning to the spiritual ideal, the recognition of any external spiritual personage who has ever lived helps us to determine our own inner spiritual nature. These ideals are like mirrors that reflect back to us what we are. Different spiritual persons throughout history may reflect different pieces of what our inner spiritual nature has become over many lifetimes. So building your own Personal Spiritual Mosaic is a sacred task. It will ultimately provide a platform from which you can see yourself. It is holy work. And it is profoundly useful, so long as you do not see competition among the pieces. The great ones whom we revere, at whatever level they exist in spirit, do not vie with one another. So if you seem to find parts of your Personal Spiritual Mosaic that do not agree with one another, keep looking for more pieces. It only means you are still looking for missing pieces of your own divine nature.

CHAPTER 31

MANTRA SUMMARY

N CASE you have become a bit dazzled by the variety of mantras presented, here is a list of mantras that will move you forward, no matter where you may be on the evolutionary path. Of course not all of the mantras in this book are listed here.

SHAIVITE

Om Namah Shivaya [or, Om Shrim Klim Namah Shivaya]
[Om Nah-mah Shee-vah-yah, or Om Shreem Kleem Nah-mah Shee-vah-yah]

Shivo Hum
[Shee-voh Hoom]

VAISHNAVITE

Om Namo Bhagavate Vasudevaya
[Om Nah-moh Bha-gah-vah-teh Vah-soo-deh-vah-yah]

Om Sri Rama Jaya Rama Jaya Jaya Rama
[Om Shree Rah-mah Jah-yah Rah-mah Jah-yah Jah-yah Rah-mah]

BRAHMA

Aham Brahmasmi
[Ah-hahm Brah-mahs-mee]

Sat Chid Ekam Brahma
[Saht Cheed Eh-kahm Brah-ma]

TIBETAN

Om Mani Padme Hum
[Om Mah-nee Pahd-meh-Hoom]

Om Ha Ksa Ma La Va Ra Yam Swaha
[Om Hah Ksah Mah Lah Vah Rah Yahm Swah-hah]

Om Tare Tuttare Ture Swaha
[Om Tah-reh Too-tah-reh Too-reh Swah-hah]

Om Ah Ra Paht Sa Na Dhih Dhih Dhih
[Om Ah Rah Paht Sah Nah Dhee Dhee Dhee]

HINDU SHAKTI

Hrim Shrim Klim Param Eshwari Swaha
[Hreem Shreem Kleem Pah-rahm Ehsh-wah-ree Swah-hah]

Sahasrara Im
[Sah-has-rah-rah Eem]

General

Om Bhu Om Bhuvaha Om Swaha

Om Maha Om Janaha Om Tapaha Om Satyam

Om Tat Savitur Varenyam

Bhargo Devasya Dhimahi

Dhiyo Yonaha Prachodayat

[Om Bhoo Om Bhoo-vah-hah Om Swah-hah

Om Mah-hah Om Jah-nah-hah Om Tah-pah-hah Om Saht-yahm

Om Taht Sah-vee-toor Vah-rehn-yahm

Bhahr-goh Deh-vahs-yah Dee-mah-hee

Dhee-yoh Yoh-nah-hah Prah-choh-dah-yaht]

Om Namo Narayanaya

[Om Nah-moh Nah-rah-yah-nah-yah]

CHAPTER 32

WHILE WE ARE STRIVING AND EVOLVING, WHERE CAN WE STAND?

 STAND ON THE LAW OF CYCLES. Whether it is sunspots or seasons, we find cycles in everything. We know that eventually upturns will be followed by downturns. The continued upturn of the stock market cannot continue indefinitely. The *I Ching* says that to be sparing and economical in times of plenty helps one survive times of scarcity.

There are also great cosmic spiritual cycles in our lives. If we live our ideals, our future good karma is assured, as well as our eventual liberation from the round of rebirth.

2. **Stand on the Knowledge of continuing divine intervention.** For thousands of years, we can see that if things get out of balance, we get help. It has happened many times and will happen again. In Christianity it is taught that Jesus "died for our sins." If true, it means he balanced the negative karma created by millions of people over many centuries. The Buddha came to help us discover what was wrong with our way of thinking and behaving in the world. The Vishnu avatars came to solve specific problems. The great ones devoted to Shiva have left a tremendous legacy of teaching, writing, and personal example, as well as serving as channels for divine grace.

3. **Stand on Faith.** By this I do not mean an empty hoping that things will just somehow get better. Faith in this context is a certainty that

God is moving surely and certainly in human affairs at all times; that God is fulfilling a plan made eons ago, which the divine ones labor to complete with constant devotion and infinite patience. Stand on Faith that you are part of the plan. If there are divine ones working for fulfillment of the Plan, then they have come from some place. Most of the information we have from various sources today indicates that some of the Masters were once human and transcended and then chose to join the path of service. This means that we, you and me, can also reach that point. We are now, and will be, part of the plan, so long as we choose to be so. There is sufficient evidence to take that view on faith. This kind of faith leads naturally to service of some kind.

4. **Stand on Service.** Serve God in your family. Serve God in humanity, on the job, or in the home. Feel that you are serving God even in the seemingly mundane business community, by dedicating through prayer all that you do for the benefit of mankind in some way. Serve through organizations that do the work you think is important. If we can do this, even in jobs where it seems difficult to make a difference, we will eventually bring about needed change to those circumstances.

5. **Stand On Your Own Sense of the True and the Good.** In India, a young man named Gautama compared the luxury of his youth to the squalor finally revealed to him on the streets. Standing on his own truth, he renounced his status and wealth and sought to follow some of the ways of the Hindu mystics. Living among them, he found corruption and misunderstanding of spiritual teachings, so he stood on his own truth and became the Buddha. He changed an entire nation and the world.

Mahatma Gandhi practiced *ahimsa*, nonviolence, and *satyagraha*, devotion to truth. He stood on these ideals and changed an entire nation. But even more than that, he left us an example of the *possible*, if we can but find the right place to stand within.

Martin Luther King also practiced a form of nonviolence and he too changed a nation. We are quite a different place today than we were before he stood on his own sense of inner truth and moved forward.

Mother Teresa defied her order of nuns and followed and then stood on her own truth, practicing devotion and service to the poorest of the poor. In so doing, she demanded that everyone who wanted to follow her example, do so joyfully. No long faces allowed. By her works and example, she inspired the world and even the Roman Catholic Church.

6. **Stand on Devotion and Love.** If Love is the ultimate end of our common journey, then Devotion is a vehicle on that path. Devotion invokes the power of the heart. Combined with proper understanding, devotion links the mind to the heart, giving it incredible power beyond even that which we can imagine.

I want to end my book with the mantra that declares "I Am Divine Love." By chanting this mantra, you invoke that quality of energy into you in a tangible way.

Aham Prema
[Ah-hum Preh-mah]

May you want for nothing in your great journey. May you find your Personal Spiritual Ideal and be given the grace to attain it all. May you shine as an example affirming the ancient truth, "Yes, one can become enlightened and liberated while still living in the body."

SUMMARY OF THE CHAKRA PETALS AND QUALITIES

MULADHARA

Four Petals: Vam, Sham, Sham, and Sam

Vritti (Qualities): Four Forms of Bliss: Yogananda (Bliss of [through] Yoga), Paramananda (Supreme Bliss), Sahajananda (Natural Bliss) and Virananda (Vira Bliss)

Principle: Earth

Seed Sound: Lam

Devata: Devi Kundalini

Shakti: Red, four-handed Shakti Dakini

Deities: Indra, also Brahma and Savitri

One who achieves mastery over this chakra acquires beginning knowledge of the motive power of kundalini and the means to awaken it. When the kundalini awakens in this chakra one gets Darduri Siddhi, the power to rise from the ground. The breath and reproductive fluids come under control. Much karma is burned and one acquires some knowledge of past, present, and future. One can approach Sahaja Samadhi, the natural state.

SWADISTHANA

Six Petals: Bam, Bham, Mam, and Yam, Ram, Lam

Vritti (Qualities): Credulity, Suspicion/Mistrust, Distain, Delusion, False Knowledge, Pitilessness

Principle: Water

Seed Sound: Vam
Devata: Varuna
Shakti: Rakini
Deity: Maha Vishnu and Saraswati

One who achieves mastery over this chakra conquers fear of water. Many psychic powers come to you, intuitional knowledge manifests, and one gains control over the senses. One gains full knowledge of astral entities and enemies such as lust, greed, anger, jealousy and attachment are destroyed.

MANIPURA

Ten Petals: Dam, Dham, Nam, Tam, Tham, Dam, Dham, Naam, Pam, Pham
Vritti (Qualities): Shame, Fickleness, Jealousy, Desire, Laziness, Sadness, Dullness, Ignorance, Aversion—disgust, fear, and the opposite of all these
Principle: Fire
Seed Sound: Ram
Devata: Agni
Shakti: Lakini
Deity: Rudra and Badra Kali

One who achieves mastery over this chakra becomes free from all diseases and has nothing to fear from fire, even if thrown into a blazing fire. Hidden treasures come to such a one.

HRIT PADMA OR HRIDAYAM

Eight Petals: The eight cardinal directions
Deities for Each Petal: Indra, Agni, Yama, Niruta, Varuna, Vayu, Kubera, Ishana
Seed Sound: Hrim
Shakti: Any and all. There is a wonderful mystical relationship between the fundamental shaktis and the *atman*. It defies description and exists on its own terms.
Deity: The Atman or Self

The Beloved of the devotee appears to one in the form one desires. The Ego-Mind-Personality becomes permanently divine. Higher mysteries of shakti begin to be revealed.

ANAHATA

Twelve Petals: Kam, Kham, Gam, Gham, Mam, Cham, Jam, Jham, Nyam, Tam, Tham

Vritti (Qualities): Hope, Anxiety or Care, Endeavor, Sense of Mineness, Arrogance or Hypocrisy, Languor, Conceit, Discrimination (in the positive sense), Covetousness, Duplicity, Indecision, Regret

Principle: Air

Seed Sound: Yam

Devata: Vayu

Shaktis: Kakini and Kala-ratri

Deities: Tri-Kona Shakti and Narayana as Vishnu (also Hiranyagarbha) in the pericarp of the Hrit Padma. In the Main center Ishwara and Kakini Shakti

One who attains mastery over this chakra gains full control over the wind. One can fly in the air. One can enter into another's body. One attains divine love and all peaceful qualities.

VISHUDDHA

Sixteen Petals: Am, Aam, Im, Iim, Um, Uum, Rim, Riim, Lrim, Lriim, Em, Eim, Om, Aum, Amm, Ah

Vritti (Qualities): Here are the seven musical notes, followed by a venom-like quality. Then comes nectar (*amrit*) and the sound Hum

Principle: Ether

Seed Sound: Hum. There are also other seed sounds that are seen here —Phat, Vaushat, Vashat, Swadha, Swaha, and Namaha

Devata: Saraswati

Shakti: Shakini

Deities: Shiva as Ardha Narishwara

One who attains mastery of this chakra becomes immortal and will never perish, even when the time of great dissolution comes at the end of the life of Brahma. One is automatically successful in anything. One gains knowledge of the four Vedas.

LALANI CHAKRA OR KALACHAKRA

Twelve Petals with Vrittis: Shraddha (Faith), Santosha (Contentment), Aparadha (Sense of error), Dama (Self command), Maana (Anger, as between two close people), Sneha (Affection), Shoka (Sorrow, Grief), Kheda (Dejection), Shuddhata (Purity), Arati (Detachment), Sambhrama (Agitation), Urmmi (Appatute or Desire)

Time is surpassed as a limiting quality. Through initiation, one may be reborn in the company of a Bodhisattva or similar entity for the purpose of service and/or liberation.

AJNA CHAKRA

Two Petals: Ham and Ksham
Principle: Divine Mind
Seed Sounds: Om
Devata: Guru or Dakshina Murti
Shakti: Hakini
Special: There is a triangle with a form of Shiva, and his consort Siddha Kali. Brahma, Vishnu and Shiva sit in the corners of this triangle

One who attains mastery of this chakra destroys all karma in any previous lifetime. Rudra Granthi, the knot of Shiva, is pierced here by the kundalini. One becomes a Jivan Mukta, or one who is liberated even while living in the body. Words are incapable of describing the benefits of mastery here. One acquires the eight major powers and the 32 minor ones.

MANAS CHAKRA

Six Petals: (Jnana here means true knowledge) Shabda Jnana, Sparsha-Jnana

Vrittis: Hearing, Touch, Sight, Smell, Taste, Sleep—and the absence of any of these

Higher powers of the mind are achieved here. One's consciousness can live anywhere without the need of a physical body.

SOMA CHAKRA

Sixteen Petals with Vritties: Kripa (Mercy), Mriduta (Gentleness), Dhairya (Patience, Composure), Vairagya (Dispassion), Dhriti (Constancy), Sampat (Spiritual Prosperity), Hasya (Cheerfulness), Romancha (Rapture, Thrill), Vinaya (Sense of Propriety, Humility), Dhyana (Meditation), Susthirata (Quietude, Restfulness), Gambhirya (Gravity in demeanor), Udyama (Enterprise, Effort), Akshobha (Emotionlessness), Audarya (Magnanimity), and Ekagrata (Concentration). Transitory State and Place Leading To the Sahasrara

GURU CHAKRA

12 Petals: Part of the Sahasrara Chakra in the form of an umbrella on the underside of the crown chakra. The place of Great Decision
Devata: Guru

SAHASRARA CHAKRA

Thousand Petals with all Vritties: In each of the petals are found all of the individual letters of the Sanskrit alphabet. All of the levels and layers of the universe exist here in a potential rather than manifest state. The name of this place varies according to the path of the seeker: Shaivites—Shiva Sthana; Vaishnavas—Parama Purusha; Shaktas—Devi Sthana; Sankhya Sages—Prakriti Purusha Sthana. Other names are Shakti Sthana, Parama Brahma, Parama Hansa, Parama Jyothi, Kula Sthana and Parama Shiva Akula
Devata: Parama Shiva and Paramatma (Supreme Spirit)
Shakti: Adya (first) Shakti
This is not technically a chakra. It is beyond all the chakras.

GLOSSARY

Advaita   Refers to a philosophy of nondualism where everything, including all souls, is the same Being. This philosophy posits no difference between a soul and God.

Agastya   A great sage who was a foremost discipline of Sage Hayagriva, said to be a part manifestation of Vishnu. Agastya kept scrupulous records so that the teachings were largely preserved even into the present day.

Ahamkara   Ego, in the sense of "I Am." For example, "I am aware of myself, thus I exist. I am."

Akasha   Ether, the fifth element in creation, after earth, water, fire, and air. (The sixth is mind.)

Akashic Records   The place in the universe where all information, especially pertaining to people and events, is stored and available to adepts who can access it.

Ananda   Bliss. Also the final word in names of monks who have taken Sanyas, or monastic vows, that are directly or indirectly related to the original Adi Shankarachayra who completely reorganized the monastic system in India.

Arati   Literally, "The waving of the light." It is a short ceremony conducted in five forms (as compared to the sixteen forms of a complete Hindu ritual). It is similar to Vespers in Christianity.

Asura   Demons in humanlike form. Also sometimes called the *daityas*, they are the sworn enemies of the celestials or *devas*.

Atman   The divine flame burning in the Hrit Padma, that goes by many names, including soul or self.

Avatar   A divine being with no karma whatsoever who comes to Earth to perform specific beneficial tasks for humanity. There are many types of avatars.

Bharata	Sanskrit term for India. Also the brother of the Avatar Rama, who, as a faithful steward, ruled Ayodhya when Rama was banished to the forest for fourteen years.
Brahma	Personified Vedic God representative of the known universe and all of its contents. Also called the creator of the universe in ancient story-based scriptures called the Puranas.
Brahmarishi	A sage (*rishi*) who has reached one of the highest possible states of knowledge by being at one with the universe yet is still an individual being. Similar to Subramanya consciousness. Reaching this state is possible only through a combination of effort and grace.
Buddha	Prince Gautama, the Ninth Avatar of Vishnu. Also, a state of consciousness.
Buddhi	The mind in a transformed state, sometimes referred to as an enlightened state. Metaphorically, one of two wives of Ganesha-Ganapathi.
Chakra	Literally, "wheel" in Sanskrit. However, its common meaning refers to various spiritual centers located in the subtle body. Although there are dozens of chakras in the subtle body, the six located along the spine and the seventh at the top of the head are most commonly discussed.
Clairaudience	The psychic ability of subtle hearing. One may obtain information about the past, present, and future with this ability.
Clairvoyance	The psychic ability of subtle seeing. In a way similar to clairaudience, one may obtain information about the past, present, and future with this ability.
Dattatreya	The first Sadguru, operating in a state of being and consciousness called *Avadhuta*, he is the author of the *Avadhuta Gita*.

Deva   A term for a celestial. It also refers to classes of sentient, non-human entities that are on an evolutionary path somewhat different from humanity. Occasionally, there may be movement of souls from one evolutionary line to the other.

Dhanvantari   The celestial healer who appeared at the churning of the ocean of consciousness just as Lakshmi did. He distributed the Nectar of Immortality while giving discourse on the healing properties of plants, gems, and other remedies.

Dharma   Divine Law. It also refers to the proper progression of events and persons according to a divine order.

Durga   Personified feminine power of protection. Member of the Hindu Feminine Trinity.

Dvaita   Dualism. This philosophical school posits that there is a subtle but important difference between the soul and God.

Gana   Power in one context, sometimes personalized and given a name. Group in another context.

Ganapathi or Ganesha   The personified power of unity that removes obstacles and assigns order to various spiritual powers and abilities.

Garuda   The vehicle of Vishnu in the form of a divine eagle.

Gayatri   The feminine name given to the spiritual energy that comes to earth through the sun from the higher realms. It is a personification of spiritual light. Also, a particular rhythm or cadence given to a class of mantras.

Gayatri Mantra   The mantra often called "The Essence of the Vedas." This mantra on universal spiritual light and sound is practiced by Hindus and some branches of Buddhism who work with mantra.

Granthis   Spiritual knots, three in number, located along the spine in the subtle body that prevent premature entrance of kundalini energy into centers on the spine above the sacral center (Swadhisthana Chakra). Were this energy to travel up the spine before the spiritual vehicle is ready, harm to the physical body could result.

Guna   A quality of nature. Three are generally discussed. *Tamo Guna* the inert, *Rajo Guna* the active, and *Sattwa Guna* the tranquil. Earth elements are *Tamo Guna*, Humanity is generally *Rajo Guna*, and the celestials or *devas* are *Sattwa Guna*. In a twist, certain negative forces are also composed of *Sattwa Guna*, which makes them hard to defeat.

Guru   Literally, "that which dispels darkness." In this case, it is the darkness of ignorance. Although many teachers hold that the true guru is not a person but a principle, the term "guru" is often used colloquially to denote an advanced spiritual teacher (also see *upaguru*). An enlightened spiritual teacher with the ability to transmit spiritual energy by one or more methods.

Hayagriva   A sage who had two well-known students: Agastya in Hinduism and Atisha in Tibetan Buddhism. Hayagriva was a foremost teacher of the secrets of Shakti, sometimes called Tantra.

Hylozoism   Greek word meaning life at every level of creation.

Ida   The masculine current in the subtle body. One of the serpents shown in the Caduceus.

Jagad Guru   An enlightened world teacher. Those spiritual figures around whom the world's great religions have formed are examples of Jagad Gurus. There are also Jagad Gurus with broad-reaching spiritual authority in specific geographical districts in India. These divine "precincts" are called *maths*. Jagad Gurus exist in the Shankarachayra lineage and the Madvacharya lineage.

Japa   The repetition of mantras in an ongoing discipline or as a lifestyle. *Japa* can be audibly vocal, muttered, or completely silent. Sometimes *Japa* can occur spontaneously, without any conscious effort. This is referred to as *Ajapa Japa*.

Kailas	Mountain in the Himalayas where Shiva is said to dwell.
Kala	Sanskrit for "time."
Kali Yuga	Spiritual Winter. This time period, lasting 432,000 years, began just over 5,000 years ago according to calculations based upon data in the *Maha Bharata*. This date for the inception of *Kali Yuga* is used by the Brahmin Priest Class, the Shankaracharyas, and other Hindu spiritual authorities.
Kama	Carnal desire and sometimes any desire. In the mythic Hindu stories, the character Kama is similar to Cupid, but with far-reaching abilities to create illusions that appear absolutely real.
Karma	The Law of Cause and Effect. The sum total of actions and thoughts that cause a reaction or return of like energy to the source that generated it. Reincarnation or rebirth continues until all karma is balanced or neutralized. *Sanchita Karma:* To total all karma from all lifetimes. *Prarabdha Karma:* Karma for one life, including planetary karma represented by the natal birth chart is a particular birth or incarnation. *Agami Karma:* Returning karma from this and other lifetimes. *Kriyamana Karma:* Immediate results from present actions.
Kashyapa	Sage who is the "father" of several sentient race of beings. He is said to have mated with the feminine of several species to gain this title. The offspring of those unions have formed different races of intelligent beings.
Krishna	Eighth Avatar of Vishnu. Born more than five thousand years ago, Krishna is said to be the most complete incarnation of divinity to come to Earth. He left when *Kali Yuga* or Spiritual Winter began.
Kundalini	The coiled, serpentine feminine energy laying in repose at the base of the human spine. Although powering all activities in the physical and subtle bodies, it is still characterized as dozing or being asleep in most people. When it awakens, new spiritual abilities manifest in individuals. Eventually it moves as an energy force up the spine in the subtle body, usually over more than one lifetime, until it reaches the crown chakra at the top of the head. At each chakra located along the spine, it releases

energy leading to increased spiritual knowledge and abilities. Once the energy has reached the top of the head, one becomes "Shiva" and is liberated from the necessity of rebirth, although one may choose rebirth for the purpose of service to mankind. All forms of shakti are generated here: Kriya, Jnana, Iccha, Para, and Mantra, to name but a few.

Lakshmana	Rama's younger brother who traveled with him when Rama was banished to the forest for fourteen years.
Lakshmi Tantra	A text in which Lakshmi explains her relationship with Narayana and gives teachings about the nature of the universe and its creation. She teaches in great depth and provides mantras for working with her energy.
Laya	Dissolution.
Laya Yoga	Yoga that achieves its goal by dissolving into the supreme. Through mantra, *pranayama*, or both.
Lila and (Lila the game)	Drama. The game is played representing the "drama'" of our evolution and life. There are places where one advances quite high, only to slide back down many levels due to some fault or flaw. The modern game of Chutes and Ladders is derived from this ancient game.
Loka	A plane or level of existence. There are said to be seven upper luminous *Lokas*, only three of which are physical in existence, and seven dark or nether *Lokas*. Spiritual beings occupy the luminous *Lokas* while negative spirits inhabit the lower *Lokas*. The Earth is said to be the first or bottom of the upper spheres of light. Thus, negative spirits are constantly trying to get here, where they can cause havoc.
Madvacharya (Madva)	Enlightened sage who taught *Advaya Tattwa* or Unity in Diversity. Many followers of Advaita said he followed Dualism because he said that there was not only a difference between souls and God, but that there were different classes of souls with varying destinies. Like Shankaracharya, he never lost a debate. They lived in different eras.

Maha	Great. Also a spiritual plane (*Maha Loka*) in the nonphysical universe where sages and saints of high attainment are said to dwell.
Mala	Hindu Rosary.
Mandala	A divine design.
Manjushri	Bodhisattva of wisdom and knowledge, usually shown holding the sword of discriminating wisdom. Tibetan spouse of Saraswati.
Mantra	A spiritual formula producing specific results, previously tested and verified by an ancient sage. There are millions of mantras in the oral and written records.
Mantra Siddhi	The power one attains when one has unwrapped the power of the mantra through repetition. *Mantra Siddhi* is generally recognized as beginning at 125,000 repetitions of a mantra, and increases as more repetitions are completed
Markandeya	A 16-year-old sage who was liberated from the necessity of rebirth by a cry to Shiva that subsequently became known as the *Maha Mrityunjaya Mantra*. Markandeya is the Seer of this mantra practiced to combat disease and death.
Math	Geographical spiritual district which is presided over by a lead Jagad Guru and his handpicked successor, a second-in-command Jagad Guru.
Matrika	Name given to the Sanskrit Alphabet. Esoterically referred to as "She who binds and She who sets free." If you know her secrets, combinations of her letters (mantras) can free one from the round of rebirth. If one is ignorant of the letters, one will continue to be karmically bound by ignorance.
Mudra	Divine gesture. Exact placement of arms, hands, and fingers are said to produce specific energy effects if practiced by an Adept or spiritually advanced individual.
Nadis	Astral nerve tubes, similar to veins, which run through the subtle body.
Nandi	A bull who is the vehicle of Shiva.

Narayana   Personification of the source of all of this reality, including the
                   creation of Brahma the Creator. Also concurrently, the three-fold
                   flame burning in the Hrit Padma. This seeming duality is intended
                   to demonstrate that we may seem parted but are never really
                   separated from God or the Divine.

Padma   Lotus in Sanskrit. Also a name that is given to women as a slang
                   form of Lakshmi.

Paramahansa   The supreme swan. The swan here is another name for the self
                   in the Hrit Padma. Paramahansa is a title given to a person who
                   has demonstrated exceptionally high spiritual attainment.
                   In modern times, Paramahansa Muktananda, Paramahansa
                   Yogananda and Paramahansa Ramakrishna are well-known
                   examples.

Parama Shiva   The Supreme Consciousness in which all is contained: All
                   consciousness, all energy, everything.

Parasurama   The sixth Avatar of Vishnu. He was instructed in the mysteries
                   of the Great Feminine as part of his preparation for his avataric
                   work by the Avadhuta, Sadguru Dattatreya.

Parvati   Spouse of Shiva. In other guises she is also Durga, Kali, and
                   Chamundi.

Pingala   Feminine energy channel in the subtle body. One of the serpents
                   shown in the Caduceus.

Prana   A life force that exists in the subtle body. There are five divisions
                   of this life force: *Prana*—Situated in the region of the heart, this
                   energy move the lungs for inhalation and exhalation; *Apana*—
                   this energy, situated below the navel, is associated with elimi-
                   nation of spent energy and waste products from the physical
                   body; *Vyana*—this energy pervades the whole body and gives
                   rise to the sense of touch; *Udana*—an energy centered in the
                   throat that provides connection and disconnection of the mind
                   from the body during deep sleep or when engaged in advanced
                   yogic practices. It does this by closing off the throat while leav-
                   ing a chord or strand attached to the traveling subtle body;
                   Samana—this energy at the navel center digests food and dis-

tributes the energy derived to all parts of the body, permeating the subtle body equally in every part.

Pranayama Scientific breathing. There are breathing techniques that produce a variety of specific results, including activating the kundalini.

Puranas Indian prehistory, myth and stories all mixed up together. Vast amounts of spiritual information and teachings exist in the many Puranas that still exist.

Puja Generic Sanskrit term for ceremonial worship.

Purusha Transcendental overself. The aggregate spiritual soul-mind of humanity and yet more as well.

Rama Seventh Avatar of Vishnu. He came to show how potential nobility can actually manifest. He was the perfect ruler, husband, sage, friend, and brother.

Rig Veda One of the four foundational scriptures of Hinduism that deals with matters of cosmology and creation of the cosmos.

Sadguru A God-realized teacher beyond the realms of energy-identified existence or mind-identified existence. A being firmly established in a form of enlightened activity that appears similar to daily human life. The Sadguru has a specific job of leading souls to spiritual freedom. Sadgurus have no karma in the normal sense of the word. Any seeming karma, called "Yoga Yoga Samskaras," is created by Sadgurus to help hide their true nature and aid their work.

Sadhana Any regularly practiced spiritual discipline.

Samadhi Mind merged, absorbed in the divine. There are several types of *Samadhi*. With form: where one is merged with a form of the divine beloved. Formless: where the meditator is one with the great principles that formed and operate the universe at all levels.

Sanatana Eternal.

Sanskrit Ancient language sometimes called Deva Lingua, or language.

of the gods. Also referred to as the Mother of Tongues since so many modern languages are derived from it.

Shaivism The study of consciousness and its attributes through Shiva, commonly known as the masculine principle in the universe. In this country Kashmiri Shaivism has become popular as a way to intellectually explore cosmogenesis and personal evolution.

Shakti See Kundalini.

Shankara-charya An enlightened sage who reorganized the swami (monk) order in India. He may have single-handedly rescued the intellectual traditions and knowledge base of Hinduism, saving it from disappearing under the sweeping force of Buddhism at the time he lived.

Shatrugna Younger brother of the Avatar Rama who always was in the company of another brother, Bharata.

Shiva Personification of consciousness in a male form. This personification is used in myths and stories to make complex ideas easier to understand.

Shiva Sutras Revelations that reportedly appeared carved into a rock, the location of which was revealed in a dream to a sage. This scripture is a foundation of *Kashmiri Shaivism*.

Shushumna The spine in the subtle body, an energy body that interpenetrates the physical. The subtle body contains the chakras.

Subramanya Son of Shiva and Parvati. Some stories place his birth prior to Ganesha while others place it later. Also goes by Karttikeya and Skanda. Esoterically, Subramanya consciousness is the highest possible stage of consciousness while still identified as an individual. The next step is merging into the divine state in which there is no "self and other." Only unity exists.

Siddha One who has attained *siddhis*. One who is on a path of perfection of the Divine Vehicle—the physical and subtle body.

Siddhi A seemingly magical spiritual ability or gift. Plural is *siddhis*.

Suktam Hymn, usually to a specific deity, such as the Narayana Suktam or the Purusha Suktam.

Turiya	The highest category or state of consciousness. Most Hindu scriptures from different points of view agree on this word and this definition.
Turiyatita	A division of *Turiya* state of consciousness that is particular to the Shiva Sutras.
Upaguru	Literally, "the enlightener without form." The omnipresent "teacher without form" that can manifest in seemingly bizarre ways. It can appear as "the magazine article that seems like it was written just for you," or "a statement by an actor in a televised drama that is so powerful for you that it nearly brings you out of your chair." These are examples of how the *upaguru*, a principle residing in everyone, may teach and lead.
Upanishads	A series of scriptures which are all that remain of a much larger, older body of scriptures. Originally written on palm leaves many centuries ago, the number of scriptures became so unwieldy that they were summarized. Some *Upanishads* are actually summaries of summaries.
Vahan	Sanskrit term for Vehicle, as in the vehicle of Shiva which is a bull.
Vaishnavite	A follower or scripture pertaining to Vishnu.
Vedas	Four central scriptures from the *Upanishads* that were never summarized and remain intact. They are the *Rig Veda*, *Sama Veda*, *Yajur Veda*, and *Artharva Veda*.
Vishnu	The Vedic god of preservation. It is said that all true spiritual leaders and teachers from any religion carry the energy of Vishnu.
Vishwa	Universal.

Yuga   Spiritual Age, or period of time in the life of the universe. There
are Yugas and Maha Yugas. Here is a short summary:

Winter (*Kali Yuga*):	432,000 years
Spring (*Treta Yuga*):	1,296,000 years
Summer (*Satya or Krita Yuga*):	1,728,000 years
Autumn (*Dwapara Yuga*):	864,000 years
A Complete Yuga	
Revolution: (*Mahayuga*)	4,320,000,000 years

It continues from there: 1,000 revolutions is a *Manvantara* and
is 4,320,000,000 years long. This amount of time is also called
a "Day in the Life of Brahma." It is followed by a "Night of Equal
Length." Three hundred and sixty days and nights of Brahma
are called "one year of Brahma." One hundred such years
constitute the life of this universe, or a *Maha Kalpa* —
311,040,000,000,000 years.

There is also a short 24,000-year cycle in which the axis of
the earth spends 2,000 years in each sign of the zodiac. It is this
cycle that astrologers are referring to when they say that we are
in the Age of Aquarius.

NOTES

1 Shyam Sundar Goswami. *Laya Yoga*. (Rochester, Vermont: Inner Traditions, 1999) page 38.

2 Shyam Sundar Goswami. *Laya Yoga*. (Rochester, Vermont: Inner Traditions, 1999) page 38.

3 Blavatsky, H.P., *The Secret Doctrine*. 1888, Pasadena, California: Theosophical University Press, 1977

4 Sivananda, Swami. *Lord Siva and His Worship*. (The Divine Life Society, Yoga Vedanta Forest Academy, U.P., Himalayas, Tenth Edition, 1996), page 18.

5 Shyam Sundar Goswami. *Laya Yoga*. (Rochester, Vermont: Inner Traditions, 1999) page 124.

6 Ganesh Pranama, *Ganesha Gita*, vs. 1: 21-29; 3: 9-11.

7 There is also a Feminine Trinity composed of the spouses of the Masculine Trinity: Lakshmi for Vishnu, Saraswati for Brahma, and Durga (or Kali, as well as Parvati) for Shiva.

8 Those who are very devoted to their spiritual teacher sometimes chant a Guru Mantra first, such as "Om Sri Gurubhyo Namaha," and then chant a Ganesha mantra. But this is the exception, not the rule.

9 Singh, Jaideva. *Siva Sutras* (Motilal Banarsidass: Delhi and other cities 1979, 1988) Summary of pages 40–47.

10 Keshavadas, Sant. *Lord Ganesha*. (Vishwa Dharma Publications: Oakland, California, 1988), pages 28-29.

11 This concept is given substantial treatment in the mystical classic, *The Fourth Way*, by P.D. Ouspensky.

12 Of course in the case of Tibetan Lamas, survival did become an issue when the Chinese decided to annex the country and slaughtered hundreds of thousands of monks and nuns. But this is not usually the case with monasteries.

13 Rodgers, William. *THINK*, New York: Stein and Day, 1969, pp. 249-50.

14 Baba, Meher. *Discourses* Vol III. San Francisco: Kinsport Press, Suifism Reoriented, 1973, p. 15.

BIBLIOGRAPHY

Ashley-Farrand, Thomas. *The Ancient Science of Sanskrit Mantra and Ceremony Vols I-III.* Pasadena, CA: Saraswati Publications, LLC, 1995, 2001

———. *Healing Mantras.*New York: Ballantine Wellspring Books, 1999.

———. *Shakti Mantras.* New York: Ballantine Books, 2003.

———. *True Stories of Spiritual Power.* Saraswati Publications, LLC: 1995.

Avalon, Arthur pen name Sir John Woodroffe. *Maha Nirvana Tantra: The Tantra of Great Liberation.* New York: Dover Publications, Inc, 1972.

Baba, Meher. *Discourses*, Vols I-III. San Francisco: Kinsport Press, Suifsm Re-oriented, 1973.

Bailey, Alice. *Initiation, Human and Solar.* 4th Edition New York: Lucis Trust, 1980.

Blavatsky, H.P., *The Secret Doctrine.* Pasadena, California: Theosophical University Press, 1970.

Board of Scholars. *Mantramahoddadhi.* Delhi, India: Sri Satguru Publications, 1984.

Dalai Lama The. and Jeffery Hopkins. *The Kalachakra Tantra.* Boston, MA: Wisdom Publications, 1985.

Dowson, John. *A Classical Dictionary of Hindu Mythology and Religion.* Calcutta, India: 1982.

Festinger, Leon. *A Theory of Cognitive Dissonance.* Stanford, CA: Stanford University Press, 1962.

Goswami, Shyam Sundar. *Laya Yoga.* Rochester, Vermont: Inner Traditions, 1980.

Grimes, John. *Ganapati—Song of the Self.* Delhi, India: Sri Satguru Publications, 1996.

Gupta, Sanjukta. *Laksmi Tantra.* Leiden, Netherlands: Brill 1972.

Harshananda, Swami. *Hindu Gods and Goddesses.* Mysore, India: Sri Ramakrishna Ashrama, 1982.

Keshavadas, Sant. *Gayatri—The Highest Meditation.* New York: Vantage Press, 1978.

———. *Liberation from Karma and Rebirth.* Virginia Beach, Virginia: Temple of Cosmic Religion, 1970.

———. *Healing Techniques of the Holy East.* Oakland, California: Vishwa Dharma Publications, 1980.

———. *Dattatreya: The First Guru.* Oakland, California: Vishwa Dharma Publications, 1986.

———. *Lord Ganesha.* Oakland, California: Vishwa Dharma Publications, 1988.

Kapture, Bradley. *The Sounds of Silence; Healing Body, Mind and Spirit with Ancient Meditatons.* Bloomington, IN: Author House, 2004.

BIBLIOGRAPHY

Ashley-Farrand, Thomas. *The Ancient Science of Sanskrit Mantra and Ceremony Vols I-III.* Pasadena, CA: Saraswati Publications, LLC, 1995, 2001
———. *Healing Mantras.*New York: Ballantine Wellspring Books, 1999.
———. *Shakti Mantras.* New York: Ballantine Books, 2003.
———. *True Stories of Spiritual Power.* Saraswati Publications, LLC: 1995.
Avalon, Arthur pen name Sir John Woodroffe. *Maha Nirvana Tantra: The Tantra of Great Liberation.* New York: Dover Publications, Inc, 1972.
Baba, Meher. *Discourses,* Vols I-III. San Francisco: Kinsport Press, Suifsm Re-oriented, 1973.
Bailey, Alice. *Initiation, Human and Solar.* 4th Edition New York: Lucis Trust, 1980.
Blavatsky, H.P., *The Secret Doctrine.* Pasadena, California: Theosophical University Press, 1970.
Board of Scholars. *Mantramahoddadhi.* Delhi, India: Sri Satguru Publications, 1984.
Dalai Lama The. and Jeffery Hopkins. *The Kalachakra Tantra.* Boston, MA: Wisdom Publications, 1985.
Dowson, John. *A Classical Dictionary of Hindu Mythology and Religion.* Calcutta, India: 1982.
Festinger, Leon. *A Theory of Cognitive Dissonance.* Stanford, CA: Stanford University Press, 1962.
Goswami, Shyam Sundar. *Laya Yoga.* Rochester, Vermont: Inner Traditions, 1980.
Grimes, John. *Ganapati—Song of the Self.* Delhi, India: Sri Satguru Publications, 1996.
Gupta, Sanjukta. *Laksmi Tantra.* Leiden, Netherlands: Brill 1972.
Harshananda, Swami. *Hindu Gods and Goddesses.* Mysore, India: Sri Ramakrishna Ashrama, 1982.
Keshavadas, Sant. *Gayatri—The Highest Meditation.* New York: Vantage Press, 1978.
———. *Liberation from Karma and Rebirth.* Virginia Beach, Virginia: Temple of Cosmic Religion, 1970.
———. *Healing Techniques of the Holy East.* Oakland, California: Vishwa Dharma Publications, 1980.
———. *Dattatreya: The First Guru.* Oakland, California: Vishwa Dharma Publications, 1986.
———. *Lord Ganesha.* Oakland, California: Vishwa Dharma Publications, 1988.
Kapture, Bradley. *The Sounds of Silence; Healing Body, Mind and Spirit with Ancient Meditatons.* Bloomington, IN: Author House, 2004.

Ouspensky, P.D. *The Fourth Way.* New York: Vintage Books, 1971.

Pargiter, F. Eden, B.A. *The Markandeya Purana.* Delhi, India: The Asiatic Society of Bengal, 1981.

Rodgers, William. *THINK.* New York: Stein and Day, 1969.

Rokeach, Milton. *The Open and Closed Mind.* New York: Basic Books, 1960..

Singh, Jaideva. *Siva Sutras.* Delhi: Motilal Banarsidass, 1979, 1988.

Sivananda, Swami. *Japa Yoga.* U.P., Himalayas: The Divine Life Society, Yoga Vedanta Forest Academy, 1972.

———. *Kundalini Yoga.* U.P., Himalayas: The Divine Life Society, Yoga Vedanta Forest Academy, Tenth Edition, 1994.

———. *Lord Siva and His Worship.* U.P., Himalayas: The Divine Life Society, Yoga Vedanta Forest Academy, Tenth Edition, 1996.

Various. *The Holy Bible,* King James Version or the Jerusalem Bible.

Walker, Benjamin. *The Hindu World: An Encyclopedic Survey of Hinduism,* Vols I & II., New York: Frederick A. Praeger, 1968.

THOMAS ASHLEY-FARRAND
NAMADEVA

THOMAS ASHLEY-FARRAND (NAMADEVA) has practiced mantra-based spiritual disciplines since 1973 and is an acknowledged expert in Sanskrit Mantra spiritual disciplines.

He has received initiations and blessings from a number of prominent spiritual teachers, including Jagadguru Shankaracharya Jayendra Saraswati, Jagadguru Shankara Vijayendra Saraswati, the Jagadguru of Pejowar Math in the Madvacharya lineage, the Dalai Lama, the 16th Gyalwa Karmapa, Kalu Rimpoche, Sakya Jetsun Chiney Luding, and Christian mystic Dr. Leon Wright. His guru is the late Sadguru Sant Keshavadas from Bangalore, India. He follows Guru Rama Mata, Sant Keshavadas' widow and lineage holder.

Vedic Priest, author, and international lecturer and storyteller, Mr. Ashley-Farrand has made presentations in the U.S. and Canada, as well as India. He was a priest at the Temple of Cosmic Religion in Washington, DC, and has taught at George Washington University and Chaffee College.

Ashley-Farrand is a Kriya Yoga Initiate and a member of Astara. He is president of Sanatana Dharma Satsang.

Thomas currently lives near Portland, Oregon, with his wife Margalo (Satyabhama), an attorney and mediator in private practice who often performs the ancient Vedic ceremonies with him. Thomas Ashley-Farrand's Web site is *www.sanskritmantra.com*.

TO OUR READERS